Health Politics in Korea

Health Politics in Korea
The Political Dynamics of Healthcare Reform

Printed in Seoul, Republic of Korea
ISBN 978-89-521-1776-2 93350

Seoul National University Press
1 Gwanak-ro, Gwanak-gu, Seoul 08826, Republic of Korea

E-mail: snubook@snu.ac.kr
Home-page: http://www.snupress.com
Tel: +82-2-880-5252
Fax: +82-2-889-0785
First Printing: May 25, 2016

HEALTH POLITICS IN KOREA

The Political Dynamics of Healthcare Reform

Soon-yang Kim

SNUPRESS
Seoul National University Press

Acknowledgements

This book analyzes the political dynamics of South Korea's healthcare reform, through the case study on the debate to inaugurate the single payer system of health insurance, which had been practiced for two decades since the early 1980s. During this period, South Korea had undergone unprecedented political and economic turmoils. Through this book, readers will be able to gain valuable insight into how these turbulences had impacted healthcare reform in a politically and economically transitional country. This book also grants opportunities for readers to compare the different paths taken by South Korea's healthcare reform which reflects the changing dynamics of its political regimes.

The book's key theoretical perspectives are underpinned by the policy network perspective and new institutionalism. This combination allows the book to establish more integrative and stereoscopic analytical framework linking environmental context, institutional constraints, policy network, and policy outputs. Through this framework, the book comparatively explores four case studies that had developed in different political regimes. This will allow the readers to grasp how undergoing political and economic turmoils in South Korea subsequently shaped its political dynamics of healthcare reform.

In writing this book, I am indebted to a large number of people. I am very grateful to all those who have contributed to the publication of this book. My particular thanks are due to Professor Elias Mossialos of The London School of Economics and Political Science (LSE). He has been remarkably generous with his assistance during my studies at LSE. Without drawing on his sincere consideration, this book would not have been possible. I also extend my gratitude to Professor Chung-gil Chung who guided me throughout my graduate school days at Seoul National University. Words cannot express my gratitude towards them.

On a more personal level, I would like to thank my family members who have given me a boost. This book could not have been written without their loving support and encouragement. My special gratitude goes to my parents who had sacrificed their entire lives to educate me and my siblings. This book is dedicated to the memory of my parents, to acknowledge their unconditional love and sacrifices they have made for me. Thank you very much indeed.

Soon-yang Kim

Contents

Chapter 3

Bureaucratic Politics in a Closed Terrain:

The First Merger Debate in the Early 1980s

Chapter 4

Democratisation but Frustrated Health Insurance Reform:

The Second Round of Merger Debate in the Late 1980s

Chapter 5

Pushing the First Button:

Accomplishment of Partial Merger in the 1990s

Chapter 6 Unfinished Symphony:

Accomplishment of Full Merger in the 2000s

Chapter 8 Conclusion

Chapter
1

Introduction

1. Republic of Korea: Whirlpool Politics and Miracle Economy

1) Republic of Korea: a profile

The Republic of Korea (South Korea) is a small peninsular country (100,284 square kilometres) situated in East Asia. Before being divided into the two Koreas, it was surrounded by three faces of the Pacific Ocean and two large rivers, the Amnok (Yalu) and the Tuman (or Tumen). Korea has largely been ethnically homogeneous since its inception in 2333 B.C.

Although Korea has suffered from many invasions from neighbouring powers and the Korean War (1950-53), modern Korea has been triumphantly journeyed towards political democracy, social diversity and economic expansion.

Currently Korea's basic socio-economic indices (based on the formal statistics of 2013) are as follows: 50,220 thousand citizens, 12.2 percent of whom are above 65 years old, 84.6 years of female life expectancy at birth (males 77.9), 8.6 crude birth rate and 5.3 crude death rate per thousand people. Economically, Korea's GDP stands at $1,304 billion, translating into a per capita GDP of $26,205, and a low 3.1 percent of the population are registered as unemployed. Its main industry consists of heavy and chemical, high-tech and service industries (Ministry of Health and Welfare Statistical Yearbook 2014, The Bank of Korea (http://ecos.bok.or.kr)).

Politically Korea follows a presidential system. The President is elected

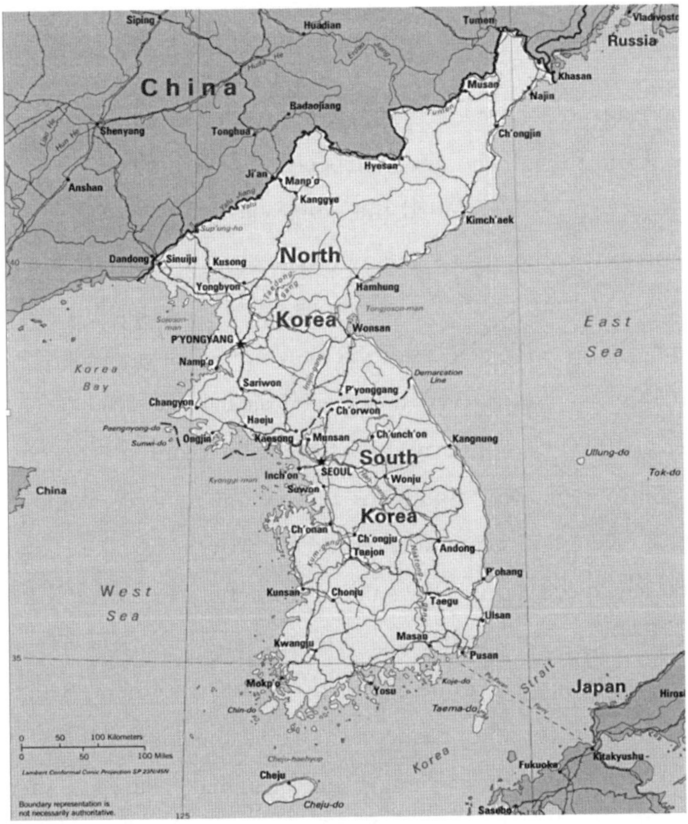

Source: http://www.wintranslation.com/languages/korean.html

directly and serves a five-year single term. Korean Parliament has a unicameral legislative system and holds rights to make law, review the government budget and investigate state affairs. Party politics is well established under the multi-party system and the local autonomy system was introduced in the early 1990s. Interest groups freely articulate their interests in the policy-making process. Since the successful popular protest of the late 1980s, civic groups have become key players in Korean politics.

2) Whirlpool politics

Since liberation from colonial rule in 1945, Korea had consistently suffered political chaos. Even though the new independent government (1948-60) of President Rhee Syng-man copied the American political system — presidential system, bicameralism, and four-year term for the President and lawmakers — Western political institutions failed to sympathise with Korea's traditional culture. Ideological conflict and animosity between rival politicians made the new country very unstable (Hoare and Pares, 2000: 72).

The Korean War (1950-53) devastated Korea's burgeoning economy. In the 1950s politics remained tumultuous and became more ideologically rigid. Political corruption contaminated the country. A rigged election of March 1960 led to the April 1960 student revolution. President Rhee stepped down and the short-term democratic government (1960-61) of Premier Jang Myoun was inaugurated. But the new government, which adopted the cabinet system and bicameralism, failed to suppress political chaos. In May 1961 General Park Chung-hee led a military coup, and after two years' military rule, was elected the President (Robinson, 2007: 128). The first Park administration (1963-72) chose the presidential system and the unicameral legislative system.

From the late 1960s Park's politics followed that of dictatorship. The Constitution was revised in 1969 to make the third-term presidency possible and a state emergency was declared in 1971. Park proclaimed *Yushin* (revitalisation) in October 1972 to rewrite the Constitution and dissolve Parliament (Shim, 2004: 227). The second Park administration (1972-79) showed a typical form of dictatorship. The President was indirectly elected by the puppet National Conference for Unification without competition and appointed one-third of all lawmakers, making Parliament seemingly untrustworthy. Civil society was also tightly controlled.

After the assassination of President Park in October 1979, General Chun Doo-hwan led a series of military coups between 1979 and 1980, leading to his eventual presidency. The Chun administration (1980-88) also adopted the presidential system and the unicameral system, harshly suppressing civil society and opposition parties. But from the mid 1980s, politics became even more disordered, triggering the June 1987 popular protest. Following this successful protest, Korean politics was transformed from dictatorship to democracy. Although the ruling candidate Rho Tae-woo won the 1987 presidential election, his power base was very fragile from the beginning. Opposition parties dominated Parliament and civil protests overturned governmental authority. The presidency was subsequently shortened to a five-year single term (Heo and Roehrig, 2011: 40-41).

The Kim Young-sam administration (1993-97) enforced political and economic reforms and advocated globalisation as a political agenda. Korea affiliated to the OECD in 1995 to open up its capital and commercial markets widely. But from 1997, the lame-duck presidency was unable to properly manage the economic crisis. In December 1997 opposition candidate Kim Dae-jung was elected the new President. The Kim Dae-jung administration (1998-2002) restructured labour market and business sector and pursued flexible inter-Korean 'sunshine policy' to alleviate the tension between the two Koreas (Buzo, 2002: 188). Under the Kim administration, civil society power was significantly increased. The Rho Moo-hyun administration (2003-07) was the most progressive government in Korean history. Civic groups and trade unions became key political players and the general public were encouraged to participate in state affairs. However, Korean politics returned to conservativism in the Lee Myung-bak administration (2008-12) and Park Geun-hye administration (2013-present) and governing conservatives tried to erase the ten years' traces of progressive governments.

In sum, modern Korean politics has undergone very turbulent times. There were several military coups. For many years, authoritarian political leadership dominated Korean politics and civil society was heavily repressed. However, Korean politics has incessantly marched towards democracy and openness. The state goals have moved on from economic growth and bureaucratic efficiency to distributional justice and political democracy. Empowered civil society has improved the transparency of politics and bureaucracy (Kihl, 2005: 275).

3) Miracle economy

When Korea was liberated in 1945, its economy was devastated. Inflation was high, natural resources were scarce and the population swelled by the return of migrants from abroad. After the division into the two Koreas, almost all heavy industries and energy suppliers were in North Korea. In addition, the Korean War destroyed nearly two-thirds of the country's productive capacity. The Korean economy in the 1950s was largely sustained by foreign aid (Robinson, 2007: 123).

From the 1960s, the economy started to grow and prosper. Under the situation where the domestic market was weak, the Korean government adopted export-driven industrialisation. In the 1970s farming sectors introduced the Semaul-undong (New Village Movement) that aimed to increase rural incomes and promote a positive and enlightened spirit. The size of exports jumped from $40.9 million in 1961 to $1,624 million in 1972 (www.

kostat.go.kr).

The government successfully transformed the economic framework from a labour-intensive light industry into a capital-intensive heavy and chemical one, dramatically changing Korea's impoverished past into a successful economy. The government encouraged exports by providing companies with many preferential benefits, such as tax exemptions and supplies of credit. Protectionist measures on foreign imports were erected to look after burgeoning domestic industries. The developmental nexus linking big companies and the government played a pivotal role in the rapid economic growth of Korea (Hoare and Pares, 2000: 104).

During the 1970s average economic growth rate was 9.4 percent, whereas the unemployment rate was only 3.8 percent. Per capita GDP jumped from $319 in 1972 to $1,687 in 1979. The economy grew seven fold during this period. But the heavy reliance on foreign loans and budget deficits destabilised economic fundamentals. Average growth rate of consumer price index was 15.7 percent during the period and the income gap was greatly widened.

But in the early 1980s, the Korean economy stagnated due to political instability and the deteriorating world economy. Inflation was very high and trade balance fell into the red. Average growth rates of consumer price indices in 1980 and 1981 were 28.7 percent and 21.3 percent, respectively (Statistics Korea, 1998: 113). To break through the deadlock the government championed economic stability as its top goal. In 1986 Korean economy went into the black, thanks to low oil prices, low interest rates and low commodity prices. However, with the progress of political democracy from the late 1980s, labour strikes were intensified. International pressure to open up its market resulted in the Korean government pursuing economic liberalisation (Kihl, 2005: 273).

Meanwhile, economic globalisation and a neo-liberal economic ideology, advocating privatisation and deregulation, prevailed in the 1990s. But sweeping capital liberalisation and the Asian economic crisis depleted Korean foreign currency reserves and ended in an IMF bail-out fund. Thus, the Kim Dae-jung administration (1998-2002) restructured the economy in order to deal with economic insolvency. While labour market flexibility increased, big companies were forced to exchange production items and lines to avoid overlapping investments (Kim S.-y. 2015: 8). The financial market was also rebuilt by forcefully liquidating insolvent banks and securities companies. In contrast, the Rho Moo-hyun administration (2003-2007) emphasised economic redistribution and a larger proportion of the government budget was directed towards social welfare. Meanwhile, the Lee Myung-bak administration (2008-12) positioned itself as business-friendly and loosened government regulations on market and business activities. The Lee administration successfully dealt with the 2008 global financial crisis.

To sum up, Korea has built its economy from scratch following liberation in 1945. Furthermore, the Korean War of the early 1950s completely destroyed Korea's economic infrastructure. Until the mid 1960s Korea was one of the world's poorest countries and its economy was mainly reliant upon aids from international society. However, since the late 1960s, educated and diligent workers, effective politico-administrative leadership, and Korean people's can-do spirit have all contributed to achieving extremely speedy growth, propelling Korea into 14th place in the world economy (as of 2014).

4) Progress of health status and healthcare

Almost all health-related indices in Korea have continuously improved in recent three decades, thanks to a growing economy, advanced medical technology and improved nutrition. Above all else, the volume of key healthcare professionals, including physicians, dentists, pharmacists and herbal medical doctors, has increased several times. The increase in healthcare facilities is also worthy of close attention. Compared to 1980, hospitals/clinics, dental hospitals/clinics, and herbal medicine hospitals/clinics increased 375 percent, 640 percent, and 443 percent respectively by 2013. Moreover, as the number of healthcare facilities rose, inpatient care beds were continuously replenished. As of 2012, there were 12.0 hospital beds per one thousand people, indicating a 606 percent increase since 1980 (MOHW Statistical Year Book 2013, 2013).

The average life span of Koreans has increased every year. While Korean women's life expectancy at birth was 70.0 years (male 61.8) in 1980, it was 84.6 years (male 77.9) in 2013, similar to those of the United States and the United Kingdom (as of 2011, male 76.3 and female 81.1 of the United States and male 79.1 and female 83.1 of the United Kingdom) (OECD Health Data 2013, 2013). Crude death and crude birth rates were reduced to 5.3 persons and 8.6 persons per one thousand in 2013 from 7.3 persons and 22.6 persons in 1980, respectively. While the infant mortality rate was 23 persons per one thousand in 1985, it was dramatically decreased to 3.0 in 2013 (Statistics Korea, 2013 Annual Report on the Vital Statistics, 2014).

Meanwhile, Korea is facing an ageing society. In 2013, 12.2% of the population were aged 65 and over, equalling the rate of developed countries. It is projected to be 24.3 percent in 2030, making Korea a super ageing society where a quarter of its total population is elderly. With this, the age dependency ratio is also sharply increasing every year. While the aged dependency ratio and ageing index were 16.7 percent and 83.3 percent in 2013 respectively, and are expected to be 38.6 percent and 193.0 percent in 2030 (MOHW Statistical Year Book 2014, 2014).

Conversely, since the mid 1980s population growth has radically slowed, mainly due to the government's effective birth control programs, the rise of age at marriage, and the high financial burden of private education. Currently Korea's population growth rate is in the world's lowest band by recoding 0.43 percent growth in 2013 (Statistics Korea, The Future Estimated Population, 2013).

From 1977 compulsory health insurance began to take root in Korea. At first, health insurance only covered those who worked in companies with 500 and more employees. From 1979 the health insurance program covering government officials and private school teachers also went into effect. Throughout the 1980s the health insurance program was gradually extended to cover workers in small and medium sized companies.

Meanwhile, efforts to introduce a health insurance scheme for the self-employed were made from the early 1980s. Between 1981 and 1983, the pilot health insurance programs for the self-employed were launched twice, as a preparatory step to extend health insurance coverage to the self-employed. The government introduced a compulsory health insurance to the rural self-employed in 1988 and to the urban self-employed in 1989, achieving the universal health insurance coverage only in 12 years. As of 2013, 49,990 thousand persons of total beneficiaries of medical security are covered by a health insurance program, while 1,459 thousand people living under the poverty line benefited from Medical Aid (MOHW Statistical Year

Book 2014, 2014).

2. Research Purpose

Social policy-making in Korea has experienced unprecedented turbulence, with a wide variety of actors who have greatly influenced the way policy has been shaped. Both Korea's policy outputs and contents have undergone significant changes recently. Within the field of social policy, health policy — an area that covers health insurance — has been one of the most controversial areas. Derthick (1979) characterises health policy as a 'boundary issue' of the welfare state, and points out that 'issues of principle' often stir passions and mobilise interest groups on a massive scale. From this perspective, health policy in Korea has been highly politicised, attracting the attention of academia, often with conflicting views.

Korean compulsory health insurance began in 1977 with the revision of the Medical Insurance Act. 12 years later, in 1989, a nationwide health insurance scheme was launched. However, there have been several controversial issues in the development of the health insurance programme, such as the level of insurance premiums and the managing systems associated with the programme. Amongst them, the debate on the merger of health insurers has been one of the most prominent and durable policy agendas. Since the early 1980s, it has been an issue that has continuously attracted public attention, and several attempts have been made to transform a system of multiple insurers into a single insurer system. During this process, there have been serious conflicts of interest between proponents and opponents of the merger. Original policy goals often have remained unattained and the policy process has been paralysed several times because of irreconcilable differences between policy actors.

Keeping these events in mind, this book aims to develop a comprehensive analytical framework of Korean health policy by combining new institutional and policy network perspectives. This framework will be employed to longitudinally investigate the dynamics of health politics in Korea, focusing on the two decades of the debates on the merger of health insurers. The analytical framework looks closely at the dynamic interaction between four major components of policy context, institutional features, policy networks, and policy outputs. In this regard the analysis in this book is conducted from a systemic and process-driven point of view.

In this book, policy context encompasses environmental elements which influence the attributes of the other three components, whereas the idea of institutions outlines the factors that constrain policy-making. Policy networks are related to both relational structure and patterns of interaction in policy-making. Finally, policy outputs examine the end results of policy-making. The following are the five main areas that this book will cover.

- The extent to which policy context influenced institutional features and policy networks over time
- Similarly, how have institutional features constrained the characteristics of policy networks over time?
- How, and why, have the attributes and types of health policy networks changed over time? Which interests have dominated policy networks?
- To what extent do the differences in health policy networks explain the difference in policy outputs?

- Finally, the investigation into the interaction between the four analytical components — policy context, institutional features, policy networks and policy outputs.

This book consists of eight chapters. The first chapter deals with the research context, briefly examining the modern politics of Korea, its healthcare and health insurance system. The development of key debates on the merger of health insurers is discussed. Chapter 2 examines policy-making dynamics and presents theoretical views. This book predominantly uses new institutional and policy network perspectives. The analytical framework for reviewing health politics is also established in this chapter. Four case studies that cover health politics in Korea are empirically analysed from Chapters 3 through to Chapter 6. Chapter 3 examines the first merger attempt in the early 1980s. Chapter 4 details the second merger attempt of the late 1980s whilst Chapter 5 looks at the argument surrounding the partial merger in the 1990s. Chapter 6 covers the debate on the full merger of health insurers which occurred between the late 1990s and the early 2000s. Each of these four chapters is subdivided into six headings:

- introductory comments
- policy context
- institutional features
- policy networks
- policy outputs
- conclusion

Chapter 7 longitudinally compares and contrasts the findings in Chapters 3-6. Chapter 8 summarises findings and deliberates on the theoretical and empirical implications of this research for a better understanding of health politics in Korea. The Chapter concludes with a discussion on the limitations of the book and suggestions for further research.

3. Key Debates on the Health Insurance System: Case Synopsis

The Medical Insurance Act was enacted in 1963, but the program, dependant on voluntary affiliation, was destined to failure in light of economic conditions at the time. The government completely revised the Act in 1976 to make it compulsory from July 1977, offering obligatory coverage to employees in companies with over 500 workers. From then on, the government gradually extended insurance coverage to include all companies with at least 5 employees by 1988.

From the start, Korea adopted a national health insurance system rather than a National Health Service (NHS) system, taking into account the limited supply of health institutions in the public sector and the government's reluctance to shoulder financial responsibility. In 1979, the health insurance program covering government/private school employees came into effect. The government extended compulsory coverage to the rural self-employed in January 1988 and to the urban self-employed in July 1989, thus, achieving the nationwide introduction of health insurance. In the 1990s, the government started to gradually integrate health insures by enacting the National Medical Insurance Act and the National Health Insurance Act (NHIA), respectively. A timeline of Korean health insurance policy development is summarised below:

- 1963 Enactment of the Medical Insurance Act
- 1976 Second amendment of the Medical Insurance Act
- 1979 Medical insurance program for government and private school employees
- 1981-82 Pilots for self-employed medical insurance program
- 1988 Medical insurance program for the rural self-employed
- 1989 Medical insurance program for the urban self-employed
- 1989 Medical insurance program for pharmacies
- 1997 Enactment of the National Medical Insurance Act
- 1999 Enactment of the National Health Insurance Act
- 2000 Separation of dispensary from medical practice
- 2000 Establishment of the National Health Insurance Corporation
- 2003 Accomplishment of the merger of health insurance funds

In relation to the debates on the health insurance system, when a compulsory health insurance programme was launched in 1977, the government adopted the multiple insurer system, giving administrative and financial autonomy to each insurer. At the time, the government had expected the multiple insurer system to be more effective in gradually extending health insurance coverage and reducing its financial burden. But, unfortunately, the multiple insurer system reduced equity between policyholders from different socio-economic strata and created inequalities in terms of insurance benefits. Moreover, small-sized insurers were less efficient in delivering insurance services.

With the introduction of health insurance for government/private school employees in 1979, the government formed the Korea Medical Insurance Corporation (KMIC) as a single insurer. Meanwhile, health insurers for company employees and the self-employed were managed by a multiple insurer system. Thus, until the organisational merger of health insurers in July 2000, the health insurer system in Korea had maintained a dual management system consisting of the KMIC and multiple insurers for company employees and the self-employed.

However, as the health insurance programme was extended to cover the self-employed in the 1980s, heated debates arose regarding the nature of the health insurer system. Since, the most challenging and durable concern has been whether the country's health insurance programme should be administered by multiple insurers or by a single insurer. While the advocates of the single insurer system insisted on the merits of an integrated system in achieving a balance between health insurance benefits and premiums, the proponents of the multiple insurer system placed more emphasis on the benefits generated by the autonomy of each insurer.

Diverse socio-political factors have also been engaged to shape the health insurer issue into an ideological conflict between policy actors with different perspectives. With the progress of democracy from the late 1980s, the number of participants in the debate has increased dramatically, fundamentally changing the nature of health insurance policy-making and outputs.

The first merger debate started with the announcement by the MHSA minister, in September 1980, that the system would move towards the establishment of a single insurer, with the aim of laying the foundation of a nationwide health insurance program. The ruling party also advocated the merger. But staff in the Office of the President (henceforth, OP) persuaded the President to oppose the merger plan, stressing the potential problems of a single insurer system. Employee health insurers and business associations also championed the multiple insurer system currently in operation by emphasising its contribution to labour/ business cooperation and the difficulty of an equitable collection of insurance premiums between policyholders. Despite such debates between 1981 and 1982, the issue did not make any additional headway, given the opposition from the OP. In November 1982, the President halted the debate by siding with the opponents of the merger.

The second merger debate was initiated by the introduction of the rural self-employed health insurance programme in January 1988. In extending health insurance coverage to the self-employed, the government preferred to continue a multiple insurer system, taking into account the sharp income gap and unequal distribution of medical institutions between regions. Unlike the first debate, the ruling party and government departments supported a multiple insurer system.

From the mid 1980s, Korea's political system rapidly transformed itself from one dominated by authoritarian politics into a democratic system. Numerous interest groups were formed to articulate their interests. Although the ruling party won the 1987 presidential election, opposition parties held the parliamentary majority. Farmers' groups and progressive healthcare professionals played key roles in triggering the second debate.

Meanwhile, the National Medical Insurance Bill was passed in an opposition-dominated Parliament in March 1989. This legislation sought to merge health insurers but the President vetoed the Bill following a recommendation from relevant government departments. Despite protests from proponents of the merger, the government extended insurance coverage to the urban self-employed in July 1989, again through a multiple insurer system.

In the 1990s, proponents of the merger formed a united front to demand healthcare reform, but the government responded to their demands by advocating the enlargement of health insurers on the basis of a multiple insurer system. Confronted by the tenacious attachment of the governing bloc to the multiple insurer system, civic groups pressured opposition parties and staged protests, taking advantage of the 1996 general election, to promote their goal. Two main opposition parties responded by proposing a merger bill in 1996, even though it was blocked by the objection of the ruling party which held a parliamentary majority.

Approaching the 1997 presidential election, the political situation changed in favour of merger proponents. The ruling party now altered its position to back the merger, hoping to reap the benefits in the forthcoming election. In any case, Parliament passed the National Medical Insurance Act in November 1997, and this partially merged 227 insurers for the self-employed with the KMIC. As a result, the National Medical Insurance Corporation (NMIC) was established in October 1998. But 142 employee insurers still retained their autonomous status.

The Kim Dae-jung administration, which was inaugurated in the midst of national economic insolvency, formed the Korea Tripartite Commission (KTC) as a way of coping with the on-going economic crisis. In February 1998, the KTC proposed the merger of health insurers, thereby pushing the issue as a major political agenda. President Kim supported the merger as one of his main presidential election pledges, and opposition parties also did not block the merger. But counter-attacks from opponents of the merger were ongoing. From mid-1998, the employee insurers union and the

FKTU led a wave of anti-merger protests.

Despite the intensified resistance from opponents of the merger, Parliament passed the National Health Insurance Act (NHIA) in January 1999 to set up a single insurer by incorporating 142 company employee insurers into a single body with the NMIC. But the government requested a postponement of the merger under the pretext of difficulties in defining the income level of the self-employed. In December 1999, the NHIA was revised to postpone the organisational merger of health insurers until June 2000 and the financial merger until December 2001. However, the organisational merger between the NMIC and company employee insurers was achieved by June 2000, as scheduled.

Unlike the organisational merger, the financial merger of insurance funds was challenging because of the difficulty in developing a common criterion from which to derive insurance premiums. The government and the ruling party wanted to delay the financial merger, while opponents of the merger argued that the financial merger should be cancelled altogether. During the 2002 presidential election campaign, the ruling party promised to proceed with the merger, as agreed, whereas main opposition candidates supported the idea of splitting the finances between different types of policyholders. As the ruling candidate Rho Moo-hyun won the election, the financial merger was finally implemented in July 2003.

Chapter 2

Dynamics of Health Politics

1. Politics as the Context of Policy

Public policy is greatly constrained by the policy context or environment and is subject to policy-making dynamics. Moreover, changes in policy context make its impact on policy processes and outputs more complicated and unpredictable. Peters (2004: 14) summarises the importance of the policy context when examining policy dynamics: “Policy is not constructed in a vacuum; it is the result of the interaction of all these background factors... neither individual decision makers nor the nature of the system appears capable alone of explaining policy outcomes. Instead, policy emerges from the interaction of a large number of forces, many of which are beyond the control of decision makers.”

Concern about the impact of policy context on public policy was examined in the 1950-60s under the name of policy determination theory, and Dye (1998) suggested a very simple classification on the variation of policy determination theory. While economists claim that public policy as a government activity is closely related to the condition of economic resources in society, political scientists emphasise the direct bearing of the political system, particularly party competition and voter participation and institutions, on policy outputs.

In detail, political scientists have developed a ‘political competition model.’ While the model accepts that economic resources determine the level of party competition and voter participation, it emphasises that these political factors in turn determine public policy. The model emphasises the importance of political factors in producing policy outputs. Meanwhile, economists suggest an 'economic resource model' which proposes that economic development variables are more influential than political system characteristics in shaping policy outputs. Economic resources shape both political system characteristics and policy outputs, but characteristics of the political system have no direct effect on policy outputs (Dawson and Robinson, 1963).

Political scientists Cnudde and McCrone (1968) challenged the economic resource model by developing the so-called 'hybrid model'. Dye (1998: 308) explains the model: "... in this model economic resources shape public policy both directly and indirectly by affecting political factor, which in turn affect public policy. This model appears to be more appropriate for the study of welfare policy, which the conflict between haves and have-nots exist, than other fields of policy."

The policy determination perspective has greatly contributed to raising attention to the importance of policy context in studying public policy. However, it fails to describe the reciprocal relationship between policy context and policy outputs, by overstating the unilateral impact of policy context on policy outputs, and cannot properly illuminate the dynamic world of policy-making. It also tends to emphasise the constraints of economic factors on political system and policy outputs, ignoring their possible interactions.

The systems approach tries to revise the narrow focus of the policy determination perspective. Easton (1979) proposed an open systems model to emphasise the openness of political systems and the interactive relationship between context, political systems and outputs. Dye (1966) suggested a model for analysing public policy by introducing three variables:

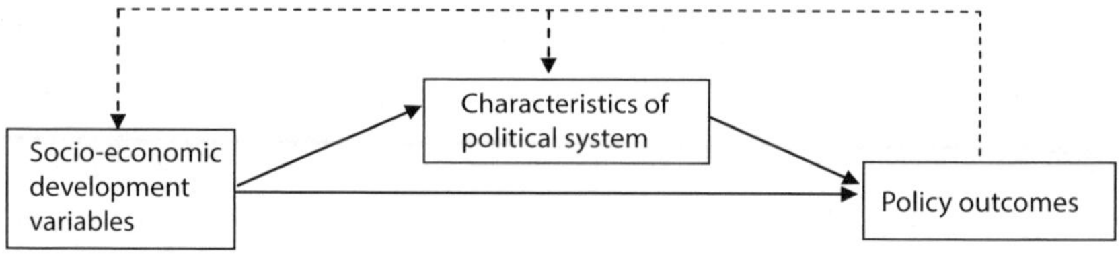

Figure 2.1 Dye's policy system model

socio-economic development variables, the characteristics of the political system and the policy outcomes (or outputs). Socio-economic variables function as an input - composed of demand and support factors that shape the political system, and in turn, the characteristics of the political system determine policy outcomes. To him, political system variables have important independent effects on policy outcomes by mediating socio-economic conditions and outcomes. On the other hand, socio-economic variables may affect public policy directly. Policy outcomes also have a reciprocal impact on both socio-economic condition and system characteristics in a feedback loop. Figure 2.1 shows Dye's (1966: 4) interactive policy system.

Currently, most policy scientists acknowledge the huge impact of policy context on the policy process and its outputs as well as their reciprocal interaction. Although researchers show differences in the specific variables of policy context and the degree of their impact on public policy, it is becoming the norm in policy studies that the policy process is occurring within the complicated realm of policy context (Hill, 2014: 12-15). Further, policy outputs are not unilaterally influenced by policy context and policy process. They can adversely affect each other in the form of a feedback loop.

2. Policy Process and Participants

Policy scientists are more interested in policy processes than policy substance. It is usual to divide policy processes into four larger categories including: agenda-setting, policy-making, policy implementation and policy evaluation. Figure 2.2 presents dynamics of policy process.[1]

Agenda-setting is the process of transforming social problems into government agendas to solve dynamic social issues. It includes following sub-stages: private problems, public problems, issues, systemic agendas and institutional agendas. According to Cobb and Elder (1983: 151-59), systemic agendas are "all issues that are commonly perceived by members of the political community as meriting public attention and as involving matters within the legitimate jurisdiction of existing governmental authority," whereas institutional agendas are defined as "those sets of items explicitly up for the active and serious consideration of authoritative decision makers."

Once policy ideas receive political endorsement they are fed into the system for detailed deliberation. The policy-making stage begins with the establishment of policy goals, which include several steps such as defining policy problems, setting priorities amongst policy goals, and specifying and amending these policy goals. The next step is to choose possible policy alternatives, even if they are not optimal. Finally, each policy alternative is compared and evaluated to select the most desirable alternative under given conditions. The policy-making process is very much a political, though not

1 Policy outputs mean the end result of policy making, whereas policy outcomes designate the result of policy implementation (Palumbo, 1994: 20).

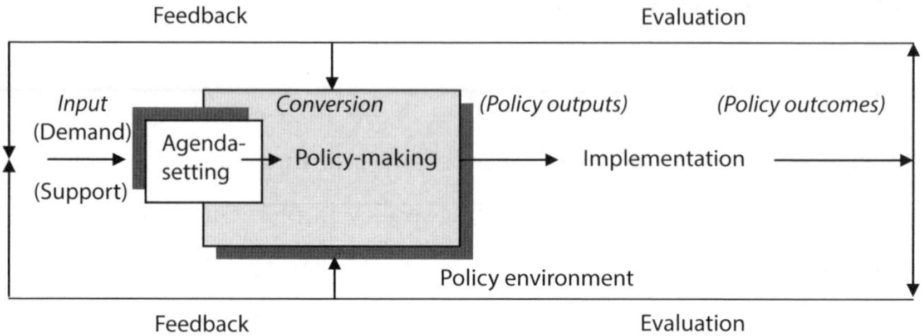

Figure 2.2 Dynamics of the policy process

necessarily a partisan, activity (Dorey, 2005: 12). Moreover, the implementation process is also political and unpredictable. Implementers do not mechanically carry out the policies decided by policy makers and the relationship between them is not unidirectional.

A number of political actors involve themselves in the policy process to articulate their interests. As policy problems become more complex, the policy process has become much more political and turbulent. With respect to the several types of policy actors, it seems appropriate to categorise them into official and unofficial policy actors, following Anderson's (2015) classification.[2]

In presidential democracies, official actors include the President and his/her staff, political appointees, public servants, Parliament and the judiciary. They have the official right to make and/or implement public policy.

2 Kingdon (2003) classifies policy actors into participants inside and outside government. While the former includes the President, presidential staff, political appointees, civil servants and Parliament, the latter consists of interest groups, academics, the media, election-related participants such as campaigners and political parties, and public opinion.

Meanwhile, unofficial actors consist of political parties, interest groups, the mass media, academics and policy analysts. They exert an influence on the policy process from outside the official policy arena (Dorey, 2005: 128).

Some unofficial actors who own valuable resources needed by official actors are more influential on the policy process, enabling them to be insider groups (Jones, 1998: 170), while the actors who do not have significant resources remain outsiders. But often, the boundary between official and unofficial actors is blurred, permitting many unofficial actors to formally participate in the policy process.

3. Institutions Matter: The New Institutional Perspective

Old-style institutionalism, as a formal-legal approach, was indifferent to informal aspects of politics, and its normative orientation obstructed any adoption of empirical methods in analysing political reality. It plainly described formal institutions, at best juxtaposing institutions in different countries, without any explanatory comparison. It also failed to develop intermediate-level categories linking individuals with the macro structure.

The behavioural revolution of the 1950s was a reaction against old institutionalism. In behaviourism, the property and behaviour of individuals are the main explanatory variables, and political results are regarded as the aggregation of individual actions (Blom-Hansen, 1997: 674). But it does not answer the question of why policies and behaviours differ from one country to another. The actor-centred approach obscures the intermediate institutions that structure politics.

On the contrary, new institutionalism tries to determine if differences indeed exist, and what differences they make with regard to the performance of the system. New institutionalists also focus on the institutional difference between advanced countries, to understand why similarly industrialised countries adopted different policy options in coping with the 1970s' economic crisis. They regard institutions as an independent variable, which is capable of explaining the different policy options in similarly industrialised countries. Their key notion is that institutions can shape both actors' objectives and the power distribution among them (Hudson and Lowe, 2004: 158).

New institutionalism emphasises the dynamic relationship between institutions as a research object and includes informal institutions like procedures, customs and culture, as well as formal legal institutions. With respect to research methods, new institutionalism seeks dynamic relations between institutions and policy options, contrary to the static description of the political phenomena in old institutionalism.

1) Institution: its meaning and dynamism

New institutionalists commonly believe institutions matter and explain the difference in policy options. Thus, institutions are historically formulated problem-solving mechanisms and the system of 'nested rules' designed to reduce costs associated with uncertainty (Goodin, 1996: 23). However, each discipline focuses on a different concept of institutions and picks out different characteristics as their defining features. Among them, the two most popular definitions are those made by March and Olsen (2006) and Hall (1986).

March and Olsen (2006) define institutions as "the rules of conduct in organisations, routines, and repertoires of procedures" and political institutions as "collections of interrelated rules and routines that define appropriate actions in terms of relations between roles and situations." Hall (1986) broadly defines institutions as "formal rules, compliance procedures, and standard operational procedures (SOP), which structure the relations between individuals at various levels of polity and economy." According to Hall, institutions include both formal organisations and informal rules and procedures.

Although institutions tend to be stable,[3] the process of their creation and change is very dynamic. Institutions change due to deliberate political strategy or gradual institutional evolution. In relation to the emergence of institutions, economists take institutions as given, or as something that can be easily created, as a result of an individual's rational and strategic choice. Meanwhile, political scientists tend to emphasise the asymmetric power relationship between actors, with institutions created by political coercion for long-term benefits. Sociologists, in the meantime, are concerned with the process of creating values and cognitive frameworks (Koelble, 1995: 232).

With regard to the change of institutions, economists contend that institutional change may occur when the existing institution fails to meet the requirements for which it was originally formed, and thus, goal-oriented individuals attempt to change it. Political scientists seem to be much better suited to explain the continuity of institutions than to explain institutional change. Institutional crisis, usually emanating from the changes in external

3 According to Ikenberry (1988), institutions are inclined to be stable because beneficiary groups do not want institutional change, so any acquired norms and values do not change easily, and organisational members stay with established institutions to preserve their tasks.

environment, causes the breakdown of old institutions, and precipitates intense conflict over shaping new institutions. Meanwhile, sociologists look at institutional change in a more functionalist way, with the notion that institutions must adapt to environmental changes, and attempt to mould their environment to meet their own needs, rather than passively responding to it (Powell and DiMaggio, 2012: 64-74).

2) Varieties of new institutionalism

New institutionalists are not a single cohesive unit, exhibiting sharp differences in terms of the meaning and role of institutions, according to their academic background. The most widely accepted classification is to divide into three broad categories: rational choice, historical and sociological institutionalism (Koelble, 1995: 231-45).[4]

Rational choice institutionalists in economics regard institutions as an aggregation of rules that shape individual behaviour. For them, an institution is an intervening variable capable of affecting an individual's choices, strategies and actions (Thelen and Steinmo, 1992: 7). They also assume the central role of individuals in the political process and emphasise individuals' intentions in the formation and operation of institutions. The principal reason why individuals create institutions is to reduce transaction costs and to facilitate exchange. They argue institutions are created on the basis of the nature of these incentives and constraints of the present (not the past), and

4 Meanwhile, Peters (2011) confirms six types of new institutionalism: normative, rational choice, historical, empirical, international, and societal institutionalism. Thelen and Steinmo (1992: 7) simply split new institutionalism into two types: rational choice and historical institutionalism.

regard preferences as exogenously given.

Historical institutionalism in political science stresses the historical context in which institutions are built. Krasner (1984) describes it as 'path dependency', depicting the constraints of past policy upon a following path; once actors make their initial policy and institutional choices, the patterns created will persist. They argue that preferences are formed by the institutional context within which they emerge. Hence, institutions play much greater roles in shaping choices than suggested by economists. For them, institutions are a crucial factor that formulates an actor's strategy and influences policy options (Béland, 2005: 3). Methodologically, they prefer a qualitative historical approach and this curtails the possibility of generalisation of research outcomes (Smith, 1993: 355).

Sociological institutionalism focuses on the way in which individuals' actions are 'embedded' within the context of collective institutions, and are therefore shaped by the institutional context in which they are set. It argues that individual decisions are affected not only by institutional setting, but also by a much larger frame of reference. Individuals are structurally embedded in social, economic and political relationships beyond their control. Unlike rational choice theorists, they believe individuals are not free to choose among institutions. As Koelble (1995: 232) asserts, "the quip that rational choice institutionalists attempt to show how people choose and sociological institutionalists try to show how people do not have choices to make still appears to hold true."

3) Limitations and implications

Despite revitalising the importance of institutions in analysing policy choice, new institutionalism also exhibits some limitations. First of all, it lacks consistency and concreteness in using the concept of institutions. Definitions are different in each discipline and even from scholars within the same discipline. It also fails to explain institutional change within the same country over time, despite its merits in explaining the stability and continuity of institutions and comparing the difference in policy options across countries (Béland, 2010: 617-19).

Economic explanations overemphasise the capacity of actors to create institutions and are excessively functional in explaining the creation and maintenance of institutions. However, historical institutionalism is ineffective in explaining institutional dynamics and lacks the development of systemic and general theories by overlooking the possibility of a universal model. Meanwhile, sociologists are too vague in defining the concept of an institution. Also, they belittle the choice of individuals in decision-making by rigidly holding onto the influence of institutional context, leading them to adopt a form of institutional determinism (Abrutyn and Turner, 2011: 289-292).

New institutionalism, nevertheless, has advantages in connecting an actor-centred microanalysis with a structure-centred macro one, by delving into institutional arrangements that intermediate between them. Institutions constrain the preferences, behaviours and choices of policy actors in several ways (Sitek, 2010: 574). Accordingly, this book puts a great deal of emphasis on the fusion of new institutionalism with the concept of policy networks in order to create a more solid analytical framework. By regarding the institution as an independent variable constraining behaviours, new institutionalism provides researchers with valuable knowledge about the relationship between institutions and policy networks and their combined impact on policy outputs.

Of the several strains of new institutionalism, the notion of 'path dependency' in historical institutionalism and the idea of the institution-actor interaction in rational choice institutionalism may be useful for providing the analytical framework that captures the dynamics of health policy-making and outputs. Yet, concepts developed by sociological institutionalism are too broad and abstract to apply to empirical research in this book. Thus, this book will attempt to interpret the constraint of previous policies on current policy networks and their resultant outputs, by borrowing ideas from historical institutionalists and rational choice institutionalism may be beneficial for analysing the motives and preferences of policy actors and understanding the dynamism of policy choices.

4. Policy-making Structure and Interaction: The Policy Network Perspective

The policy network perspective, a confluence of two research traditions of network analysis in sociology and policy analysis in political science, is derived from the notion of sub-government in America and the idea of policy community in Britain (Smith, 1993: 57). The emergence of the network idea, since the 1970s, has been an inevitable response to changes in political realities. The increased participation of competing actors in the policy process has led to 'over-crowded policy-making,' and has blurred boundaries between public and private sectors. To cope with the growing importance of information and the complexity of government affairs, the necessity of inter-dependence between the state and private actors has become apparent.

Lowi's (1969) concept of sub-government is a criticism of the pluralist view on decision-making and power distribution. He regards sub-government as "a coalition of interest groups, public administrators and members of Congress serving on relevant committees that control the administration of public policy for the benefit of those within the sub-government." The most well known label of sub-government is the 'iron triangle' which emphasises the closed terrains of the policy-making system consisted of government departments, parliamentary standing committees and relevant recognised interest groups. In contrast, Heclo (1978: 88), an American pluralist, asserts, "fairly open networks have replaced the closed circles of control." His issue networks imply a loose and larger collection of players whose impact depends on both what and who they know (Hague and Harrop, 2001: 158).[5] In issue networks the power of interest groups varies by topic, depending on their expertise.

German and Dutch scholars view policy networks as a new form of governance, in contrast to the hierarchy and market. For them, policy networks involve a loose structural coupling and an interaction between autonomous actors that produce a negotiated consensus (Marsh, 1998a: 8).[6]

However, the concept of policy networks has been systematised more in Britain than in any other country. It has become one of the more dominant approaches for policy-making studies in Britain, as an alternative model of interest intermediation to pluralism and corporatism. Richardson

5 McFarland (1987: 146) defines an issue network as "a communications network of those in policy in some area, including government authorities, legislators, businessmen, lobbyists, and even academics and journalists…"

6 Börzel (1998) distinguishes the policy network as a typology of interest intermediation (policy network) from the policy network as a specific form of governance (network governance).

and Jordan (1979: 74) emphasise the disaggregated nature of government and the fragmentation of society by adopting a policy community idea. To them, "the policy making map is in reality a series of vertical compartments or segments — each segment inhabited by a different set of organised groups and generally impenetrable by unrecognised groups or by the general public." Policy networks can exist either at a sectoral or sub-sectoral level, affecting policy outputs. Marsh (1998b: 194) also examines the dialectic relationship between network structure and interaction, and between policy networks and policy outputs.

1) Policy networks: meaning and dynamism

Even though there are many different definitions of policy networks, the concept of policy networks can be applied to all kinds of relationships between public and private sectors (Groenendijk, 2001: 18).[7] A policy network idea is characterised by a mixture of public and private actors who work together to overcome formal differences.[8] All participants connect with each other to work together as a system. Actors within policy networks depend

7 For example, Kickert et al. (1997: 6) define the policy network as "(more or less) stable patterns of social relations between interdependent actors, which take shape around policy problems and/or policy programmes." Börzel (1998: 254) describes policy network as "a set of relatively stable, non-hierarchical and interdependent relationships linking a variety of actors who share common interests with regard to a policy and who exchange resources to pursue these interests…" Meanwhile, Rhodes (1997) sees inter-dependence, a continuous exchange of resources, autonomy and game-like interactions as the four core characteristics of policy network (Hudson and Lowe, 2004: 130).

8 Williams (2004: 97) contends: "Policy networks consist of a variety of public, private and societal actors that converge around a particular policy issue…They often consist of several sub-groups of actors or advocacy coalitions. Each shares a common set of normative core values or beliefs."

on one another for resources such as information, expertise, access and legitimacy. A relationship of mutual support is necessary "in the case that any one actor does not possess sufficient resources to act alone (Smith, 1993: 58)."

Albeit taking into account any discrepancies about the usefulness of the policy network idea,[9] the majority of network theorists see the idea as an alternative or superior notion to pluralism and corporatism with regard to the state-interest group relation. When compared to traditional perspectives, policy networks clearly have a number of advantages, as it is much more flexible and comprehensive and is capable of accounting for variations in state-interest group relations.

Methodologically, a multi-level theoretic approach is necessary for an adequate understanding of policy networks. The policy network, as a meso-level concept on the relationship between policy actors, is closely connected to the broader macro context, like power distributions in society. Micro-level interpersonal relations within policy networks should also be included in analysis.

Policy networks change according to their composition and external environment. Therefore, Enroth (2011) emphasises the necessity to adopt a dynamic approach to review any network change, looking at the origin, development and termination of policy networks. The causes of network change are various and complex, and the durability of policy networks against the pressure for change differs depending on the nature of policy networks. Tight policy communities are more resistant to change than open issue networks (Marsh et al., 2001: 190).

9 Particularly, Dowding (1995) asserts the concept of policy networks has no theoretical basis and explanatory power, because they are merely used as a heuristic device or a metaphor.

Changes in international relations are one of the primary causes of network change. Economic and social changes also affect actors' relationships and induce network change. Value change, for instance, creates new policy issues such as peace, environment and sexual equality. Governmental change and a subsequent change of political ideas are another important source of network change. The Thatcher years in Britain witnessed the collapse of the existing policy networks, excluding trade unions from the policy-making process (Coxall, 2001: 70).

The growth of new technology or knowledge also creates new interest groups, and thus changes the constituent units of policy networks. For example, with new technology in agricultural policy, the stable agricultural community faces competition from new environment, animal welfare and consumer groups (Smith, 1995: 89). Individual actors can also initiate network change. In particular, government actors ultimately determine the rules of the game and are able to break up policy networks.

2) Two contrasting types of policy network

Of the many different classifications of policy network types, the most frequently quoted classification is derived from Marsh and Rhode's (1992) simple categorisation into policy community and issue network, identifying them as opposites. To them, the two types function as an ideal type and help in the process of analysing and comparing the reality of interest intermediation. Smith (1993: 65) writes: "It is a seldom case that networks will exist which conforms to all dimensions mentioned in two types."

Policy communities have a limited number of participants with some groups consciously excluded. There are game rules that actors have to abide by in order to gain entry to policy communities (Cope, 2001: 8). Usually economic and/or professional interests constitute well-established insider groups and dominate policy-making. There are frequent and high quality interactions between members on all policy issues. Its membership, values and policy outputs tend to persist over time. Participants share broad policy preferences and accept the legitimacy of the outputs.[10] They possess resources so the relationship between them is one of exchange, and the basic interaction is a bargaining mechanism between members (Hill, 2014: 69).

In general, policy communities develop where "governmental actors want to achieve particular goals, and need to create the means to achieve their goals" (Smith, 1993: 225), because they are advantageous to the government. They make the policy process predictable and enable the government to smoothly implement policy. Policy communities also tend to have a core (primary) community and periphery (secondary) one. But policy communities may downgrade the quality of the decision-making process, owing to limited participants. Also, they may obstruct policy change by excluding critical or disagreeing actors (Dorey, 2005: 133).

In contrast, issue networks consist of a large number of participants. There is no intended exclusion of particular groups from the networks.[11] As Heclo (1978: 102) points out, issue networks comprise "a large number of participants with quite variable degrees of mutual commitment or of

10 The notion of policy communities does not imply that there are no conflicts between community members. Heclo and Wildavsky (1974: 15) note: "Community refers to the personal relationships between major political and administrative actors — sometimes in conflict, often in agreement, but always in touch and operating within a shared framework."

11 But issue networks are not completely open because participants must have some interest in the area, a minimum degree of knowledge, and minimal resources to exchange (Smith, 1993: 64).

dependence on others in their environment, and participants move in and out of networks constantly." The contacts between participants fluctuate in frequency and intensity, and access to the networks varies significantly. New actors are constantly entering and leaving the policy arena (Cope, 2001: 7).

It is usual to disagree over the nature of policy problems and available solutions between actors. Many access points and a large number of decision-making centres make it difficult to establish a consensus. In the areas where issue networks develop, there are conflicts over policy direction and no clear policy goals, leading to unpredictable policy outputs (Fawcett and Daugbjerg, 2012: 201-206).

3) Limitations and implications

The policy network idea is a useful meso-level framework to explain the relationship between diverse kinds of policy actors. It helps researchers to understand not only formal institutional arrangements, but also the highly complex informal relationships in the policy process. But despite its strengths, the policy network perspective also has several limitations. Above all else, there is too high a degree of confusion in using and defining the concepts. Although Rhodes (1990: 311) suggests that "definitional problems should be left aside and attention turns to matters of substance," the basic agreement on the main concepts is a necessary step to start research.

It is also undeniable that there are serious shortcomings where policy network ideas try to explain policy outputs and policy change, despite its strength in describing policy networks per se. In addition, the usefulness of network analysis for policy study has been questioned because some political relationships are merely symbolic. Sometimes the considerable effort spent collecting and analysing data yield very little result (John and Cole, 1998: 137).

This book presents a policy network perspective by bringing together network structure and interaction. Both structural arrangements and policy actors' interaction patterns are considered in anatomising policy networks. This book also explores the practical utility of the policy network perspective for analysing policy-making dynamics. It is asserted that the perspective has explanatory power in explaining differences in policy outputs, in line with recent significant findings of Marsh (1998b: 186).

5. Linking the Two Theoretical Perspectives

Limitations in traditional theories in examining the dynamic realities of policymaking have led to a new approach to be taken in this book. Specifically, two theories of new institutionalism and policy network perspectives are utilised. Up to now, neo-Marxist views have been popular in the field of political science, but they fail to fully analyse the role of the state, largely due to their propensity to seek answers in class orientation. They also restrict policy debates to the relationship between the state and an economic ruling class, emphasising the homogeneity of their interests. Therefore, they cannot explain the diversity of policy interests and the multiple roles of the state in the policy process. Neo-Weberians mainly focus on the capacity of state bureaucracy, neglecting the vital roles of other possible actors in policy-making. They also overstress the state bureaucrats' monopoly of policy-making power, and thus, fail to understand the importance of relationships between policy actors (Nordlinger, 1987: 371).

Both pluralists and corporatists have focused on the state-interest group relationships in policy-making, suggesting the middle-range paradigm on the system of interest intermediation. But pluralists put too much stress on the free competition between interest groups, mainly by emphasising the neutral role of the state (Hill, 2003: 168). In contrast, corporatists emphasise the active role of the state, and depict the stable relationship between the state and particular interests in policy-making (Minnich, 2003: 28). But corporatists also fail to adequately explain the diverse types of relationships, and overstress the state as a planner of the entire system of interest intermediation. No serious roles for Parliament, political parties and the mass media are expected in corporatism. Both pluralism and corporatism lack comprehensiveness and flexibility as theoretical frameworks to analyse the dynamic, political and complicated reality of policy-making. Also, while corporatism has strengths in examining structural relationship among policy actors and pluralism is useful to analyse behavioural aspects, neither consider both aspects together.

In contrast, new institutionalism has distinctive advantages in explaining the stability and continuity of institutions and in comparing the differences of policy options among countries. Of its three strains, the rational choice school explains the origin and preservation of institutions with the notion of utility maximisation by the individual actors. Historical institutionalism evaluates the role of preceding institutions as a constraint on actors' contemporary behaviours and on current institutions (Béland, 2005: 3), while sociological institutionalists accentuate the broad institutional context and its constraint on actors' behavioural patterns. In general, new institutionalism provides a useful way of examining the constraining power of institutions on policy-making and policy choices. From this perspective, researchers can understand how differences in institutions generate the differences in policy outputs and how previous decisions constrain options available to policy actors. New institutionalism also explains well the stability of the policy-making system and the incremental changes in policies (Skocpol, 1995: 103-6).

But new institutionalism alone cannot clarify the interaction of policy actors and the possible impact of key actors on institutional change and policy outputs. The dynamics among institutions, actors and policies can be more adequately examined by combining the new institutional perspective with the policy network one. The intentional explanation of rational choice institutionalism, however, over-emphasises actors' capacities to create institutions and overlooks the possibility of an unbalanced power relation on the creation of institutions. Meanwhile, historical institutionalism is ineffective in explaining institutional dynamics, although it does satisfactorily describe institutional stability and policy continuity through the concept of path dependency (Sitek, 2010: 573). It also insufficiently anatomises the causal relationship between institutions and policy choices as it lacks microanalysis on individual behaviour. Sociological institutionalism is too vague in defining the concept of institutions to apply to reality.

The policy network perspective has advantages compared to other approaches. Firstly, it helps researchers to understand not only formal features but also highly complex informal actions in the policy process. Also, shared decision-making between public and private actors and the way in which actors exchange resources to achieve their goals can be examined. The perspective, furthermore, enables a more flexible adaptation of the theoretical framework to the reality of policy-making, by comprising several subtypes under the same label. It does not assume the pre-defined relational patterns of actors and their roles, giving it particular strength in describing reality as it is. Its nature of comprehensiveness and flexibility as a theoretical approach enables researchers to take into account diverse actors, such as civic groups, political parties and unorganised interests. It also renders both cross-sectional and longitudinal comparisons possible (Hudson and Lowe, 2004: 132-34).

But the policy network idea also has weak points, and other more coherent theoretical frameworks should reinforce it. For instance, policy networks struggle to explain casual relations between variables despite its ability to describe reality (Marsh and Rhodes, 1992: 260). It also does not adequately relate the differences in policy networks with influencing policy context. Its indifference to the constraining nature of institutions on policy networks is also criticised.

Thus, in order to grasp the dynamic nature of policy-making and outputs, it is imperative to blend several versions of new institutionalism and to link them together with the policy network perspective.[12] Frequently, an eclectic approach is more useful for social science than the strict adherence to a single approach. As Koelble (1995: 243) points out, "each theoretical lens has its advantages and disadvantages; each may be criticised as faulty from the perspective of the other approaches, but each also has a set of features superior to its competitors, depending on the research questions."

New institutional and policy network perspectives are arguably complementary to each other, sharing common ideas. For instance, the concept

12 Béland (2005: 4) remarks; "Even such a flexible vision of institutional patterns cannot allow historical institutionalism to explain fully the specific content of key political decisions that shape social policy outcomes."

of transaction costs, which is a key term in rational choice institutionalism (Goodin, 1996: 9), is also adaptable to the policy network perspective. By making and/or entering policy networks, participants can reduce transaction cost and stabilise their relationship. Interest groups save the cost of making repeated efforts to gain access, while the government spares the cost of information collection and the effort to acquire assistance. According to the idea of path dependency in historical institutionalism, interests in policy networks are influenced by history, which in turn is important in shaping policy networks and policy choices (Ham, 1999: 5)

By linking new institutionalism with policy network perspectives, this attempts to examine the relationship between institutions and the politics within policy networks and analyses how institutions constrain the strategies and choices of participants working in these policy networks. By drawing on the institutional perspective, which emphasises the intermediate role of institutions between individual actors and the political context, the policy network perspective can relate the macro framework with the micro interactions among participants. As a meso-level perspective on the relationship between policy actors, the policy network perspective should be combined with both macro- and micro-level perspectives to be useful as an explanatory tool. Particularly, a more complete depiction of policy-making is possible by combining the policy network perspective with microanalysis on the behaviour of individual actors (Blom-Hansen, 1997: 673).

The ideas developed by historical institutionalism, one of the three disciplines of new institutionalism, will largely contribute to the formation of the analytical framework. The institutions in historical institutionalism mainly operate as constraints on policy networks, particularly in terms of network structure. The established policies, nested interests, political institutions, decision-making rules, and power relationships can all constrain policy networks and policy outputs. But the constraints of institutions are not unidirectional and deterministic, as policy actors can respond or interpret them differently, according to their peculiar knowledge, experiences, interests and preferences (Hudson and Lowe, 2004: 132-39). Thus, historical institutionalism has to be combined with rational choice institutionalism and the policy network perspective if it is to depict the dynamism of policy-making adequately.

Meanwhile, rational choice institutionalism can be combined with the interaction patterns within policy networks. Its creative ideas can provide useful insights in exploring the variables of network interaction and interpreting realities upon which they are based. In nature, rational choice institutionalism emphasises the rational calculation of individual actors, aiming to maximise their self-interests, in making institutions and selecting policies (Oliver and Mossialos, 2005: 16-18). But, unlike the propositions of rational choice institutionalism, policy actors cannot always pursue rational calculations, as they are forced to consider the political situation and power relationships. In many cases, the policy-making process becomes more political rather than rational or economic (Dorey, 2005: 12-14). Also, institutions are not easily altered; informal or custom-based rules, in particular, tend to persist. Thus, rational choice institutionalism by itself has limitations in explaining policy-making dynamics, and needs to be combined with the policy network perspective and the other disciplines of new institutionalism.

6. Analytical Framework: Institutions, Policy Networks and Policy Outputs

1) Policy context

This book constructs the analytical framework from a process-driven but inter-related point of view, by combining the following four components — policy context, institutional features, policy networks and policy outputs — in order to examine the health politics of Korea. To begin with, the influence of the policy context on policy-making and outputs is commonly acknowledged in public policy studies. As mentioned previously, policy is not made in a vacuum. It is constructed and implemented under the context of distinctive environment. Policy context is the broader political, social, cultural and economic environments, which constrain or enable participants' actions. Historically, social scientists emphasised the unidirectional impact of policy context on policy-making and outputs. But nowadays, as Anderson (2015) contends, it is common to suggest the interactive relationship between policy context and policy-making.

In this book, the policy context denotes the environmental factors that affect the attributes and types of institutional features and policy networks, and again policy outputs. This book introduces political and social contexts as the components by drawing extensively from preceding studies (Lipson et al., 1995; Dye, 1998; Cochran et al., 2003; Dorey, 2005; Anderson, 2015). Amongst these accepted components, however, the economic context has been excluded, owing to the non-economic nature of the case studies analysed in this book. With regard to the political context, political ideology, political power and leadership are all important elements. The international political context is also influential in an era of globalisation. From these facets this book selects governing ideology, political events, politics and political leadership styles as the main variables of political context, in order to make the concept easier to adopt.[13]

This book explores ideologies of governments which guide the direction of policies over a specific time. Ideology serves as a constraint in choosing policy options, and affects the scope of policy network participants and policy-making patterns.

Political events, such as presidential and parliamentary elections, the emergence of new political leadership and military coups, bring about changes to existing institutions and policy networks (Rushefsky and Patel, 1998: 21). The attributes of politics and political leadership styles are mainly related to the work of politics and the ways political leaders are selected. If politics is managed in an open and democratic way and political leaders are selected through competition, policy networks are inclined to be more open and institutions also have a chance to be more democratic.

Meanwhile, the social context and the function of civil society are counted as a demand side of policy (Cochran et al., 2003: 13). Strong civic groups and powerful trade unions may open up policy networks more widely and contribute to the shaping of institutions. The following are the variables and indicators used to examine the policy context:

13 Among the researchers who have examined Korean policy-making, Lee J. (2000) introduced variables such as changes in policy actors, political power, and political events in analysing political context. While Lee H. (2000) referred power distribution between the ruling and oppositional parties, elections, and international factors as variables of political context, Kang (2002) listed political ideologies and political power structure as political factors. Meanwhile, Shin (2004) emphasised political system, party competition, and election cycle as political context variables.

- Political context
  - Governing ideology: stated national goal
  - Political events: emergence of new leadership and existence of particular political events
  - Politics and political leadership styles: democratic/competitive vs. authoritarian/ non-competitive
- Social context
  - Vitality of civil society: activity of civic groups and trade unions

2) Institutional features

Hall (1986) defines institutions as "formal rules, compliance procedures, and standard operational procedure (SOP), which structure the relation between individuals." As a set of rules, institutions are relatively stable and structured naturally. Institutions influence policy networks as they constrain the structure and interaction patterns of policy networks. Differences in institutions can explain a considerable amount of the difference in policy network characteristics. Blom-Hansen (1997: 669) states the necessity of new institutionalism in the analysis of policy networks in a following way:

> Policy network analysis must incorporate an explicit model of the actor if the concept is to enable the analyst to move beyond mere description and into the more interesting field of policy explanations. To this end, the use of new institutionalism is proposed.

But, of the three strains of new institutionalism, combining sociological institutionalism with the policy network perspective is generally difficult.

The concept of the institution in sociological institutionalism is too broad and vague to be utilised in analysing the reality of policy-making. Also, sociological institutionalism over-emphasises the institutional constraints on actors' behaviour and thus preventing a proper understanding of the interaction between them.

This book therefore mainly draws on historical and rational choice institutionalism in combining the institutional concept with the policy network idea. Together, ideas of constraints produced by path dependency and actor-centered rational choice are combined to form the new institutional perspective which provides us with a useful tool in capturing the interaction between institutions and policy networks (Lowndes, 2009: 95-101). Historical institutionalism, which emphasises the continuity and path dependency of institution, is helpful in exploring the influence of institution on the interaction patterns within policy networks and tracing the impact of previous decisions. It explains why it is difficult to change the established structures of policy networks and the privileged policies of a certain group of participants (Wilsford, 2010: 668-70).

In contrast, rational choice institutionalism is mainly beneficial in explaining the impact of actors' motivation on making and changing policy networks and in depicting how the actors' interactions in policy networks generate changes in institutions. It is also useful in exploring the change of institutions and policy networks per se. Rational choice institutionalism can provide insights into the policy-making process in a dynamic society, like Korea, where actors' roles are more important than the established rules. It is also useful to examine the preferences and strategies of network participants.

On the concept and scope of institutions, Ikenberry (1988) argues that the range of institutions extends from the specific features of government institutions to the more overarching structures of the state, and to the nation's normative social order. Ikenberry's narrowest definition of institutions refers to legal, administrative and regulative rules mediating the conflict between policy actors, whereas the middle level definition connotes the concentration and diffusion of power within the state. The broadest meaning of institutions describes the norm related to a belief system and defines the relationship between the state and civil society. However, almost all institutionalists are ambiguous in defining the concept and scope of institutions. Accordingly, it is necessary to specify the concept and scope of institutions if one is seeking to adapt the idea to an analysis of policy-making (Peters, 2011: 28).

New institutionalists include both formal aspects — such as constitutional rules, government organisation and formal ways of conduct — and informal game rules, routines and procedures within the concept of institutions. Institutions can be both unwritten codes of conduct, which underlie formal rules, and formally written rules (March and Olsen, 2006: 21-26). But the broad and abstract understanding of the concept and scope of institutions give rise to difficulties in adapting an institutional idea to a real-life situation.

Referring to earlier studies covering the concept and scope of institutions,[14] this book classifies institutions into four categories: i) institutionalised power relations between the state's political organisations; ii)

14 As an example, Hudson and Lowe (2004) include following components into institutions: election rules and voting systems; party systems and structures; relations between branches of government; structure and organisation of key economic or interests groups; and welfare state agencies and delivery systems.

institutional properties of political system regarding to governing, political party and election systems; iii) the rules on decision-making and conflict resolution, and iv) previously established policies that regulate current policy-making and options. According to Hall (1992),[15] the institutionalised power relationship corresponds to middle level institutions, "which are concerned with particular characters of political economy and basic organisational structure of the state and society in each country." Middle level institutions influence the power relationship between individuals and groups in society and can explain the differences in policy options in each country. The structure of trade unions, the organised pattern of capital, the relationship with international economy and the nature of the political party system are included in this level of institutions. Decision-making rules fall under lower level institutions or micro-level definitions, which refer to standard operational procedure and rules, whether are formal or informal. The following suggest the variables and working indices this book employs to anatomise institutional features.

- Power relationship between the state's political organisations
  - Relative power distribution between main political organisations
- Institutional properties of political system: governing, party and election systems
  - Formal institutions on governing, political party and election systems and their practical operation

15 Amongst the three levels of institutions classified by Hall (1992), the upper level institutions as 'the basic organisational structure related to democracy and capitalism' include constitutional provisions on elections and economic institutions prescribing the private ownership of productive means. It is a broader structural constraint framing policy directions.

- Rules on decision-making and conflict resolution
  - Formal rules on decision-making and conflict resolution in Parliament and government, and their practical operation
- Previous policies or programs
  - Influence of established policies or programs on the current policy debate and policy-making

3) Policy networks

This book assumes that the nature of policy networks explains a larger part of the differences in policy outputs. But a policy network concept alone cannot explain constraints that operate outside policy networks. Here, institutional factors must be taken into account when explaining the interaction in policy networks. The behaviour and choices of various policy actors are quite often constrained by institutions (Jordana and Sancho, 2005: 522).

Some researchers include almost all of the theoretical models of interest intermediation within the policy network perspective. But, of the various network types, this book prefers two ideal types of policy community and issue network, which were suggested by Marsh and Rhodes (1992). By using this simplified classification, it is possible to situate policy networks on the continuum between the two network types and compare the changing patterns of policy networks. Moreover, Smith (1993) divides policy communities into the core community that determines a community's membership and goal, and the periphery community, which lacks the required resources. This book also realises that different policy networks are not mutually exclusive in the same policy agenda (Bulkeley, 2000: 729), as shown in Figure 2.3.

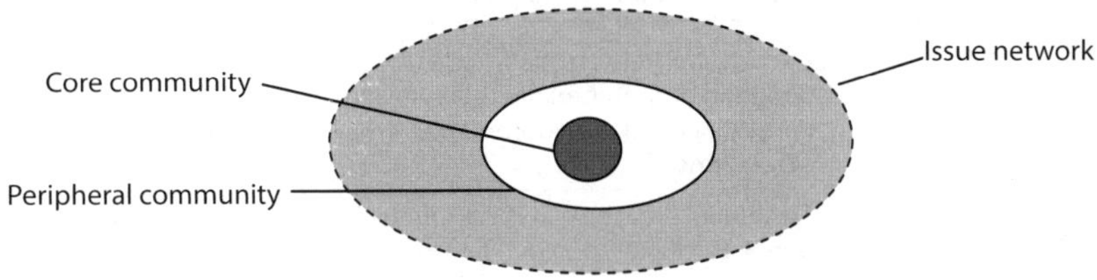

Figure 2.3 Tiered policy networks

Marsh (1998b) divides the policy network into network structure and network activity, even though the distinction is relatively blurred along the continuum of continuity, repetition, predictability and stability. In general, if the exchanges and transactions between actors are repeated and institutionalised, they may turn into a network structure (Waarden, 1992: 31). Thus, the structure is more stable, continuous and predictable with regard to the activities of actors (see Figure 2.4). Additionally, Marsh (1995) emphasises the dialectical relationship between structure and actors. While structure shapes and facilitates actors' preferences, it does not mechanically constrain or enable actors, because actors are capable of interpreting and restructuring structural constraints.

To prescribe the nature and type of policy networks, researchers need to develop variables and indicators based, in part, on previous studies. Table

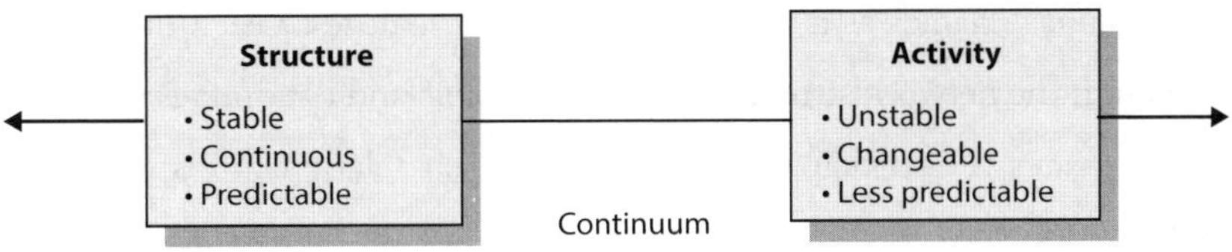

Figure 2.4 The continuum of structure and activity in policy networks

Table 2.1 Dimensions or variables for analysing policy networks

Analysts	Selected variables
Collins (1995)	Boundaries, membership types, linkage pattern, intensity and density of relations, coordination types, centrality, stability, nature of relations
Cope (2001)	Continuity (or instability), membership (limited vs. wide and open), resources, power balance
Daugbjerg (1998)	Membership, integration, institutionalisation
Döhler (1991)	Network structure, actors and coalitions, governance structure, patterns of interaction, strategic selectivity of networks
Jordan and Schubert (1992)	Level of institutionalisation, scope of policy-making arrangement, number of participants
Knoke et al. (1996)	Policy domain, policy actors, policy interests, power relations, collective actions, policy outcomes
Marsh and Rhodes (1992)	Membership, integration, resources, power
Montpetit (2005)	Multiplicity of networks, capacity distribution, interconnection, cohesion
Rhodes (1988)	Constellation of stable interests, membership, vertical independence, horizontal independence, resource distribution
Ripley and Franklin (1991)	Actors, relationships between actors, stability of relationships, the degree of influence
Yishai (1992)	Exclusion of networks, dependence between actors
Waarden (1992)	Actors, function, structure, institutionalisation, rules of conduct, power relations, actor strategies

2.1 shows variables which appear in previous studies.

Referring to the previous remarks on policy network variables, this book separates the policy network, at first, into two broad dimensions of network structure and participants' interactions, and then introduces several component variables as a way of reviewing the nature of each dimension. Although the network structure has a more stable and continuous character and regulates the participants' interactions, their relationship is reciprocal and dialectical.

The first dimension, the network structure, is related to fundamental features of the making and maintaining of policy networks. On the one hand, network structure is affected by the policy context and institutional features, but on the other, it influences the patterns of participants' interaction and the resultant outputs of policy (Jordana and Sancho, 2005: 521). This book shapes network structure with variables that reflect the nature of participants, their interests in the issue, and resource dependency between them.

Network membership refers to the number of participants, who dominates and those who are consciously excluded from policy networks. On the number of participants, a very limited number of actors will be accepted to enter a policy arena in closed policy communities, whereas in open issue networks a larger number of actors can enter freely (Grant, 2000: 50). The type of dominant actors refers to which participants play a leading role in making and maintaining policy networks. It is held that economic and professional interests dominate policy communities, whereas issue networks encompass a wide range of related interests. But in most cases, the resource distribution between the government and other actors is asymmetric, since the government monopolises legitimacy and regulatory power. The exclusion of membership depends on the existence of barriers to entry to policy networks for particular actors. While policy communities might exclude those who flout game rules, issue networks includes all affected actors, irrespective of their characteristics (Richardson, 2000: 2-3).

Participants' interests in the issue are fundamental in forming policy networks (Börzel, 1998: 254). In closely knitted policy networks, participants share a large amount of interest, making policy networks stable and their relationships intimate. But, a degree of interest sharing is generally very low in loosely coupled networks. This book intends to measure this variable by investigating the stated and practical objectives of each network participant.

Resource dependency is important because the relationship in policy networks is generated from the need to exchange resources (Bomberg, 1998: 168). This is affected by resource distribution, and is intimately related to the power relationship, which is a function of the positions occupied by network participants. If the degree of resource dependency is great, policy networks will be more of a closed type. This book confirms, initially, the amount of resources each participant possesses, and then goes on to evaluate the relative importance of these resources with regard to each of the case studies. Finally, the degree of resource dependency is analogised by examining the resources each participant needs and the mutual dependence of resources.

The second dimension, the interaction between participants, refers to the operational aspect of policy networks. It is unstable when compared to the nature of network structure, and is also constrained by network structure. However, they are not determined by the structure unilaterally because participants can selectively accept the influence of the network structure. So, the three variables included in this dimension are: the basic nature of interaction, the frequency of interaction and the participants' mobilised strategies.

Regarding the nature of interaction, the participants' co-sharing of values and interests is high in policy communities, and this makes the basic interaction in policy communities consensus-oriented. In contrast, the conflictual relationships between participants are constantly witnessed in issue networks (Daugbjerg, 1998: 44).

On the frequency of interaction, policy communities have frequent and high quality interaction between its players, but the interaction between actors in issue networks fluctuates in terms of its frequency and intensity

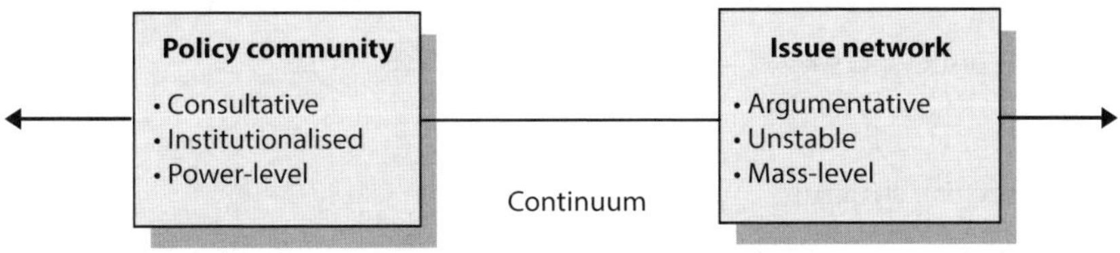

Figure 2.5 Participants' strategies on the continuum of the two network types

(Cope, 2001: 8-9). This book measures the frequency of interaction by confirming the existence and type of communication channels and the process of coalition building between participants.

The strategies adopted by network participants are a crucial element affecting the attributes of policy networks and policy outputs.[16] Participants make strategic judgements in light of their subjective perceptions of the costs and benefits involved. Participants adopt diverse strategies to maximise their preferences and to reach the choices they prefer. It is possible, therefore, to situate the mode of participants' strategies on the continuum of consultative versus argumentative, institutional versus unstable, and towards power-level versus mass-level activities, largely by referring to the mode of interest inputs, which have been mainly developed by pluralists. Generally, participants in policy communities adopt this strategy while participants in issue networks confront each other (Grant, 2000: 50). Figure 2.5 contrasts participants' strategies of the two different types of policy networks.

16 According to Kickert et al. (1997: 184), "The concept of strategy means that actors attempt to influence the collective action. Strategies and the underlying goals are not fixed and unchangeable. Goals and strategies develop over time due to interactions and to the strategies and goals of other actors and due to learning processes in interaction."

The following outlines the dimensions and variables that portray the nature of policy networks.

- Network structure
  - Nature of participants (number, dominant actors and exclusion)
    - ¤ Change in number of participants and dominant actors in policy-making
    - ¤ Intentional exclusion of particular actors
  - Participants' interests in the issue
    - ¤ Each participant's stated and practical interests in the issue
  - Resource dependency between participants
    - ¤ Each participant's resource to exchange and the degree of resource dependency between participants
- Participants' interaction
  - Basic nature of interaction
    - ¤ Nature of relationship between participants (consensual vs. conflictual)
  - Frequency of interaction
    - ¤ Frequency of relatively-patterned interaction between participants
  - Mobilised strategies of interaction
    - ¤ Properties of interaction strategies between participants (consultative, institutionalised, power-level vs. argumentative, unstable, mass-level)

4) Policy outputs and feedback

In theory, policy outputs are different from policy outcomes, although many scholars conflate the two. While policy outputs are the end result of policy-making, policy outcomes are related to policy implementation. Cochran et al. (2003: 9) regards both policy outputs and policy impact as a result of implementation; "policy outputs are tangible manifestation of policies, the observable and measurable results of policy adoption and implementation." Meanwhile, "policy impacts are the effects that policy outputs have on society". In nature new institutionalism regards policy outputs as a dependent variable of institutions by postulating that the varying institutions generate differences in terms of policy outputs. The policy network perspective also tries to link with policy outputs in an explanatory sense.

Although policy networks do not determine policy outputs, they privilege certain interests and shape policy outputs. Differences in network types cause different policy outputs. The existence of closed policy networks is more likely to result in policy continuity, preserving the intended policy goals and protecting the interests of community members, because participants have a common ideology and a similar policy preference. Conversely, policy outputs in issue networks are likely to be more varied, reflecting constantly changing policies (Hudson and Lowe, 2004: 133-34).

Of the network theorists, Marsh and Rhodes (1992) adopt a structural explanation, emphasising the impact of network structure on policy outputs while an intentional explanation contends that network structure per se has no influence on policy outputs. But as mentioned above, this book regards the policy network as a complex entity, which comprises both aspects of the network structure and actors' interactions. They interact with each other and affect policy outputs together.

In the open system policy outputs are fed back to preceding variables: policy outputs affect policy networks in the manner of reformulating them. In this regard policy outputs are both a dependent and independent variable. In theory, they can destroy existing policy networks and exclude some participants from these networks.

Employing two variables will be sufficient to show how differences in policy networks generate differences in terms of policy outputs. Firstly, the originally intended policies are compared with the final policy outputs to measure the change of policy content as a result of policy-making. The differences between intended and final contents of policies tend to be small whenever the government has strong power and the network is made up of tight policy communities (Bulkeley, 2000: 729).

The second variable to estimate is a measure of those whose interest are reflected in final policy outputs. It is hypothesised that policy actors who have key resources will be more valued in outputs. In policy communities, members' interests will be reflected more in policy outputs, excluding those of intermittent participants. Out of policy community members, the interests of a core community will benefit more than those of a peripheral one. There is also a clear trend that professional and business interests are more privileged than others (Shively, 2003: 273).

So far, this chapter has mentioned the components and variables that this book adopts to examine and compare the dynamism of health politics in Korea. By fusing different theoretical perspectives and putting policy networks into systematic relationships with other components, this book establishes a comprehensive analytical framework, shown in Figure 2.6, ranging from policy context, via institutional features and policy networks, through to policy outputs. Their relationships are basically interactive, although in some cases, preceding components in the analytical framework constrain those following.

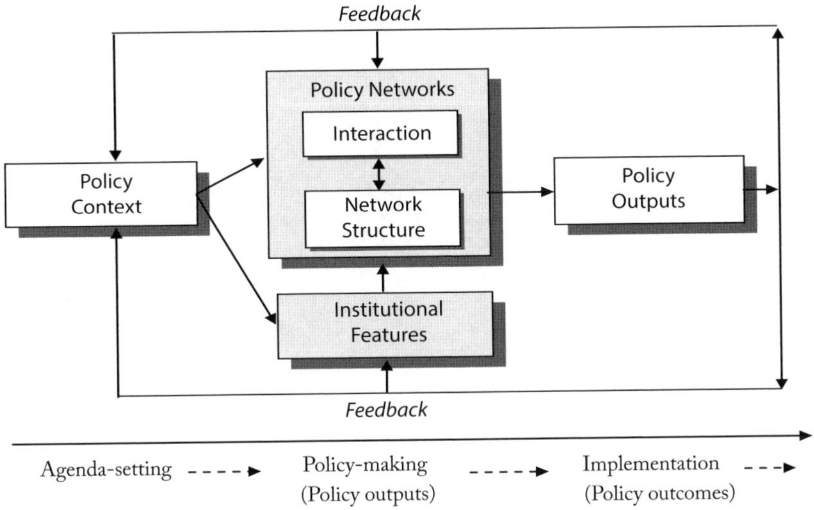

Figure 2.6 The basic analytical framework of this book

Chapter
3

Bureaucratic Politics in a Closed Terrain

The First Merger Debate in the Early 1980s

1. Introductory Comments

The compulsory health insurance programme, started in July 1977, was based on a multiple insurer system, which endowed each health insurer with managerial autonomy, in order to reduce the government's financial burden. However, several problems with the multiple insurer system became clear once this coverage was extended to smaller companies, such as the financial instability of small-sized insurers, the limited risk pooling among them, and the inequity of insurance premiums and benefits between policyholders. To cope with these problems, the government decided, in February 1980, to merge small-sized insurers (with those under 3,000 policyholders) to make larger and more stable insurers. The first amalgamation plan was completed in August 1980.[1]

However, in September 1980, newly appointed Minister Chun Myung-kee of the Ministry of Health and Social Affairs (MHSA) suspended the ongoing amalgamation programme and proposed a more radical transformation of a single insurer system (Wong, 2004: 90). He was driven by the idea that a single insurer system would ease health insurance coverage to the self-employed, by transferring the accumulated funds of established insurers to a newly extended program, ahead of the introduction of na-

1 The MHSA started to integrate the then 603 employee health insurers from July 1980 in order to make 423 bigger ones, and they themselves transformed into 185 health insurers by May 1981 (MHSA *White Paper*, 1982).

tionwide health insurance. Politicians and the Korean Medical Association (KMA) supported the merger of health insurers (henceforth, the merger) out of political expediency.

However, the MHSA plan to set up a single unified insurer met with strong opposition from advocates of the multiple insurer system, especially business interests and employee health insurers. Staff in the Office of the President (OP) were negative to the merger and played a key role in upsetting the MHSA plan. President Chun Doo-hwan was passive on this matter at first, partly because of his lack of knowledge about health insurance. Gradually his attitude towards the merger plan turned more negative, thanks largely to the continuous flow of negative advice from his staff, who suggested that the government would have to raise the subsidy if the merger proposals were allowed to proceed. At the time, President Chun's top priority was economic stability, and control over government expenditure was crucial.

Having met with strong resistance from the OP, the MHSA then turned its attention towards proposals for a follow up, or second, amalgamation programme and the pilot self-employed insurance programmes from 1981. However, the results of these pilot self-employed insurance programmes ignited a further debate on the merger once again, as the programmes only highlighted the inability of the self-employed to bear the costs of insurance premiums.[2] Although some people identified low-level

2 The rate of health insurance premium collection in three counties, which the first pilot self-employed insurance program was enforced, remained 61.9 percent for a year from July 1981 (Kim J., 2002: 68), largely due to the lack of policyholders' concerns about the program.

insurance premiums as the main reason behind the failure of the programs, proponents of the merger attributed it to the economic incapability of the targeted self-employed and claimed that only mergers could solve the financial deficit of these self-employed health insurers. From late 1981, political parties and Parliament took the initiative to replace the MHSA (with single insurer schemes). In particular, the ruling party urged the MHSA to submit a timetable of the proposed merger plan. But unlike her predecessor, new Minister Kim Jeong-rye from May 1982 was passive in supporting the merger. So, despite intensified pressure from the ruling party, the MHSA started to dissipate in the debate.

President Chun ended the heated debate on 2nd November 1982 by taking sides with opponents of the merger. From then on, the MHSA and politicians stopped debating the matter. Strong opposition from the President and his staff frustrated the first merger attempt, which was backed by the MHSA and politicians. Some MHSA officials who had backed the merger were ousted from office in February 1983, on the pretext of corruption (NFMI, 1997: 271-73). The chronology of the first merger attempt is, thus, summarised:

1980

- MHSA decided to amalgamate small and medium-sized health insurers and completed the first phase by August 1980 (February)
- Chun Myung-kee was appointed as MHSA minister (September)
- Minister Chun ordered MHSA officials to suspend the second amalgamation programme and to draw up a single insurer system (September 30)
- Minister Chun reported the MHSA merger plan to the President, but failed to get his backing (October 15)

- MHSA confirmed its merger plan and received prime ministerial approval (November 4)
- Minister Chun resubmitted the merger plan for the President's approval, but the President ordered a deeper review of the plan (November 17)

1981

- MHSA decided to go ahead with the second amalgamation programme (April)
- MHSA referred its plan to integrate inspection bodies and computer systems, instead of driving forward with its original merger plan (July)
- Parliament urged the MHSA to merge multiple insurers. But Minister Chun answered that the MHSA would submit a merger bill by the next parliamentary session (October 22)
- Parliament adopted a resolution urging the MHSA to submit a merger plan, and formed a standing sub-committee to review the merger (November 23)

1982

- MHSA agreed, with the ruling party, to submit a revised merger bill during the 1982 parliamentary session (January)
- Mrs Kim becomes new MHSA minister (May 21)
- Mrs Kim revealed that it was impractical to keep to the timetable of promises made last year. The Prime Minister also stated that any reform would require more detailed consideration before proceeding (October 13)
- Parliament decided to introduce a merger bill by 18 December 1982 (October 27)

- High-level figures supporting the merger called on the President to sound out his views on the proposed merger. The President rebuffed the approach (November 2)
- MHSA and the ruling party decided to submit multiple proposals, including a plan to set up a single insurer system, to Parliament (December 8)
- MHSA announced that the merger would be a practical impossibility (December 18)

2. Policy Context

1) Political context: authoritarian politics and non-competitive leadership

The key stated national goals of the Chun administration included the embodiment of a just society; the building of a welfare society; and the promotion of culture. To meet the goals of a just and welfare society, Chun stressed social equity and redistribution, a contrast to the emphasis on economic growth and efficiency in Park Chung-hee's 1970s administration. This gave some impetus to those in favour of the merger, as they believed that a single insurer system would be more conducive to achieving nationwide health insurance. Unlike the official governing ideology, however, Chun's real top priority was economic stability. Chun's New Year Address of 1981 accentuated economic stability: "The government will best serve in stabilising basic prices. This stabilisation will increase exports and make continuous economic growth possible by strengthening the international competitiveness of our products…". President Chun's secretary Kim Jong-dae confirms the big impact of Chun's emphasis on economic stability upon the debate:

> President Chun worried that the merger of health insurers might increase the burden on both employers and employees. In nature, the increasing rate of medical treatment fees outstripped the rise in commodity price. Thus, the merger of health insurers could turn out to be a burden on the national economy, and so, the President worried about the negative impact of merger on the management of economic stability. (Interview on 15 December 2004)

It is commonly acknowledged that political events, such as elections or the emergence of new leadership, influence policies to please the general public. They influence the policy-making process by constraining the policy agenda-setting (Kingdon, 2003: 165-68).

The first debate on the merger coincided with an unprecedentedly turbulent time, marked by the sudden death of dictatorial leader Park Chung-hee in October 1979. A group led by General Chun Doo-hwan carried out a military coup in December 1979, and proclaimed martial law in May 1980. Chun was elected the 11th President in August 1980 by the rubber-stamp National Conference for Unification (NCU) (Oberdorfer, 1997: 133). A national referendum to revise the Constitution was held in October 1980, resulting in a 95.5 percent turnout with 92.9 percent approval, to lay down a seven-year single term presidency and an indirect presidential election through an electoral-college.[3] Chun was re-elected to launch the

3 The revised Constitution laid out the framework of a seven-year single term presidency

5th Republic in February 1981. The general election was also held in March 1981. But these elections were not hugely influential as they mostly took place in the early stages of the merger debate. Under single term presidency, Mr Chun was not worried about re-election, claiming "I don't adhere to popularity and I will put forward the right policies, in spite of being ill spoken of by the people." (Monthly *Chosun*, January 1993).

As a result of these changes, the ranks of politico-administrative leaders were now filled with fresh faces. Rebellion leader Chun became President and many military officers had suddenly turned into politicians and high-level administrators, and sympathisers of the military coup formed the ruling Democratic Justice Party (DJP) in January 1981 (Monthly *Chosun*, January 1993). In the wake of these changes, opposition parties were forcibly reshaped and the March 1981 general election produced new political leaders. Administrative leaders were also newly recruited with the inauguration of a new government, and MHSA ministers were replaced twice during the first round of merger debate.[4]

Politics and the political leadership style in the early 1980s were authoritative and non-competitive. Parliament was dissolved by force in October 1980, transferring its functions to the pro-government Legislative Council for National Security, whose members were nominated by the

---

and prohibited the extension of presidential term. A single term presidency was introduced as a consequence of the longevity of former Presidents (President's chief secretary on Public Relations Lee Jong-ryul's interview with Monthly *Chosun* in January 1993).

4 MHSA ministers during the first debate were Chun Myung-Kee (Sep. 1980-May 1982) and Kim Jeong-Rye (May 1982-Feb. 1985) (MHSA *White Paper*, 2001). Remarkably, both of them were recruited from the ranks of opposition politicians. At the time, MHSA ministerial roles were set aside for opposition politicians as compensation for their political degeneration. But politicians could not but rely upon political judgement, or court popularity, in decision-making.

President (Kihl, 2005: 77). Hard-line opposition politicians were purged and trade unions were strictly controlled. The media were widely censored and domesticated, through the forceful merger of newspapers and broadcasting stations in 1980.

The presidency was set up in a non-competitive fashion. Mr Chun was elected President in August 1980, by the pro-government NCU, recording a figure of nearly 100 percent in terms of turnout in his favour, and he was re-elected in February 1981 by revised Constitution, securing another overwhelming polling score.[5] The 1981 general election followed similar non-competitive lines, as key opposition politicians were denied candidacy and a medium electorate system was introduced. The ruling party scored 97.8 percent wins except in only 2 cases where candidates dropped out (Shim, 2004: 337).

2) Social context: an inactivated civil society

For many years, Korea had maintained the state-dominant system over civil society under authoritarian politics. The dictatorial government of the 1970s tightly regulated freedom of assembly and association and rigorously controlled civil society. Government control of society was strengthened with the military coup in May 1980. Under this new framework the government selectively backed some groups' participation in state affairs with approval and financial support. One goal was to weaken trade unions. Compliance

5 The nature of the electoral-college system was not that different from the NCU election system. Although college members were elected, unlike the NCU, they were all pro-government. Unsurprisingly, Chun was re-elected by the overwhelming support of 90.2 percent, defeating three puppet candidates (Jee et al., 2001: 346).

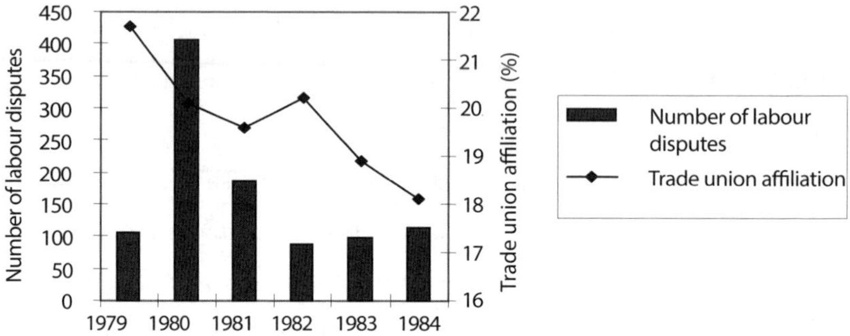

Note: The abrupt increase of labour disputes in 1980 was due to the political thawing of 1980 spring season just before the May 1980 military coup.
Source: Ministry of Labour (2003), *Labour Union Summary*.

Figure 3.1 Trade union activities around the early 1980s

from them was secured through such measures as intervention in leadership selection, the forceful clampdown on the labour movement, and the provision of financial subsidies (Koo, 2007: 75-77).[6] Figure 3.1 shows how much the labour movement was incapacitated at the time.

The power relationship between the government and business associations, such as the Federation of Korean Industries (FKI) and the Korea Employers Federation (KEF), had also become unbalanced. The government had retained several measures to control the business sector under the authoritarian system of the 1970s. Professional interest groups were also supervised by the government through the authorisation or cancellation of

6 In the early 1980s, the government purged trade union leaders under the pretext of corruption and agitation, and the trade union system was changed from an industrial guild system to a company-based one to ease government control over individual trade unions (Kim Y.-m., 2003: 253).

licenses,[7] and civil protests and student activists were discouraged.

3. Institutional Features

1) Power imbalances between the state's political organisations

The power distribution inside Korea's public sector in the early 1980s was highly imbalanced, with power concentrated within political organisations. Developmental dictatorship in favour of rapid economic growth from the 1970s reinforced this (Seth, 2010: 173-74). Figure 3.2 simplifies the power imbalance in terms of the relationship between the diverse kinds of political organisations.

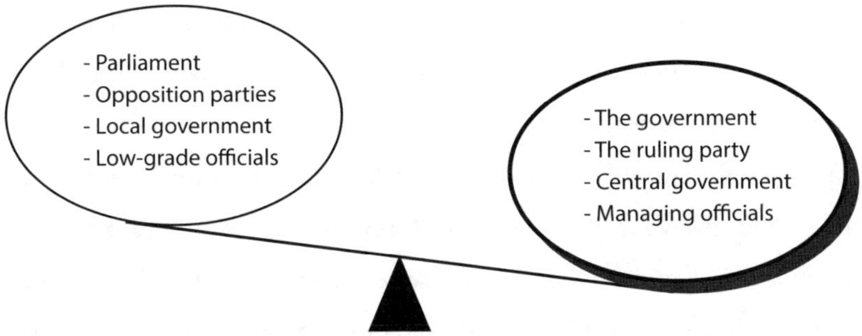

Figure 3.2 Power imbalances between and inside political organisations in Korea

7 With regard to healthcare sector, the Medical Service Act and the Pharmaceutical Affairs Act detailed the processes on forming medical and pharmaceutical associations, the approval and suspension of certificates, and the observance of defined criteria in prescribing and dispensing medicine.

Table 3.1 Parliamentary legislation under the Chun administration (cases, %)

	Proposal			Approval		
	Total	Parliamen-tarians	Ministers	Total	Parliamen-terians	Ministers
11th Assembly (1981-85)	489	202	287	340 (69.5)	83 (41.1)	257 (89.5)
12th Assembly (1985-88)	379	211	168	222 (58.6)	66 (31.3)	156 (92.8)
Total	868	413	455	562 (64.7)	149 (36.1)	413 (90.8)

Note: Numbers in parentheses indicate the ratio of approved bills, compared to those proposed.
Source: Secretariat of the National Assembly (1996), *The National Assembly Statistics*.

In detail, the strong presidential system concentrated a large proportion of political power in the hands of government. The government, headed by the President, manipulated Parliament through the ruling party which held a parliamentary majority. The ruling party was a sort of vanguard for the President, who both formed and held its presidency concurrently (Breen, 1998: 217). The high approval ratio of government bills in Table 3.1, compared to Parliament initiated bills, clearly shows the power imbalance between the two institutions.

The power relationship between the ruling and opposition parties was severely tilted in favour of the former.[8] Opposition parties were rebuilt by the permission of military leaders and were under strong political surveillance by intelligence agencies like the National Security Planning Board (NSPB, Korean CIA) (Hoare and Pares, 2000: 85). Disrupted and docile major opposition parties, the Democratic Korea Party and the Korea National

8 In the 11th National Assembly, the approval rate of the ruling party-proposed bills amounted to 83 percent while that of opposition parties remained just 4.0 percent (Chai, 2001: 192).

Party, could not compete with the stronger ruling party.[9]

Within the government, the President effectively controlled departments by appointing key public officials and exercising the authority to inspect and supervise public work. Powerful departments like the Board of Audit and Inspection and the NSPB were under the President's direct control. The OP itself was the most powerful government agency and had several measures to command and control public affairs (Shin, 2004: 24).

Decision-making power was also concentrated in the hands of central government. Where local autonomy system was not permitted, central government ruled local government through the control of budget and personnel. Against an authoritative organisational backdrop, upward communication and participation from below were unusual, concentrating decision-making power mainly on managerial-level officials (Cha, 1991: 500).

2) Undemocratic political party and election systems

The Chun administration continued the tradition of a strong presidential political system. Above all, the transcendental power was constitutionally endowed to the President. The President could proclaim a state of emergency and could take particular measures to restrict basic rights by declaring martial law whenever there was an emergency. The President had powers to dissolve Parliament, when there were good reasons to do so, in the interests of the people as a whole. S/he could also veto parliamentary decisions. Ad-

9 It was after the formation of the Consultative Committee for the Promotion of Democracy in May 1984 and the successful debut of the New Korea Democratic Party in the 1985 general election that opposition bloc began to be in a position to check ruling power (Buzo, 2002: 157).

ditionally, the President controlled Parliament through the ruling party that he founded.

The Prime Minister, appointed by the President, assisted the President on state matters and supervised government departments. S/he requested the appointment and dismissal of ministers to the President. However, in reality, the PM power was very restricted and largely ceremonial.

Parliament officially checked the government by making laws and deliberating the budget. Important government policies and the appointment of key public figures, like the Prime Minister, were consulted with Parliament in advance. It investigated government actions and could vote for the dismissal of cabinet members. Parliament also had powers to impeach the President and cabinet members. In theory, therefore, Parliament's counter-balancing power against the President and the government was guaranteed, though it was not equivalent in terms of political muscle. But the reality was far from theory. Parliamentary rights outlined in the Constitution and relevant laws were unlikely to be realised, as the situation was so tightly controlled by the President. The length of a parliamentary extraordinary session was limited to just 30 days and the total session was confined to 150 days in any one year (Min et al., 1996: 194).

Meanwhile, the President's right to declare a state of emergency and martial law was very visible in the light of President's indulgence of the time.[10] It was hard to block the dissolution of Parliament by the President in an emergency situation, and bills vetoed by the President could not be easily reconsidered in the situation where the ruling party controlled Parliament.

10 In the 1970s President Park Chung-hee declared a state of emergency and martial laws several times to face down oppositional demonstration (Kim Y.-m., 2003: 205).

Politicians in the early 1980s, in particular, were mostly very compliant, having recently survived a political purge carried out by the military junta (Heo and Roehrig, 2011: 35-36).

Regarding the political party system, the Constitution and related laws championed a multi-party system by ensuring the free establishment of political parties (the Constitution, Article 7). The government was obliged to protect a free party system and to subsidise political parties. But in practice, political parties were in a very weak position vis-à-vis the government, as the government could ask for the disbandment of political parties if it felt that their purpose ran counter to the basic order of democracy. Such abstract constitutional prescriptions left open enormous possibilities of abuse.

Even so, Korea's political party system had been a two-party system until the 1970s, consisting of the ruling party and one main opposition party. The National Assembly Act accepted parties that had 20 seats or more as a parliamentary negotiation body to prevent factions and disorder in Parliament. Small-sized opposition parties were less well placed to stand up against the government oppression during the 1970s. However, the Chun administration adopted a divide-and-rule strategy and allowed the setting up of smaller opposition parties. As a result, the political party system in the Chun administration was basically composed of the ruling party and two major opposition parties (Shim and Kim, 2002: 158).

The ideologies of political parties in Korea were conservative and anti-communist, irrespective of their parliamentary positions. All major political parties advocated the national interest, first and foremost, and sought to represent the views of the entire economic strata. Until the 1970s, a socialist party had been illegal in Korea in view of the political situation confronting communist North Korea (Cho, 2003: 335). But the Chun government instigated the setting up of the left-wing New Socialist Party (NSP) as a means of promoting cooperation with Western socialist governments and propagandising the political openness of the regime.[11] But the NSP was not allowed to promote socialist ideology, and it functioned as a pseudo political party manipulated by the ruling power.

With regard to the election system, the President in the 1970s was indirectly elected by the NCU, whose members were nominated by the President himself, making the presidential election completely ceremonial (Hwang, 2010: 237). Initially, in August 1980, President Chun was elected in the same way. But he then revised the Constitution to adopt an electoral-college system. Although electoral-college members were elected, almost all of them were filled with pro-government people.[12] Electoral institutions were one thing, and their operation was quite another. Meanwhile, a presidency was restricted to a single seven-year term to prohibit consecutive runs in term.

The new 5th Republic Constitution adopted the unicameral system of Parliament and lawmakers were recruited from both local constituencies and the proportional representation system. The new electoral system selected two lawmakers in a constituency, thus, making the ruling party's success even more of a formality (Shim and Kim, 2002: 150). The proportional representation system selected one-third of total lawmakers and two thirds

11 The government helped the NSP president to win a seat by not putting up a ruling candidate in his constituency, and as a result the NSP secured 2 seats in constituency (Shin, 2002: 84).

12 The ruling party occupied 69.6 percent of college members and 21.8 percent of college members were pro-government independent delegates, while opposition college members were only 8.6 percent (Oh, 2003: 409).

Table 3.2 Result of the 1981 parliamentary election

Political parties	Number of seats	Proportion of seats (%)	Polling score (%)
The ruling DJP	151 (regional 90+ proportional 61)	54.7	35.6
Democratic Korea Party	81 (57+24)	29.3	21.6
Korea National Party	25 (18+7)	9.0	13.3
Independents and others	19 (0)	7.0	29.5
Total	276 (92)	100.0	100.0

Source: adapted from the National Assembly homepage (www.assembly.go.kr).

of these representatives were set aside for the leading party.[13] The remaining one-third of seats was distributed to the parties with more than 5 seats across the constituencies, according to their total seat numbers. Above all, political funds and talented political applicants were concentrated in the ruling party, and the government's unfair intervention and money politics guaranteed victory for most ruling candidates. Table 3.2 shows the dominance of the ruling party in the 1981 general election.

3) Decision-making rules: hierarchy and top-down decision-making

Where concerns were expressed over government-initiating policies, rules on decision-making and conflict resolution, generally intertwined with each other, could be traced on four levels. At first, department decision-making followed a well-defined *ringi* system. The *ringi* system, which was formally described by the Provision on Office Regulations, was not only a deci-

13 The ruling DJP secured 54.7 percent of the total number of parliamentary seats in the 1981 general election, despite polling only 35.6 percent of the total votes, mainly because of an uncompetitive medium electorate system and an unfair proportional representation system (Shim, 2004: 337).

sion-making rule, but also a communication channel between the different levels of hierarchy within departments. The *ringi* system started with a document drafting (*kian*) by working-level officials. Drafted documents were referred to supervisors at each level for approval and finally signed off by department chiefs. Through this process, lateral communications with other department sections or bureaus concurrently occurred under the guise of circulation (Kim S.-y., 2002: 196). The conflict between sections or bureaus was coordinated by hierarchical intervention. Several levels of formal conferences were periodically held to coordinate differences, while informal round-table meetings took place on demand. In the department decision-making process, relevant interest groups influenced through a variety of channels. While many groups brought points from outside, some influential groups like professional and business associations were officially invited onto department committees.

The next step was to consult with relevant departments. Formal or informal inter-departmental meetings were held to coordinate differences between departments. Working-level informal meetings proceeded and formal consultations between higher level officers followed. Persuading the budget-controlling Economic Planning Board (EPB) was important in deciding department proposals (Shin, 2004: 26). The OPM (Office of the Prime Minister) coordinated inter-departmental differences.

Particularly in the early 1980s, the NSPB often intervened in deciding important state affairs on the pretext of collecting information. In the Chun administration the NSPB played a key role in coordinating politically important state affairs (Kim J., 2003: 235), and in reality NSPB chief Jang Sedong was a practical number two to President Chun. The State Council (Korea's Cabinet Council), a supreme deliberation body mandated by the Constitution and consisted of the President, the Prime Minister, and cabinet members of between 15-30 people, was the final arbiter of government policies and the bills decided in the State Council were sent to the President for his signature and then submitted to Parliament. But practically, there was hardly a case when the State Council opposed the President's will, because its role was no more than nominal at the time.

There were formal channels designed to coordinate the difference between the ruling party and government departments, in order to smoothly pass government bills through Parliament. The ruling party-government conference, introduced in 1963, aimed to promote a cabinet style system of governance, and it has been institutionalised since the 1980s. As it developed, the conference has also functioned as a channel to control opposition parties' objection to government policies (Chai, 2001: 193). The ruling party-government conference usually started with informal contacts between working-level staff, and the formal conferences between higher figures, including department ministers and lawmakers, followed. During the consultation process, department proposals were revised to satisfy the criteria of political desirability and feasibility, and then the ruling party would strongly support them in Parliament.[14]

Decision-making in Parliament, which had adopted a unicameral system, was largely divided into two steps: one of deliberation in relevant standing committees and a second of tabling a resolution in a plenary session. Standing committees were established to scrutinise the work of each government department and were dominated by the ruling party in the

14 During the process of consultation, lawmakers tend to insist on political feasibility, whereas bureaucrats stick to the economic rationality of policy (Parsons, 2003).

early 1980s. These bodies usually formed sub-committees to deliberate on proposals in more detail. Standing committee decisions followed the process of policy explanation, report reviewing, discussion, article-by-article consideration, and voting. Ordinary measures were decided by a quorum attendance of lawmakers and by majority approval of those present. Agreed bills were sent to the Legislation and Judiciary Committee to review their jurisprudential appropriateness. Although a plenary session was the final arbiter of parliamentary decision-making, it was very rare that it vetoed standing committee decisions. Decision-making in a plenary session followed a majority rule and rejected bills could not be suggested again during the same parliamentary session.

The President should promulgate the passed bills within 15 days in case of not raising objection to them. But s/he could ask Parliament to reconsider the bills. While the vetoed bills were confirmed as laws by the quorum attendance of at least half of the lawmakers and the approval of two-thirds of those present (the Constitution of the 5th Republic, Article 89-4), it was absolutely impossible that the vetoed bills would ever be reconsidered in Parliament, dominated by its ruling party.

4) Previous policies imported from abroad

According to historical institutionalism, established institutions or decisions have tendency to persist, constraining the pattern and content of current decision-making (Hudson and Lowe, 2004: 150). With regard to the health insurer system, a multiple insurer system was adopted from the beginning,[15]

15 While the EPB preferred the NHS system, underlining the possibility of huge financial

as the government understood it as a halfway point between the NHS system and a private insurance system, and believed it would be more advantageous in minimising the government's financial burden and gradually extending health insurance coverage. At the time, Japanese and German insurance systems were often referred to,[16] as Kim Jong-dae, head of MHSA competent section of the day, confirms:

> I was a competent official when the compulsory health insurance program was introduced in 1977. At the time, the MHSA thought long and hard about the decision to set up such a programme, but the degree of conflict among MHSA officials was not that great. We agreed on a multiple insurer system as a matter of course, because Korea's health insurer system copied the Japanese system, which had adopted a multiple insurer system, from its inception in the early 1960s. (Interview on 15 December 2004)

Once a multiple insurer system was established as an institution, it began to constrain future discussions. When the system met problems such as the financial difficulties of small-sized insurers, the government responded by introducing some small adjustments to the system (Kim S.-y., 2011: 69-70). So, from 1980, the MHSA started to amalgamate small-sized insurers, gradually extending the target.

However, the amalgamation program could not solve the basic prob-

---

losses in a multiple insurer system, the MHSA and business interests supported a multiple insurer system (NFMI, 1997: 91).

16 Ironically, the Japanese health insurance system affected institutional change, too. Minister Chun decided to pursue the merger after hearing of problems of the Japanese multiple insurer system during a talk with his Japanese counterpart (Lee Y., 2003: 52).

lems of a multiple insurer system, such as the inequality of insurance premiums between policyholders. Proponents of the merger reaffirmed that a multiple insurer system would produce the financial instability of small-sized insurers and the potential financial deficit of health insurance program. They intended to solve the problems by abolishing the current institution. But, being confronted with an attempt for fundamental change, the current institution showed its resistance to change once again.

4. Policy Networks

Participants in the first debate were divided into two according to their preferences of the health insurer system. Since the start of the debate — signalled by the MHSA minister's comments on the idea of setting up a single insurer system — the MHSA and the OP had led two blocs, respectively. But, from late-1981 when the pilot self-employed health insurance scheme was implemented, political parties replaced the MHSA as leading proponents of the merger, while the OP remained an outspoken opponent. Civic groups were not yet activated and the mass media only passively engaged in the debate. Table 3.3 distinguishes participants by their views on the merger of health insurers.

1) Network structure: a bureaucracy-led closed and exclusive network

Nature of participants: number, dominant actors and exclusion

There were many participants in the first debate. When policy actors are divided into official and unofficial ones following Anderson's (2015)

Table 3.3 Classification of participants in the first debate

	Proponents of the merger	Opponents of the merger
Official actors	MHSA, EPB, OPM	The President and staff in the OP
Unofficial actors	Political parties (ruling and opposition), KMA	FKI, employee insurers and their association (NFMI), mass media, FKTU (unclear)

Note: FKTU (Federation of Korean Trade Unions), NFMI (National Federation of Medical Insurance).

classification, official actors in the debate included the MHSA, the President and the OP, the OPM, and the EPB. The ruling and opposition parties, the FKI, the FKTU, employee health insurers, the KMA and the mass media belonged to the category of unofficial actors.

Of the proponents, the MHSA and political parties were core actors, while the OPM, the EPB and the KMA passively agreed to the merger. Although MHSA working-level officials opposed the merger at first, they changed positions to support the merger after repeated instructions from a department boss (Cha, 1992: 321). The EPB passively supported the MHSA proposal, despite its different view on the detailed method of the merger, whilst the OP, the FKI and employee health insurers led the opponent bloc to the merger. The attitude of the FKTU was equivocal and inconsistent. Accordingly, while there were not a few actors in the first debate, core participants were limited to a small number. A stable policy community had not yet been formed, at the beginning of what would become 20 years of ongoing debate.

Dominant actors in the first debate were mainly governing actors, as the authoritative political system of the early 1980s prevented the active intervention of opposition and organised interests. But the composition of dominant actors changed as the debate progressed. The MHSA led the proponent bloc in the first round until late-1981. Despite the ongoing amalgamation program, the new MHSA minister, appointed in September 1980, ordered a study of the merger plan to reduce management costs and extend health insurance coverage to the self-employed (Kim H., 2003: 101-3).[17] In due course, MHSA officials such as Lee Doo-ho and Cha Heung-bong and health insurance professionals such as Lee Gwang-chan played key roles in achieving the minister's goal, practically leading the proponent bloc. Mr Kim Jong-dae, who took charge of health insurance affairs in the OP at the time, unveils Minister Chun's motivation to propose the merger:

> Minister Chun's idea of merging health insurers originated with a small number of MHSA officials and professionals. At the time, three-year old company employee health insurers already accumulated a lot of insurance funds, as employees had little opportunity to make use of hospitals because of their hard work. Proponents of the merger began to covet these employee insurer funds as a way of extending health insurance program to the self-employed, without the need for any additional government financing. (Interview on 15 December 2004)

However, from mid-1981, when a pilot self-employed insurance program revealed that the rural self-employed could not shoulder the burden of their insurance premiums, the ruling party emerged as a leading proponent of the merger. The ruling party advocated the merger, mainly because

17 Minister Chun underlined his genuine motivation in initiating the merger attempt: "There was no political pressure to reform from other levels of government. There was no interest at all in this issue from either the public or government." (Kim H., 2003: 101).

the rural self-employed were its major political supporters. Among ruling lawmakers, Rep. Hwang Seong-kyun and Lee Chan-hyok were most passionate in proposing the merger, whilst Rep. Lee Jong-chan and Choi Young-cheol, as a floor leader and a parliamentary committee chairman of the ruling party, respectively, followed their lead.

In the meantime, Minister Kim Jeong-rye reassessed the situation, as she realised the impracticality of any merger in the presence of strong opposition from the OP.[18] Working-level officials also began to persuade her to give up the merger attempt.[19] Even though the KMA supported the merger,[20] it was not active on the issue, as its major priority lay in separating prescriptions and dispensaries. Other government departments like the OPM and the EPB passively followed MHSA's opinion.[21]

The OP was the most active in opposing the merger throughout the debate, worrying about realistic problems, such as further government budget burdens and possible direct confrontation between the government and policyholders. It openly opposed the merger in formal meetings, and persuaded the President, who was deficient of detailed knowledge on the

18 Kim Jong-dae explains: "Minister Kim Jeong-rye also preferred a multiple insurer system, as the key public officials backing the merger continuously persuaded her of its merit. But, she was politically sensible. After recognising the political infeasibility of the merger because of opposition from the OP, she became inactive on the merger." (Interview on 15 December 2004).

19 Before everything else, the most urgent issue to the MHSA at the time was the separation of prescribing and dispensing. Physicians and pharmacists staged demonstrations to block it and the MHSA should concentrate attention on solving the issue (KMA *Newsletter*, June 1982).

20 The KMA had supported an NHS-style health insurance system from the beginning of 1977, and since then had always preferred a single insurer system (Shin, 2004: 68).

21 During the merger debate, the EPB just pointed out the potential problems of a multiple insurer system instead of clearly articulating its interests. For this reason, the EPB was out of key participants in the debate (Kim Y.-m., 1996: 111).

matter, to side with it. In persuading the President, senior secretary Yoon Sung-tae and secretary Kim Jong-dae, who were very knowledgeable on health insurance matters, played key roles, while chief secretary Kim Tae-ho supported them as a supervisor. The President was gradually persuaded to oppose the merger, hearing repeatedly negative reports from OP staff. Some MHSA officials were also sympathetic to a multiple insurer system, and they clandestinely associated themselves with opponents of the merger.[22]

Business interests like the FKI and employee health insurers opposed the merger as vested interests seemed under threat. But, they were in a weak position vis-à-vis the government, and would not have been able to loudly oppose the government's merger plan. Major newspapers were also negative towards the merger, as sided with business sector who gave them large sums of advertising revenue (Kim H., 2003: 106).

Closed policy networks have a mechanism by which they intentionally limit policy actors from entering into these networks (Hill, 2014: 69). The first merger debate was led by a small handful of participants during the entire process, and the majority of leading participants were governing actors. While government bodies and the ruling party monopolised important policy-making channels, organised interests and opposition parties were excluded under the long tradition of Korea's closed decision-making system. Although the issue was crucial to some interest groups, most of them were passive and only intermittently participated in the debate.

It is undeniable that there were many government committees and formal or informal meetings to review health insurance policy. But, their

22 Kim Jong-dae admitted that he drew up a report opposing the merger with several MHSA officials in November 1982 (Interview on 15 December 2004).

membership was open only to a few privileged interest groups. In health-care sector, the KMA and the Korea Pharmaceutical Association (KPA) regularly participated in relevant committees (KMA *Newsletter*, 1979). The FKI and the KEF exclusively represented the interests of big companies. But in most cases, government committees and round-table meetings were nominal and merely provided the government with advice.

Participants' interests in the issue

Participants joined the bloc that maximised their own interests. Of the proponents, MHSA (as the competent department of health insurance) had interests in extending health insurance coverage without creating an additional financial burden on the government, a goal which was thought to be most effective under a merger. (Lee Y., 2003: 52). Professor Lee Gwang-chan who was the then advisor to MHSA minister explained:

> Minister Chun became convinced of the necessity for the merger, after both Um Ki-seop, of the Federation of Korean Medical Insurance Societies, and I recommended it. The meeting with Japanese Minister of Health and Welfare also influenced his view, because the Japanese multiple insurers system was confronted with many problems at the time. (Interview with the Monthly *Chosun* in May 2001)

Additionally, Minister Chun envisaged that the merger would be consistent with the political atmosphere of the early 1980s, when the forced integration of public and private organisations was being actively pursued. The President also advocated the building of a welfare society and saw it as part of his national agenda. MHSA officials' individual interests were different from those of the MHSA at first, and they followed the leader under the bureaucratic hierarchy of Korea. Kim Jong-dae describes the atmosphere engulfing MHSA officials:

> I think that over 90 percent of public servants in the MHSA opposed the merger at the time. In my view, almost all MHSA officials may have thought, some perhaps still do, that the decision to merge health insurers was wrong. They just cannot oppose openly. When I drew up a report for the November 1982 meeting, many working-level MHSA officials worked with me on it. It was a clear disobedience, as public servants should follow a minister's instruction. (Interview on 15 December 2004)

The major interests of economy-related departments like the EPB lay in controlling any additional government expenditure. While admitting the need to extend health insurance coverage, the EPB intended to reduce potential financial subsidies in a self-employed health insurer scheme.

Political parties had common interests in winning votes at elections, irrespective of their positions in Parliament. Extending health insurance coverage to the self-employed was a way of winning votes in rural areas, and political parties considered the merger as the better way to win support. Lawmakers' interests were highly dependent on the regional characteristics of their electoral constituencies. Politicians from rural areas had special interests in the merger, as the merger would improve the health of the rural self-employed, which was greatly inferior to that of the urban self-employed.

Of many professional interest groups, only the KMA had concerns about the merger, as pharmaceutical and oriental medical services lay beyond health insurance coverage at the time. Physicians' key stakes in health insurance was to secure medical treatment fees from health insurers (Lee J., 2000: 27). For this, a single insurer system was an easier way to obtain money to pay for medical treatment fees. In many instances, large numbers of small-sized insurers were financially unstable and went into bankruptcy under a multiple insurer system.

Meanwhile, the OP looked at policies which favoured the nation-state and always attempted to minimise any possible burden on the sovereign power of the President. It reviewed the merger and calculated that it would cause an additional financial burden and might put the government into direct confrontation with policyholders by eliminating the intermediary role of multiple health insurers. This would bring an enormous political burden to the President. Kim Jong-dae describes this reality:

> At the time, the MHSA and those in political circles proposed the merger by the logic of improving equity and extending health insurance coverage without adding further to the government's financial burden. But, the OP thought differently. In the not too distant future, the issue of increased government burden might become serious if the merger were to proceed. It was also impossible to set a single criterion by which health insurance premiums could be imposed — particularly given the fact that income declaration rate of the self-employed remained below 10 percent at the time. (Interview on 15 December 2004)

The merger of health insurers could heavily damage the vested interests of employee health insurers and its association, the NFMI, as the issue was directly linked with their very existence and would additionally harm any chances of staff job security (Kim S.-y., 2011: 84). In case of the merger, key health insurer managers and the majority of staff might lose their jobs, and health insurers would lose any right they held previously to manage their own insurance funds.

Business associations worried about the possible increase in insurance premiums of their employees, and employers were concerned about any outflow of money from the accumulated finances of employee health insurers to a unified insurer, which would then be beyond their control. The FKTU interests in the merger were not clearly expressed, since it was not so concerned with the issue. But, employee health insurers' union worried

Table 3.4 Participants' interests in the issue

Participants		Interests
Proponents of the merger	MHSA	Extension of health insurance to the self-employed Department ideology of social equity and distribution
	EPB	Minimisation of government expenditure
	OPM	Harmonisation of inter-departmental differences
	Political parties	Getting votes by extending health insurance to the self-employed Making jobs for retired party bureaucrats and influencing personnel management of health insurers (ruling party)
	KMA	Guarantee of medical treatment fees
Opponents of the merger	OP	Consideration of the President's governing philosophy Minimisation of the burden on the sovereign power of the President
	FKI	Constraints of the increase of both employees and employers insurance premiums Preservation of the right to manage insurance funds
	Health insurers	Job security of their personnel Preservation of the right to manage insurance funds
Unclear	Trade unions	Constraints of the increase of employees' insurance premiums Financial stability of employee insurers

about the possible job losing of its members through the merger. They were also unhappy about any possible increases in insurance premiums to compensate for financial shortfalls in the self-employed insurer funds in the event of the merger (FKTU Annual Report, 1999: 389). Table 3.4 summarises the interests demonstrated by the participants.

Resource dependency between participants

Relations within policy networks are connected by resource dependency between participants. Of the two types of policy networks, the participants in policy communities hold most of the important resources and are more interdependent (Hudson and Lowe, 2004: 133). Among proponents of the merger, the MHSA had the formal authority to regulate health insurance affairs and to supervise healthcare professionals through relevant laws. But, the MHSA was not influential in relation to other government departments, as it did not have budgetary rights and its jurisdiction was not key in exercising political power. The MHSA unilaterally depended on the EPB and the OP to secure department budgets or to exert influence over the President.

The EPB was a powerful department because it screened departmental programs and assigned the budget to various departments. But the EPB was also controlled by the OP and relied on its staff to win favour with the President over key economic matters. The OPM held higher status than other departments and the PM recommended prospective ministers to the President. But in reality, its power could not be fully realised in such a strong presidential system.[23]

23 The fact that seven prime ministers were replaced during President Chun's seven-year term

Of the political parties, the ruling party had resources needed by many government departments, as leading members of the 1980 military coup formed it and played core roles in making important decisions. Its key resource was derived from supporting department programs in Parliament. On the other hand, the ruling party also depended on government departments in producing tangible benefits to its electorate. Opposition parties, however, lacked important resources under the divide-and-rule strategy of the Chun administration (Kihl, 2005: 77-9). From the MHSA standpoint, the assistance of opposition parties was not considered that urgent, as the ruling party dominated Parliament.

Among the medical profession, doctors had professional knowledge and information that was vital in making and carrying out health policy (Ahn, 2003: 254). They were also in a position to offer support to the MHSA when it competed with other departments. But in relation to the merger, the MHSA was not heavily dependent on the KMA, because the issue did not require much professional knowledge or cooperation.

The OP was the most powerful body within the government under the dictatorial presidential system and influenced the President's final decision through professional advice. The secretaries to the President, Yoon Sung-tae and Kim Jong-dae, were all health policy professionals who were on secondment from the MHSA. It officially attached a 'review comment' to the government documents reported to the President, and had the right to oversee the work of public officials in each department. Just as the President was all-powerful the OP was very influential in shaping state policies (Buzo,

in office, largely for political reasons, underlines the weak position of the OPM vis-à-vis the President.

2002: 156).

Employee health insurers had plenty of information about health insurance matters and were tasked with running large-scale insurance programs. However, they were held an unfavourable position with the MHSA and their resource dependency on the MHSA was not reciprocal. The MHSA, as a supervisor, used diverse methods to control health insurers, including financial support and the promotion of key personnel. So, the MHSA was less dependent on health insurers when it came to the making of policies related to the merger.

Although business interests pressured political parties by providing political funds, they were in a weak position vis-à-vis the government. Under the bureaucracy-led economic system, the government controlled them by mobilising measures such as tax and fare trade investigations. On health insurance policy, business interests closely cooperated with the MHSA in introducing a health insurance program in 1977 and the amalgamation program in 1980,[24] but their dependence on the government diminished because of their different view towards the merger.

Trade unions had resources to provide political support during election campaigns, based on their big membership. Their cooperation, in theory, was also essential in implementing any policies that were brought forward. But in the early 1980s, a large number of union leaders were purged under the pretext of social agitation and the labour movement was tightly

24 In the 1970s, the Federation of Korean Medical Insurance Societies, a predecessor of the NFMI, was under the FKI and FKI vice-president held the Federation's chairmanship concurrently (Shin, 2004: 62). Also, in the early 1980s, the MHSA asked the FKI to re-employ forcibly retired personnel from the defunct health insurers — who had lost out due to the amalgamation programs.

controlled (Koo, 2007: 76). Thus, there was little dependence by government agencies on trade unions at the time.

2) Participants' interaction: persuasion through institutional channels

The basic nature of interaction

In policy communities, participants usually maintain friendly and cooperative relations with each other and make mutual decisions. But relations in issue networks are ordinarily based on conflict, as actors try to best maximise their benefits (Hudson and Lowe, 2004: 133). In the first debate, participants were divided into two blocs with different views on the merger and their interests clashed. In particular, the conflict between government agencies (i.e. the MHSA and the OP) with different policy orientations, were serious.

While relations within the proponent bloc were basically consensus-oriented, two major players, the MHSA and the ruling party, became increasingly more conflictual from late-1981, as the MHSA turned neutral towards the merger. Their split grew worse after the 1982 parliamentary regular session. The ruling party expressed dissatisfaction with the MHSA over its breach of promise to submit a clear timetable for the merger (NFMI, 1997: 267-73). The MHSA-EPB difference also deepened. They suggested different methods and approaches to the merger. Although conflict among merger opponents was not serious, they failed to effectively work together to block the merger and there was no overt coalition between them.

Frequency of interaction

Of the two different types of policy networks, interaction between players in policy communities is usually frequent and stable, whereas in issue networks, it is causal and unstable (Hill, 2014: 69). In the first debate, frequent interaction took place between governing bloc members, irrespective of their views on the merger, and differences were formally spoken of in formal conferences. Most organised interests were excluded from the formal decision-making system, and did not intimately interact with each other. While the MHSA, the FKI and employee health insurers were frequently involved in implementing amalgamation programs (NFMI, 1997: 239), their contact about any would-be merger was limited due to their different views on the matter.

The most frequent interaction was between the MHSA and the ruling party. The MHSA worked with the ruling party through formal meetings like the ruling party-government conference.[25] Attempts to coordinate differences between government departments were also made through formal and informal channels. Despite the different views on the merger, the OP also frequently contacted the MHSA and the ruling party. Meanwhile, minor opponents of the merger, such as the FKI and the NFMI, who lobbied the OP and newspapers to oppose the merger,[26] rarely made contact with other opponents (Cha, 1996: 107).

Mobilised strategies of interaction

In policy community-style networks, participants mainly rely upon the

25 The ruling party-government conference, for example, agreed in January 1982 to bring forward legislation on the merger in the 1982 parliamentary regular session and to start a single insurer system from July 1983 (Kim H., 2003: 113).

26 For example, NFMI chairman Kim Ip-sam lobbied newspapers to carry articles opposing to the merger through his personal acquaintance with reporters (Cha, 1992: 325).

strategies of consultation and cooperation with other participants, whereas policy actors in issue networks frequently develop a strategy to exert pressure on other parties (Bulkeley, 2000: 729). The first merger debate was largely between official policy actors and their interaction ran on stable and recognisable institutional lines. Participants' basic positions towards the debate were, by and large, consultative as they tried to achieve their goals through discussions in formal arenas. Minor actors, like employee health insurers and the FKI, resorted to moderate methods to advance their interests.

Among major proponents of the merger, the MHSA pursued its interests through formal decision-making bodies. It worked on persuading the President and other government agencies, by stressing the ideological supremacy of the merger in achieving social solidarity[27] and the practical merits of the merger in extending health insurance coverage to the self-employed (Shin, 2010: 4-8). Basically, the MHSA maintained a consensual stance along with other proponents of the merger, such as the ruling party, the EPB and the OPM.[28] But from mid-1981, the MHSA and the ruling party began to fall out over the schedule and method of the merger, and the resolve of the MHSA to propose the merger became greatly weakened. In relation to the OP, the MHSA tried to work on influencing the President,[29]

---

27 Minister Chun ordered a review of the decision to introduce a single insurer system, confirming that the President would support the merger in light of its moral supremacy (Kim S.-y., 2011: 78).

28 The MHSA formed a working-level task force team to review the merger in December 1980 and built a departmental committee in April 1982, consisting of representatives of government departments and relevant experts, to study a medical insurance system (Lee J., 2000: 38).

29 For example, the minister twice referred the merger plan to the President in 1980, and sought to win his backing by mentioning the merits of the merger in improving income redistribution and in spreading financial risk (NFMI, 1997: 235).

instead of a direct confrontation with the OP (NFMI, 1997: 271-73). The then Minister Kim Jeong-rye admitted the limitation of the MHSA in fighting against the OP:

> I tried to meet President Chun alone to persuade him the reform. Because President Chun had an aggressive and quick decision-making style, I waited for a chance to discuss seriously the issue with him. However, the President always brought Yoon, a senior secretariat and strong opponent of the reform, to every meeting, stating that "Yoon is a welfare expert." Therefore I had no chance to persuade the President. (Kim H., 2003: 118)

In dealing with unofficial opponents like the FKI, the MHSA used informal persuasion.[30] But after recognising the impossibility of the merger because of strong opposition from the OP, the MHSA strategy became one of seeking to delay the timetable of the merger and to gradually weaken its original resolve in pursuing the merger (Ahn H., 2001: 270).[31] Meanwhile, the OPM and the EPB intervened in the matter passively, permitting MHSA initiatives. Although the EPB initially had a different slant towards the merger from the MHSA, it was gradually persuaded by MHSA's claim that the merger would not be an additional budget burden.

30 In August 1981, the MHSA ordered employee health insurers to build a statutory corporation based on the Medical Insurance Act, instead of the current voluntary association structure, in order to more easily control them by putting under legal supervision (NFMI, 1997: 248-51).

31 Minister Chun reported Parliament in October 1981: "The MHSA will introduce a merger bill during the 1982 regular session under the policy of gradually driving the merger forward," in response to lawmakers' strong urge to start the merger immediately (National Assembly committee records number 5-6, 1981).

The ruling party led the debate from mid-1981. It regularly made use of institutional channels to propose the merger and tried to persuade the President directly. The merger debate in Parliament mainly took place in the Health and Social Affairs Committee. Even though the Committee was composed of lawmakers from both ruling and opposition parties, ruling lawmakers led the debate. Political parties usually adopted a strategy to pressurise the MHSA into submitting a merger bill, and set up a parliamentary subcommittee, in November 1981, to reaffirm their strong support for the merger. Mr Ju Kyoung-sik, the director of MHSA competent bureau and former MHSA vice-minister, recalls the situation:

> In the National Assembly of October 1981, ruling and opposition lawmakers pressured the minister into introducing a scheme to set up a single insurer system immediately. In response, the minister promised to submit a merger bill during the next year's parliamentary regular session, mentioning the likelihood that about 700 health insurer staff would be cut... (Park K. et al., 2001: 79)

Even though the KMA had continuously supported the merger during the first debate, it was inactive in general, because the merger of health insurers was not its major concern at the time.[32] Academics were also inactive in the first debate.

Among opponents of the merger, the OP stuck to the strategy of persuading the President by emphasising the potential risk the state would run

32 The KMA confined the activity to the participation in formal organisations like the task team reviewing the merger and the committee studying the general system of health insurance.

if the merger proceeded. It fully exercised its formal right to tag an opinion onto the departmental reports submitted to the President (Monthly *Shindonga*, August 1983).[33] It also adequately made use of established government conferences in opposing the merger. President Chun was gradually persuaded by the OP after realising the merger could harm the economic stability to which he gave a top priority (Chun, 2005: 164). His resolute opposition to the merger in the November 1982 meeting clarified everything, under the President's dictatorial leadership of the time. Kim Jong-dae, who made the report for the meeting, commented:

> The meeting on 2 November 1982 was a critical moment in the course of the debate. In the face of opposition from the OP, merger supporters in the MHSA and the ruling party tried to directly persuade the President. At the meeting, while Minister Kim, ruling floor leader Lee Jong-chan and Health and Social Affairs Committee chairman Choi Young-cheol advocated the merger, chief-secretary Kim Tae-ho and senior-secretary Yoon Sung-tae of the OP opposed the merger. Although I could not take part in the meeting, I drew up a report opposing the merger. In making the report, I called upon the help of MHSA officials and professional charter-makers. After the one and half-hour meeting the President said: "The OP's report is much more realistic. I don't make a decision simply to flatter the public." And he humiliated the minister and the lawmakers: "The department and the ruling party should put more

33 When the MHSA referred the merger plan to the President in November 1980, the OP added a negative opinion on the merger to the document (Won, 1990: 77). In February 1982, while the MHSA tried to win the President's permission on its revised proposal, the OP again blocked it, by insisting on the need for further study. In November 1982, when the MHSA and the ruling party finally passed the merger plan to the President, the OP persuaded the President to refuse it (Monthly *Chosun*, May 2001).

> time into studying the plan further." From then on, Kim buried her views about the merger and Choi commented: "From now I will not engage in this matter." Lee also never mentioned anything more about the merger. They realised their political lives might be over if they were to pursue this matter any further. (Interview on 15 December 2004)

Employee health insurers and the NFMI held significant interests in this issue, and actively opposed the merger during earlier rounds of the debate.[34] They visited the MHSA to oppose the merger and distributed a brochure explaining the merits of a multiple insurer system to the mass media (NFMI *Newsletter*, January 1981).[35] They also lobbied member companies to send letters opposing the merger to the MHSA, and formally took part in government committees reviewing the merger. But their opposition to MHSA policy had fundamental limits because the MHSA legally controlled their organisations and personnel.[36]

The activity of the FKI was confined to sending letters of recommendation to the MHSA.[37] Although the FKI worried about the potential disadvantages facing its members in the event of the merger, it did not resort to stronger methods to protect its member's interests. Usually, business

34 For example, the NFMI formed a special committee to resolutely oppose the merger in October 1980, in response to MHSA's merger plan (Cha, 1992: 324).

35 The brochure said that a multiple insurer system would be better in promoting managerial efficiency and industrial harmony, whilst any merger would cause additional budget burden and direct confrontation between the government and policyholders (NFMI *Newsletter*, November 1980).

36 In the early 1980s, almost all health insurer directors were selected from pro-government people like ruling party clerks, retiring public servants and military officers (Moon, 1992: 333).

37 In a letter delivered to the MHSA in October 1980, the FKI claimed that the merger would generate economic inefficiency and reverse income distribution (Yoon, 1984: 57).

interests tried to avoid conflict with the government and chose a path less controversial. The mass media was inactive at this early stage of the debate and most major newspapers were largely negative to the merger (Kim S.-g., 1998: 24).[38]

Trade unions were inactive on the issue. From 1977, when compulsory health insurance was introduced, the FKTU supported a multiple insurer system (NFMI, 1997: 87) and opposed the merger during the earliest stages of the debate. But, it changed policy to support the merger from August 1981, under the precondition that the merger should be limited to employee insurers. Mr Choi Chung-il, a career labour activist, outlines the ambiguity of the FKTU's views at the time:

> Until 1987 when autonomous trade unions began to build, trade unions in Korea were managed by the state through financial subsidy. Accordingly, it was impossible that trade unions intervened into hot political issues. They lacked a strong consistent opinion on government policies. Until the 1980s trade unions did not show any interest in social welfare issues like health insurance, as their main concern was expressed over the improvement of working conditions and over seeking wage increases. (Interview on 11 February 2005)

38 Minister Chun speculated about the hidden reasons why major newspaper opposed the merger: "The reform (the merger) was a sensitive issue for the major media enterprises because they were also a part of the large private sectors involved directly in the medical insurance as the insurer and as the insured. Thus anti-reformist groups and the media enterprises shared a common interest…" (Kim H., 2003: 106-7).

5. Policy Outputs

1) Final outputs: keeping the current health insurer system

The final output of the first debate was to continue the then multiple insurer system, frustrating the intention of the MHSA and the ruling party to set up a single insurer system. In over two years of debate, the MHSA had changed its policy several times and was in disagreement with other proponents of the merger, whereas the OP was resolute in pushing its view as a key opponent of the merger. While the ruling party and Parliament took the initiative on the issue from mid-1981, they could not reach the intended goal, largely because of the strong opposition from President Chun and his staff.

Within policy content, keynotes of the MHSA and the ruling party fluctuated several times during the process of debate, largely due to their lack of resolution about the shape of merger and the need to coordinate their activities with other relevant authorities. The MHSA originally intended to set up a single unified insurer, fully integrating a variety of health insurers. But, at the meeting in December 1980, the merger was discussed on the basis of a plan drawn up by the EPB, which included two alternatives: the enlargement of health insurers' size based on megalopolis regions and the setting up of a single insurer. From 1981, the MHSA changed its mind, starting up a pilot self-employed insurance program, then propelling the merger forward gradually. The MHSA softened its stance in July 1981, reporting Parliament: "The MHSA reaps the desired fruits, which rank next to the merger, by restructuring the supervisory bodies of medical treatment fees and integrating computer systems." (Won, 1990: 75).

In November 1981, the MHSA revised the merger plan by suggesting two alternatives, which included setting up the single insurer system as well as a partial revision of the current multiple insurer system. In January 1982, the MHSA and the ruling party agreed to submit a merger bill during the 1982 parliamentary regular session and to start the merger process from July 1983.[39] But Minister Kim was much less resolute in her attitude towards the merger,[40] and in May 1982, the MHSA decided to complete the amalgamation program targeting insurers with under 6,000 policyholders by no later than July 1982.

After reasserting the President's determined opposition to the merger, the MHSA finally submitted three options to Parliament on 18 December 1982: the continuation of multiple insurer system, an enlarged insurer system by administrative district, and an enlarged insurer system crossing administrative districts. Submitting the report, Minister Kim said: "The MHSA would gradually extend health insurance coverage under the current multiple insurer system and develop the most suitable system for Korea." (NFMI, 1997: 271-73). Table 3.5 shows the thinking at the MHSA.

39 But the agreement was not kept, because the MHSA committee, set up in April 1982 to study a medical insurance system, was ambiguous in its approach towards the merger (Lee J., 2000: 38).

40 Although her predecessor promised Parliament that the department would submit a merger bill during the regular session of 1982, she submitted a proposal for only improving the current multiple insurer system in October 1982. She reported Parliament that the MHSA would pursue the merger as part of a long-term agenda, worrying about any consequences that might stem from a hastily prepared merger (Records of the 1982 National Assembly, No. 11).

Table 3.5 Changing perspectives of the MHSA proposals towards the merger

Date	MHSA proposals
Before Sep. 1980	Enforced the first amalgamation program
October 1980	Proposed a plan to form a single health insurer
December 1980	Suggested two alternatives based on the EPB proposal
April 1981	Enforced the second amalgamation program
July 1981	Reported a plan to integrate the supervisory bodies of medical treatment fees and the diversified computer systems
November 1981	Reported two alternatives to the National Assembly
January 1982	Decided to submit a merger bill and to start the merger from July 1983
April 1982	MHSA Committee submitted an ambiguous merger plan
May 1982	Enforced the third amalgamation program
October 1982	Submitted a proposal to improve the then multiple insurer system
December 1982	Finally submitted three alternatives

2) Reflected interests: huge power gap and frustrated merger attempt

After two years of the debate, opponents' interests were finally reflected in policy outputs, totally frustrating the merger attempt. The opponents' win can be traced in several ways. First, the MHSA, the initiator and competent department, was unclear and inconsistent in its policy. It changed policies several times and Minister Kim did not adhere to her predecessor's decision. The MHSA split its attention by simultaneously promoting parallel issues of importance, such as the pilot self-employed insurance programs and amalgamation programs, which were contradictory to each other.

Second, proponents disagreed about the alternatives and timetable of the merger. In spite of seemingly approving the merger, some MHSA officials clandestinely tried to scupper it. Also, being dependent on an internal decision-making mechanism, proponents failed to extend an external coalition.

Third, proponents misunderstood the intention of President Chun who stressed economic stability rather than social equity, and failed to persuade him otherwise. Proponents stuck to idealistic political agendas, like the promotion of a welfare society, neglecting to address the practical problems that the merger might cause. In contrast, opponents of the merger effectively persuaded the President by resorting to more realistic approaches. Above all, it was naive of proponents to not fully coordinate policy with the OP, considering its strength in making important policies.

Finally, above all else, the power imbalance between proponents and opponents of the merger was crucial in frustrating the merger attempt. Under the all-powerful presidential system of the early 1980s, the OP overpowered the ruling party and government departments. Politicians were obedient to President Chun, and the ruling party was strongly controlled by him. Former vice-Minister Ju Kyoung-sik agreed that the MHSA was weak in terms of its relationship with the OP:

> The government authorities, including the OP, the OPM, the EPB and the MHSA, held many meetings on this issue. But we failed to reach an agreement on the merger. One day, the chief-secretary to the President summoned me and severely scolded by saying: "You are ill advising the minister and making things difficult." After that, I was demoted to an affiliated organisation… (Park K. et al., 2001: 79)

Due to these reasons, the merger attempt by the MHSA and politicians was frustrated, and some MHSA officials who supported the merger lost office in February 1983, under suspicion of corruption. While opponents regarded the event as a simple case of bureaucratic corruption, former

MHSA Minister Cha Heung-bong, who backed the merger for a long time, ascribed the accusation as retaliation by the OP:

> Even though opponents of the merger alleged that I was linked to the misuse of public money, it was not true. I was repelled by the simple case of receiving a few gift coupons. It was a clear political retaliation by opponents of the merger... (Interview with Monthly *Chosun* in May 2001)

The MHSA Social Security Deliberation Committee, which came up with the merger idea, was forcibly dissolved in 1986, and another merger attempt disappeared from inside the ruling party and the MHSA (Park J., 1996: 144). Former MHSA Vice-Minister Ju Kyoung-sik traced the reason why the merger attempt failed:

> Minister Chun acted in true politician-fashion in suggesting and propelling the merger issue. His idea was not bad, but his policy goal was unclear and lacked proper preparation. So, this gave an opportunity to bureaucrats and interests groups, accustomed to the established order, to systemically oppose the policy. As a career politician, Mr Chun was more familiar with problem issuance than with problem solving. The first merger attempt was a model example of failure, being propelled by a rough-and-ready method without defining any clear goal. (Park K. et al., 2001: 83)

6. Conclusion

The first merger debate concluded with the frustration of the merger attempt due to the strong opposition from the OP and the President's instruction to end the debate. In general, the first merger debate showed the following characteristics: first, the impact of political context was important to policy-making and outputs. Political contexts such as the President's ideological emphasis on economic stability and the non-competitive and authoritarian political leadership characterised institutional features and policy networks. Meanwhile, in relation to the social context, civil society remained inactive at the time, and therefore the participation of organised interests in the debate was passive and their patterns of interest input were muted.

Second, institutional features were largely affected by the political context and vice versa. Again, institutions constrained policy networks and policy outputs. The overwhelming power of the President over Parliament and political parties produced a closed policy network. The institutional properties of the political system were also significant in determining the shape of policy networks and outputs. The President's all-pervasive power, the unfair election system and the ruling party's dominance of Parliament made policy network stably closed. Meanwhile, decision-making rules did not work as they prescribed. In practice, the power relationship between participants, 'behind the scene' politics and prior consent from the President or ministers were more important than formal decision-making systems. The operation of various levels of veto points was ceremonial in many cases.

Third, policy networks were largely affected by both the policy context and institutional features. The reverse was trivial. Policy networks during the first debate were closer to those of policy communities, albeit not typical ones. 1) Authoritative politics and unbalanced power relationship were greatly influential in closing policy networks and in making participants depend mainly on a strategy of persuading the President. Again, the closed policy networks, which confined the participation to official actors, made interaction patterns simple and stable. 2) Each participant possessed different detailed interests in the merger, despite their assignment in the same bloc. It is unrealistic to postulate the possibility of shared interest among members of the same bloc. 3) Participants' resource dependency was very high. But the relative importance of their resources highlighted big differences. 4) Interaction patterns were crucially constrained by the network structure. Participants sought to reach answers through consultative and consensus-oriented manners.

Finally, the intended policy goal to introduce the single insurer system was frustrated by the objection of the President, who mainly listened to his staff. But, although policy outputs did not meaningfully affect the policy context, they fed back to the power relationship among political actors and the network structure relating to health insurance policy to a degree. A frustrated merger attempt undeniably changed MHSA's perspective and led to the reformation of its key members.

Chapter
4

Democratisation but Frustrated Health Insurance Reform

The Second Round of Merger Debate in the Late 1980s

1. Introductory Comments

In August 1986, when President Chun Doo-hwan publicized a plan to gradually extend health insurance coverage to the self-employed, the government launched 'a comprehensive social welfare scheme'. Efforts to reconcile differences were made between relevant government authorities including the Ministry of Health and Social Affairs (MHSA) and the ruling party, to launch a health insurance scheme for the rural self-employed based on the then multiple insurer system. They consented to a mix of megalopolis-sized insurers in metropolitan cities with county-sized insurers in small cities and rural areas. But President Chun instructed that all health insurers were to set up on the basis of county-sized multiple insurers.

Following the President's lead on the matter, the MHSA and the ruling party revised the Medical Insurance Act in October 1987 in order to introduce the rural self-employed health insurance scheme from 1988,[1] without any significant resistance from opposition parties who were firmly geared towards the December 1987 presidential election. With the ruling party's victory in the election, the compulsory health insurance for the rural self-employed was enforced from January 1988 (Chun et al., 2009: 141).

The second debate about merging health insurers was triggered by the

1 The bill suggested extending health insurance coverage to the rural self-employed from 1988 and to the urban self-employed from 1989, based on the then multiple insurer system (Lee Y., 2003: 68).

plans to extend health insurance coverage to the rural self-employed and directly followed protests from farmers and progressive healthcare professionals in 1988. That is, the merger of health insurers (henceforth, the merger) became a hot topic in response to farmers' dissatisfaction with high-levels of insurance premiums. The merger was seen as a good way of lowering farmers' insurance premium burden and solving the financial deficit of the rural self-employed insurers, by transferring accumulated employee insurance funds to rural self-employed insurers.

More specifically, shortly after the introduction of the rural self-employed health insurance scheme in January 1988, activist farmers' groups launched a series of complaints that ignited the second merger debate, which lasted until December 1989. They were protesting about farmers' high insurance premiums, an inadequate medical system in rural areas, and unfair insurance fees between company workers and farmers (Chun, 2005: 165). They returned medical insurance cards and staged signature-seeking campaigns between February-April 1988. They also held large-scale demonstrations from April 1988, in association with progressive healthcare professionals. Meanwhile, in contrast to the first debate, the MHSA led the coalition seeking to block the merger, along with the support of the Office of the President (OP) (Choi J., 2003: 183).

The 1988 main parliamentary session from September was a stormy one, with the revision of the Medical Insurance Act being debated in advance of the scheduled launch of the urban self-employed health insurance in July 1989. The MHSA and the OP supported the multiple insurer system, whereas opposition parties and civic groups, led by activist farmers and progressive healthcare professionals, insisted on the introduction of a single insurer system. The MHSA proposed a government bill in November 1988 based on the multiple insurer system, super-imposing county-sized insurers in small and medium cities whilst megalopolis-sized insurers were set up in big cities. Civic groups, two major opposition parties and the Korean Medical Association (KMA) all brought forward their own version of merger bill (Baik, 2010: 243).

However, Parliament failed to reach an agreement during the 1988 regular session on March 9th 1989, and the policy was carried forward to the February 1989 extraordinary session. During the session, opposition parties succeeded in passing the National Medical Insurance Bill, which adopted a single insurer system and absorbed Medicaid into medical insurance, with the ruling party's reluctant agreement.

The passage of the Bill, however, sparked strong opposition from opponents of the merger. They asked for a presidential veto and the President requested Parliament to reconsider the Bill on March 24, pointing to its possible violation of the constitutional right of property and the likely chaos that would be caused by the vagueness of its appendices (OP, 1989: 2-5). So, now, proponents of the merger strongly criticised the President for using his veto on the Bill. Civic groups staged large-scale protests urging the reversal of this decision to veto the Bill. Opposition parties issued communiqués demanding the resignation of the MHSA minister. Nevertheless, the urban self-employed health insurance scheme started in July 1989, under a multiple insurer system, as scheduled.

From September 1989, civic groups demonstrated their desire for the immediate merger and pressured opposition parties to be more proactive in proposing the merger. Following these civic groups' demands, opposition parties decided to amend the appendices of the vetoed Bill during the parliamentary regular session. But, the governing bloc refused to reconsider the vetoed Bill. With the emergence of a giant ruling party from the three-party merger in February 1990, the second debate faded away and the vetoed Bill was automatically abrogated by the end of the parliamentary term of office in June 1992 (Chung and Cho, 2001: 97).

2. Policy Context

1) Political context: progress towards democratic politics

Korean politics was changing directions again as the end of the Chun Doo-hwan administration drew closer. This was particularly true during the summer of 1987, which was a turning point on the pathway to political democracy. The Chun administration backed down amidst protests by adopting a direct presidential election system and permitting opposition leader Kim Dae-jung to compete in the next presidential election campaign scheduled for December 1987 (Heo and Roehrig, 2011: 37). But the ruling candidate Rho Tae-woo, picked by Chun, won the presidential election and thus inherited the military government.

Nonetheless, the governing ideologies of the Rho Tae-woo administration (1988-93) emphasised policies to pursue political democracy and social diversification.[2] President Rho hoped to distinguish himself from his predecessor, though they came from the same military background, by stressing

---

2 The Roh administration advocated the reconciliation between the people and 'the era of the great ordinary people' as two pillars of governance, suggesting national self-esteem, balanced development, democratic reconciliation, reunification and prosperity as the practical way of achieving his lasting national goals (Korea Government *White Paper,* 1988).

democracy and national reconciliation (Hong, 2001: 313), as was shown in his inauguration speech of February 1988:

> There are new map and compass before us. They are a map of democracy and a compass of national reconciliation, which all of us agreed when the people elected me as the President... Along with effectuation of the new Constitution, I declare that the 6th Republic is the government of the people, in which the people become the master of nation... We will also plough the furrow towards a goal of national reconciliation.

There were many political events surrounding the second debate. The revision of the Constitution in October 1987 and the December 1987 direct presidential election provided a defining moment to the second debate, as all political parties promised the nationwide extension of health insurance coverage during the presidential campaign.[3] The government distributed health insurance cards to farmers just two weeks before the presidential election, under the pretext of preparing for the rural self-employed insurance scheme that was due to start in January 1988. The April 1988 general election was another important political event. In response to farmers' strong protests after January 1988, the government introduced some calming measures in April 1988 in time for the coming election. Opposition parties also addressed the merger as an election pledge (Choi J., 2003: 184).

President Rho's key presidential election pledge was also another politi-

3 Although Rho also stood for the extension of health insurance to the self-employed as an election pledge, he intended for the extension to happen through the then multiple insurer system (Kim M.-h., 1999: 19).

cal event that forced the ruling party to agree to an opposition bill in March 1989. Dr Kim Yeon-myung, a career health policy activist, interprets the influence of the midterm plebiscite on the ruling party:

> Although some ruling lawmakers from rural areas preferred a single insurer system, the ruling party basically opposed the merger. But, facing the prospect of an expected presidential midterm plebiscite ahead, the ruling party changed policy to agree the opposition bill. It was impossible for the ruling party to reverse its opinion without presidential support. Afterwards, the President and opposition leader Kim Dae-jung compromised to cancel the midterm plebiscite and so the ruling party overturned its position not to oppose the merger. (Interview on 19 April 2005)

The return to a tougher stance on 'illegal demonstrations' in April 1989 was the main political event that altered the government's response to the demands from opposition parties and civic groups. The three-party merger in February 1990 was the final event that terminated the second debate by enabling the governing bloc to overwhelm opposition parties.

New political and administrative leadership had emerged during the second debate. Ruling party candidate Rho was elected as President and he kept his election pledge by extending health insurance coverage to the self-employed. The 1988 general election resulted in the opposition domination of Parliament, greatly affecting policy-making style and the government's response to external demands. MHSA ministers were changed three times during the course of the debate (MHSA *White Paper*, 2003), making MHSA policies inconsistent.

The nature of politics and political leadership during the second debate was entirely different from that of the early 1980s. From mid-1987 Korea's politics was rapidly transforming into a democracy and the process of selecting political leadership was becoming very competitive. The 1987 presidential election was widely seen as quite open and fair.[4] Rho's leadership style was also very different from that of his predecessor, despite his succession to power held by the former governing bloc (Robinson, 2007: 168-70). The Rho administration was based on the new Constitution that reinforced the strength of Parliament as counterweight to presidential power.

Opposition parties obtained a parliamentary majority at the 1988 general election and this meant that Parliament, which had always played a peripheral role under dictatorial politics, came back to a centre of policy-making. The Rho administration was a transitional period on the path towards democratic and competitive politics.

2) Social context: turbulent civil society

Civil society, which was inactive in the early 1980s, was vitalised as President Chun's term in office was drawing to a close in 1986-87. The general public, civic groups and trade unions took to the streets in June 1987 to demand political democracy. The Constitution was revised in October 1987, and it introduced a direct presidential election system and increased legislative powers. Trade unions were endowed with greater levels of freedom under new labour laws (Koo, 2007: 79).[5] Activist labour groups hurried

4 In the election, ruling candidate Rho Tae-woo polled 36.6 percent, while Kim Young-sam obtained 28.1 percent, Kim Dae-jung scored 27.1 percent and Kim Jong-pil registered 8.1 percent (Kwon H., 1999: 64).

5 Under the revision of labour-related laws in November 1987, conditions to form trade un-

to establish an alternative peak association, independently of the Federation of Korean Trade Unions (FKTU). Being confronted with the renewed strength of civil society, the freshly elected Rho administration was not yet confident in being able to control civil society. Moreover, civil society power had reached new heights with the emergence of big and strong opposition parties, who had held good relations with civil society (Wong, 2004: 69).

3. Institutional Features

1) Balanced power and opposition dominated Parliament

Approaching the end of its presidency, the Chun administration's capacity to control the political situation was remarkably weakened and the power gap between political organisations began to narrow. In particular, the emergence of a strong opposition group, the New Korea Democratic Party, at the 1985 general election and the revision of the Constitution in October 1987 rapidly corrected the power imbalance. The opposition parties' parliamentary dominance from 1988 toppled the existing power structure between the government and Parliament, enabling the latter to gain a central position in the political realm (Hahm, 2000: 110).

Parliament's increasing importance in making laws can be seen in Table 4.1, by comparing the growing numbers of Parliament-inspired bills. Although the power of opposition parties greatly increased, the President

ions were largely relaxed and the government's right to dissolve trade unions was abolished (Park J., 1996: 106).

Table 4.1 The number of bills proposed and approved in Parliament

	Proposal			Approval		
	Total	Parliamen-tarians	Ministers	Total	Parliamen-tarians	Ministers
12th Assembly (1985-88)	379	211	168	222 (58.6)	66 (31.3)	156 (92.8)
13th Assembly (1988-92)	938	570	368	492 (52.5)	171 (30.0)	321 (87.2)

Note: Numbers in parentheses state the ratio of approved bills, compared with those proposed.
Source: Secretariat of the National Assembly (1996), The National Assembly Statistics.

could still dampen Parliament's enthusiasm through the mechanism of the ruling party and exercise of the presidential veto. The fact that opposition parties asked eight times for the dismissal of cabinet members and were all abrogated in the 13th National Assembly shows that the President still held onto some considerable power even under the Rho administration (Kang et al., 1998: 478).

With regard to the relationship between the ruling and opposition parties, increased opposition power in the Rho administration was worthy of close attention. As is shown in Table 4.2, the ruling party attained 41.8 percent of the seats, leading to an opposition dominated Parliament.

Table 4.2 Results of the April 1988 parliamentary election

	Number of seats	Proportion of seats (%)	Polling score (%)
The ruling DJP	125 (regional 87+ proportional 38)	41.8	34.0
Party for Peace and Democracy (PPD)	70 (54+16)	23.4	19.3
Reunification Democratic Party (RDP)	59 (46+13)	19.7	23.8
New Democratic Republican Party (NDRP)	35 (27+8)	11.7	15.6
Independents and others	10 (0)	3.4	7.3
Total	299 (75)	100.0	100.0

Source: adapted from the National Assembly homepage (www.assembly.go.kr).

Within the government, public bureaucrats had accumulated managerial power during the government-led economic growth of the 1970-80s, but their autonomy from political appointees was limited. It was also usual that ministers who had strong political backgrounds controlled their subordinates more easily.

Despite the fact that presidential power was weakened with the general progress towards political democracy, the authority of both the President and his staff in the government remained unchanged. They controlled government departments through rewards and the use of discipline. The President had the final say in state affairs and exercised power through the control and coordination work of the OP and its investigation and inspection over the work of other government departments.

While the PM could recommend cabinet members to the President and superintend each department, it was seldom the case that the PM, appointed by the President, exercised this legally endowed authority. The PM frequently changed and his/her role remained largely symbolic in the 1980s, one of simply advising the President. Amongst government departments, the Economic Planning Board that controlled public money, the Audit and Inspection Board that supervised department expenditure, the National Security Planning Board that coordinated state affairs and the Public Prosecutors Office were powerful.

2) Towards a more competitive set of institutions

The year 1987 was a turning point in Korean politics. As a result of successful mass protests, the Constitution was amended and served to reduce the power imbalance between political organisations. Although ruling candidate Rho was elected the President, the political institutional properties of the Rho administration were very different to those of its predecessor.

The governing system of the Rho administration was entirely different from the previous regime and the revised Constitution had greatly weakened the President's power. Some presidential privileges such as being able to declare a state emergency and to dissolve Parliament were abrogated. But, even though his authority was reduced, the President still retained several institutional measures that could allow him to obtain legislative power. For example, although the right to declare state emergency was repealed, the President could issue emergency decrees with regard to issues affecting the national economy. The right to proclaim martial law was also preserved. Importantly, the President could veto bills passed by Parliament.

The Prime Minister's formal status was unchanged from the time of the Chun administration. His/her role vis-à-vis the President and Parliament stayed largely nominal, irrespective of the law. The authority of the State Council (Korea's Cabinet Council), a supreme body able to deliberate on important policies, remained untouched, too. But as mentioned earlier, its function was in reality largely ceremonial.

Despite all of this, institutions that strengthened legislative power were greatly bolstered under the Rho administration by the revision of the Constitution and further progress towards political democracy (Seth, 2010: 210). First, the parliamentary regular session was extended and restrictions on the length of a parliamentary session were abolished to boost Parliament's legislative function (National Assembly Act, Article 7-1). Second, Parliament's power over the control of state affairs was greatly increased. While its right to investigate particular state affairs was untouched, authority to inspect the work of government offices was added. Third, Parliament could file a suit calling for the impeachment of the President or cabinet members. To file an impeachment against the President required approval of at least two thirds of all registered lawmakers, while the PM and ministers could be impeached by a one-third motion/majority approval (the Constitution, Article 36). Finally, Parliament restricted the President's right to declare emergency measures and martial law by repealing them through a majority vote.

A multi-party system and the free establishment of political parties were guaranteed as before, and it was stipulated that the state should protect political parties and provide financial subsidies to parties with more than a set number of seats in Parliament. But, given that the institutions relating to the political party system in the Rho administration were identical to those of the Chun administration, the reality was very different. The freedom to set and run opposition parties was practically secured in the Rho administration, whereas the previous regime had put a tight rein on the activities of hard-line opposition politicians. Unlike the Chun administration, which attempted to disrupt opposition parties, the multi-party system under the Rho administration was governed by election outcomes (Jang H., 2001: 110).

Most major political parties' ideologies were identical in so far as they advocated liberal democracy and a market economy. Their party platforms were also not too different from each other, as parties were based not on ideological differences but on regional favouritism. While conservative parties occupied the mainstream of politics, socialist or progressive parties were discouraged due to the prospect of interference from the communist countries to the North.

The electoral system had undergone a remarkable change as a result of Constitutional amendment in 1987. The revised Constitution abolished an indirect electoral-college system and adopted a direct presidential election

Table 4.3 Comparison of the proportional representation system

	A quorum of proportional representation	Principle of distribution
The Chun administration	One-third of total lawmakers (or a half of constituent lawmakers)	Two thirds of proportional representatives were awarded to a leading party and a third were distributed to parties according to the rate of seat number.
The Rho administration	One-third of total lawmakers (or a half of constituent lawmakers)	Proportional representatives were awarded in accordance to the rate of seats won (a proviso). Where a leading party failed to win a majority, around half of proportional seats were awarded to it.

Source: adapted from Lee and Kim (1996: 180-88).

system, allowing for open competition in selecting the President. The President's term was shortened to a five-year single term to prevent the revival of any form of presidential dictatorship. In practice, the 1987 presidential election was very competitive, contested by four major figures. With the revision of election-related laws in 1987, the parliamentary election system also progressed towards more open competition as it adopted single-member constituencies and tidied up its proportional representation system. While the ruling party easily dominated Parliament under the medium electorate system of the early 1980s, it became impossible for the ruling party to secure a majority vote in a single-member electorate system, particularly when taking into account regional voting tactics (Robinson, 2007: 169). As is shown in Table 4.3, a proportional representation system also became more balanced between ruling and opposition parties.

3) Firmly embedded decision-making rules

The formal decision-making system in the second debate was basically identical to that of the first debate. The decision-making process started with a subordinate's report and followed a pattern of guidance from superiors through the official *ringi* system. Department meetings usually followed the unanimity rule and superiors hierarchically coordinated any differences between bureaus or sections. The minister ruled on the final decisions and fierce conflicts were resolved by his/her intervention (Cho, 2004: 50). Many department committees were formed to coordinate differences and to engage vested interests within policy-making. But in many cases, they were abused and simply used to justify a bureaucratic decision.

Inter-departmental decision-making or conflict resolution occurred through several levels of coordinating bodies such as working-level, vice-ministerial and ministerial meetings. Opinions of the competent department were largely adhered to at these meetings.[6] The OPM intervened in coordinating government affairs and the OP played a key role in making important decisions (Kang, 2004: 1141).[7]

The State Council was the formal institution that was able to rule on state affairs (Constitution, Article 88). But in practice, it remained as a symbolic institution simply justifying departmental decisions and discharging the

6 In 1987, 80.7 percent of all matters were not revised at the ministerial conference level, and discussion time per agenda item was just 5.1 minutes, while the vice-ministerial conference recorded 76.6 percent non-revision passage rate and 7.7 minutes' discussion per agenda item (Chung, 1994).

7 The power of the OP increased as it presided over the ruling party/government conference under the Rho administration, while the National Security Planning Board had done so under the Chun administration (Kim J.-h., 2003: 235).

President's political responsibility. The President participated in the State Council meetings only two or three times a year. Dr Gil who ran State Council affairs explains the work of the State Council in more detail:

> Ministerial and vice-ministerial meetings coordinated the agenda suggested at the State Council in advance. In most cases, the PM presided over the Council instead of the President. Although the President occasionally presided over the Council, it was impossible to actively debate state affairs in the Council under the situation where the President drew up guidelines of national governance. The Council is basically unable to make decisions on difficult questions of policy. (Interview on 18 November 2004)

The ruling party/government conference was a formal institution to exchange information and coordinate differences between governing bloc members. The OP also intervened where important political matters were involved. Once differences were resolved, the ruling party played the role of messenger, supporting government policy in Parliament.[8]

Decision-making and conflict resolution in Parliament followed established rules laid down by the National Assembly Act. At least 20 lawmakers, or political parties with over 20 lawmakers, could propose bills (National Assembly Act, Article 74-1). The government also presented proposals of bills before each standing committee. If the ruling party held a greater number of seats, the possibility of passing government bills was much higher. Mrs

8 Although each lawmaker was constitutionally independent, it was hard for ruling lawmakers to oppose party or government opinions in the situation where the President controlled the ruling party as its chairperson (Chung, 2003: 25).

Chung Soon-im, a National Assembly legislative researcher, explains the operation of standing committees:

> The Health and Social Affairs Committee did not go to a vote in most cases, as the Committee did not consider politically hot potatoes at that time. The Committee normally formed standing sub-committees to dig deeper into suggested policies. Sub-committees were made of 6-7 members in proportion to the number of seats that political parties had in Parliament and usually did not put matters to a vote either. Lawmakers detested voting, because they worried that the content of discussion might be recorded. (Interview on 27 December 2004)

The roles of the Legislation and Judiciary Committee and the general assembly were not different from those in the early 1980s. The President promulgated the authorised bills to introduce them into law or s/he could request that the bills go back to Parliament for further consideration. Accordingly, there were several points, at which a veto could be used in terms of governmental decision-making. But it was another question whether institutions were effective in reality or not. Veto points were not effective in the situation where such systems as informal consent and prior coordination or instruction (*naerak* in Korean) were more vital in making government decisions. Parliamentary decision-making largely depended more on the power relationship between political parties than on the role of established institutions.

4) Previous policy inertia, again

With a failed first merger attempt, all governing bloc members, including the MHSA and the ruling party, became supporters of a multiple insurer system. The earlier decision to preserve a multiple insurer system constrained policy-making by shaping participants' interaction patterns. Despite the intensified drive to set up a single insurer system in the late 1980s, the embedded system of health insurance and the newly established alliance of institution keepers successfully preserved the multiple insurer system once again.

In detail, the MHSA which had earlier altered its policy to protect a multiple insurer system agreed with the ruling party on the matter of gradually extending health insurance coverage from January 1988 through the multiple insurer system, and succeeded in revising the Medical Insurance Act in October 1987, as it had originally intended. Unlike their positions during the early 1980s, the MHSA and the OP stood shoulder-to-shoulder on this matter, seeking to preserve existing policy.

The second merger debate from January 1988 intensified as a result of conflict between reformists and those seeking maintenance of the status quo. Proponents of the merger, such as civic groups and opposition parties, tried to change existing institutions, whilst opponents of the merger represented by the MHSA and the OP made every effort to block change. Opponents of the merger stood by the existing institutions, although they partly accepted the formation of megalopolis-sized insurers in larger cities in response to repeated civil protests. When the merger bill passed Parliament in March 1989, the existing multiple insurer system survived again thanks to a presidential veto. While proponents of the merger continuously pursued the merger, established institutions stood firm against it. The former MHSA vice-minister Ju Kyoung-sik explained the process that led to the President's decision to veto the merger bill in March 1989:

> Three bills including the National Medical Insurance Act and two labour-related laws passed Parliament on 9 March 1989. But major newspapers were negative towards the bills and the government and the ruling party recommended using a presidential veto. At last, the President decided to veto all three bills and return them to Parliament for reconsideration and dismissed MHSA Minister, Labour Minister and Chief Secretary to the President accusing them of being responsible for the chaos. (Park K. et al., 2001: 82)

4. Policy Networks

The second debate on the merger lasted two years from the start of the introduction of a health insurance scheme for the rural self-employed in January 1988, to the end of the parliamentary regular session in December 1989. There were more participants this time, mainly due to the advance of political democracy and the enhanced vitality of civil society. Two blocs with conflicting views on the merger took shape and non-government actors initiated the debate. Civic groups and opposition parties championed the merger, whereas the government and the ruling party led the opponent bloc. In contrast to the first debate, in which the governing bloc dominated, private actors were major participants in the second debate and its principal debating arena was Parliament. As a result, the second debate marked, despite its failure to achieve its intended goal, a watershed in extending the influence of civic groups on policy-making and it laid the foundation for the introduction of a single insurer system in the late 1990s. Table 4.4 classifies participants in the second debate.

Table 4.4 Classification of participants in the second debate

	Proponents of the merger	Opponents of the merger
Official actors	EPB (at first)	MHSA, EPB (in the end), OP
Unofficial actors	Opposition parties, ruling party (at first), progressive civic groups and farmers groups, KMA, and social welfare academia	Ruling party (in the end), business interests (FKI and KEF), employee health insurers and NFMI, FKTU (trade union), mass media, and scholars from health and medicine

1) Network structure: abruptly opened non-exclusive network

Nature of participants: number, dominant actors and exclusion

Government departments and the ruling party had been working together, since 1986, to introduce plans to extend health insurance coverage to the rural self-employed. They reached a compromise[9] and revised the Medical Insurance Act in October 1987 to extend health insurance coverage under the then multiple insurer system.[10] Other policy actors were not involving during this revision process.[11]

However, more participants joined the debate from January 1988, when the rural self-employed health insurance scheme came into effect. Opposition parties started to actively take part in health insurance matters. The two

9 Of the key actors, the MHSA and the OP preferred a multiple insurer system while the ruling party supported a single insurer one, placing its faith in an appeal to the people in forthcoming elections. The EPB had not decided upon the shape of health insurer system (Park J., 1996: 121).

10 The ruling party and the MHSA agreed, in April 1987, to build the rural self-employed health insurer scheme on a county-sized multiple insurer system and to study the single insurer system as a longer-term project (Lee D. et al., 1992: 338-40).

11 Opposition parties were indifferent to the issue of health insurance at that time, because they concentrated on the imminent 1987 presidential election and other political issues like the revision of the Constitution and labour-related laws.

main opposition parties of Kim Young-sam and Kim Dae-jung, who led the initiative on state affairs from 1988, chose to rewrite the Medical Insurance Act in preparation for the setting up of an urban self-employed health insurance scheme from July 1989, as a way of showcasing their political muscle and increasing their appeal to the public. Civic groups and progressive trade unions emerged as key actors in Korean politics, going through the transitional period of 1987-88 (Bae, 2004: 404). They engaged in health insurance issues by using all possible means at their disposal in order to achieve their goals. In particular, civic groups twice formed united fronts, in June 1988 and April 1989, in order to drive the merger forward. The KMA also supported the merger.

The governing bloc, meanwhile, had continued to play a key role in maintaining the survival of the existing insurer system. Now, the MHSA led those opposing the merger (NFMI, 1997: 428). Other actors, such as business interests and employee health insurers, engaged in the debate to oppose the merger. While self-employed insurance unions began to stage strikes demanding the merger from mid-1989, the conservative FKTU's position on the matter was ambiguous. Chung Kil-oh, the FKTU Policy Bureau Director, explains why the FKTU took a neutral stance on the issue:

> Under the authoritarian rule of the1980s, the labour movement did not pay any attention to social reform, and trade unions were satisfied with the multiple insurer system. At the time, the promotion of workers' basic right was a top priority for trade unions. I candidly admit the FKTU did not have any determined perspective on the matter of health insurer system at that time. (Interview on 21 December 2004)

An unusual participant in the second debate was the academic circle. While social welfare academics largely supported the merger as a way to achieve nationwide risk and income redistribution between policyholders, scholars majoring in health and medical disciplines mostly opposed the merger, standing by liberalistic principles and purporting the managerial efficiency of health insurance. Both sides issued statements outlining their opinions in June and August 1988 respectively. The mass media's concern about the matter greatly increased. But most major newspapers, except the *Kukmin Ilbo* and the *Hankyoreh Shinmun*, were negative towards the merger, worrying about the possible increase in company employee insurance premiums (Kim M.-h., 1999: 59; Shin, 2004: 102).

Dominant actors in the second debate included civic groups and opposition parties, whereas the first debate mainly took place between governing bloc groups. Activist farmers' groups such as the National Farmers' Union, the Catholic Farmers' Conference, the Christian Farmers' Association were dissatisfied with high-level insurance premiums and staged large-scale protests across several months. They demanded slashing insurance premiums, merging health insurers and increasing government subsidies to self-employed insurers (Lee D. et al, 1992: 341).

Young progressive professionals in health and medicine, feeling let down by the conservative views of the KMA and the Korea Pharmaceutical Association (KPA), offered their support for the merger. Particularly, young physicians including Kim Rok-ho, Cho Hong-jun and Lee Sang-yi, who were passionate advocates of the merger, founded progressive organisations like the Association of Physicians for Humanism (APH). Then, there were activist pharmacists, like Lim Jong-cheol, who formed the Korean Pharmacists for Democratic Society (KPDS) to promote the merger. Healthcare trade union, led by nurses, also backed the merger.

In June 1988 these activist groups united to set up the National Conference for Medical Insurance Integration (NCMII), and since, have taken the lead in proposing the merger.[12] Dr Kim Yeon-myung, a founding leader of the NCMII, argues the leading role of civic groups in the debate:

> Progressive civic groups' active engagement in the debate became possible as a result of the political democratisation that started in 1987. So, it is fair to say that structural conditions that activated civil society came about because of the march of democracy. At first, young progressive healthcare professionals and student movement groups led the debate. Farmers' groups wanted the abolition of health insurance program at the time, as they lacked professional expertise on health insurance matters. We persuaded them to accept the merger and also urged labour activists to take part in the debate. We drove the agenda and sorted out any conflict of interests between farmers and organised labour. (Interview on 14 December 2004)

Feeling pressured by civic groups, major opposition parties also joined the debate from late-1988. They convened an extra parliamentary session in February 1989 and were eventually able to pass a merger bill in March 1989, although this was followed by the use of presidential veto. The KMA was also active in backing the merger. Since the late 1989, self-employed insurers union had led nationwide protests in favour of the merger, substi-

12 The NCMII mobilised diverse measures, such as signature-seeking campaigns, the refusal to pay insurance fees and legislative lobbying, as a way to propose the merger and nullify the President's veto (NCHIU, 1999: 955).

tuting civic groups, despite the failure to put the vetoed Bill in its place.

Meanwhile, the MHSA led the opponent bloc during the second debate, differently to the side they had previously supported. Kim Jong-dae and Moon Gyoung-tae were ardent opponents. While key opponent officials like Kim Jong-dae had served in the OP during the first debate, they returned to the MHSA in time for the second debate and continued to resolutely block the merger. The MHSA took the lead in issuing a government bill based on a multiple insurer system to Parliament in October 1988. In addition, it recommended President Rho to veto the parliamentary merger bill in March 1989. The OP stood firm in its resolve to keep the existing multiple insurer system. Although the EPB and the ruling party's positions were a little unclear, they eventually sided with the MHSA and the OP.

Opponents, such as business interests (KEF and FKI), the FKTU and employee health insurers, played peripheral roles in the debate. Their activities were confined to the issuance of press releases opposing the merger after the passage of the bill (*Jungang Ilbo*, 15 March 1989).

In the second debate, it was impossible for the government or any other principal actors to intentionally exclude unfavourable actors from entering policy networks. The number of participants had multiplied with the growth of political democracy. Since the June 1987 nationwide civil protests and the December 1987 presidential election, the power of civil society had been organised in a more systematic fashion, and the government could no longer shield itself from outside interests when making policy.

Multiple civic groups formed a united front to lead the entire process, and opposition parties took leadership in parliamentary decision-making. Activated progressive trade unions and self-employed insurers' unions promoted their interests in diverse ways. The KMA also put forward its views in a proactive manner (Chung and Cho, 2001: 97).[13]

Participants' interests in the merger

Participants formed two conflicting blocs, even though the reasons for joining one side or the other were not identical for all. Among proponents of the merger, civic groups advocated a single insurer system for the official reason that it would cut the cost of insurance premiums for the poor self-employed (KPA *Newsletter*, 8 June 1988). They also recognised that it would be an additional step along the road to further distributive justice, after which social insurance could be pursued. Additionally, they believed that the merger could make the extension of health insurance allowances possible by diverting the accumulated insurance funds of employee health insurers into the self-employed insurers. Civic groups also intended to make use of the issue as a symbolic event to bolster their organisational capacity and to unite civil society at a politically transient moment. Activist farmers groups had a real interest in cutting insurance premiums and in co-managing established insurance funds as a consequence of the merger (Kim, Yang, and Yu, 2013: 78).

In the meantime, opposition parties supported the merger as a way to make use of the issue as an opportunity to seize the political initiative. They also needed support from civic groups who emerged as a new power bloc from the late 1980s. Kim Jong-dae, the MHSA Public Affairs Director during the second debate, outlines opposition parties' interests in the issue:

13 The KMA requested the revision of the Medical Insurance Act in November 1988 to merge health insurers, and staged protests in February 1989 in favour of the merger (Choi J., 2001: 210).

> The official reason that opposition parties supported the merger was always the logic that the merger would make the extension of health insurance to the self-employed possible without additional government funding. But, in reality, they approached the issue from a purely political perspective. Particularly, Kim Dae-jung of the PPD proposed the merger, calculating the likely benefits in the forthcoming general election. Civic groups also alleged the merger on the basis of political logic. To them, the merger debate was a means to fight against anti-democratic forces. Opposition parties and civic groups did not have any expertise on health insurance matters and relied upon political expediency. (Interview on 15 December 2004)

The KMA's major interest in the health insurer system was to be sufficiently compensated in terms of medical treatment fees from health insurers and a single insurer system was more adequate for the purpose (Kim H., 2003: 159). The KMA, however, had greater concerns about increasing medical treatment fees, the voluntary contract for medical insurance treatment and the increased allocation of medical doctors in government committees (KMA *Newsletter*, 9 September 1989).

Self-employed insurers' union justified support for the merger by arguing that health insurance premiums for the self-employed was likely to be reduced as a consequence of the merger. But, it is also undeniable that practical interests lay in the enhancement of job security, the nationwide extension of the personnel management pool and the co-management of insurance funds through the merger.

Among opponents of the merger, the MHSA argued for a multiple insurer system, assuring its merits as a vehicle for smoothly extending health insurance coverage to the self-employed without administrative chaos. But practically, MHSA officials had vested interests in preserving a multiple insurer system, because it was more advantageous to make jobs for retired bureaucrats and to control health insurers (Kim S.-y., 2011: 84).[14] Mr Kim Jong-dae, however, denies this pragmatic point of view:

> MHSA officials did not oppose the merger just to protect their own benefits. They sincerely worried the dysfunctions that might be caused any rushed merger of health insurers. They took pride in the health insurance program that they had introduced and had an obligation to protect it from proponents' political expediency. In fact, the debate about the merger became largely a political one from the late 1980s. To proponents, the debate was a good chance to refute Korea's military past. Proponents asserted the people should oppose any program the military government pursued. The logic of democratic and anti-democratic dichotomy was introduced into the debate, greatly wasting national energy as a result. (Interview on 15 December 2004)

The EPB, the principal budgetary department, had always prioritised minimising the extra burden of government spending by the initiation of new programs. Although the EPB admitted the need to extend health insurance coverage, it was open to different methods and was not rigid on the form of the health insurer system (KMA *Newsletter*, 1 September 1989).[15] By

14 Rep. Park Young-sook of the opposition PPD argued: "The MHSA prefers a multiple insurer system, because about 90 percent of the senior staff of health insurers is recruited from retired public officials, ruling party's bureaucrats and discharged soldiers." (Shin, 2004: 93).

15 The EPB proposed the introduction of a medical security tax, as a way of extending health insurance at first, because it worried that it would put a strain on government budgets in case of the merger, due to the difficulty of raising a premium rate (KMA *Newsletter*, 6

the end, however, the EPB opposed the merger after being persuaded by the MHSA (NFMI, 1997: 427).

The OP was not so active in the second debate, as it had already agreed with the MHSA to keep a multiple insurer system. A key concern for President Rho and his staff was to select the easiest way to extend the health insurance program, and they preferred a multiple insurer system as a more stable way to achieve this end without causing administrative chaos (Kim J.-d., 2000: 97).

The ruling party's principal interest in the merger was to win votes in elections. The ruling party preferred a single insurer system at first, believing that its social equity appeal would attract voters. In particular, the rural self-employed were the ruling party's main supporters and a single insurer system was expected to be much more beneficial to them considering their lower income. But unlike opposition parties, the ruling party had benefited from a multiple insurer system through the allocation of jobs to retiring party bureaucrats.[16] So, the ruling party was ambivalent towards any potential merger. Dr Kim Yeon-myung interpreted on the ruling party's motivation in favouring a multiple insurer system in an unusual way:

> One important motivation that the ruling party preferred a multiple insurer system was in the fact that the then core governing power, especially pro-Park Cheol-eun clan, had vested interests in maintaining a multiple insurer system. Under the system, the pro-Park clan was able to appoint friendly retiring bu-

---

March 1986).

16 In 1989, 29.4 percent of high-level managers of health insurers were occupied by party bureaucrats, 15.4 percent by retired military officers and 44.1 percent by retired public officials (Won, 1990: 93).

> reaucrats and military officers as heads of health insurers. In the future, they might play important political roles for Mr Park who had designs on being the next President. (Interview on 14 December 2005)

Of the minor participants in the second debate, employee health insurers and business interests opposed the merger, as they felt that the merger would generate a sharp increase in employees' insurance premiums and could discriminate between policyholders due to the lower income declaration of the self-employed. But their real interests lay in preserving job security and protecting accumulated insurance funds. Business groups worried about the possible rise in employees' insurance premiums and the loss of employers' control in managing the insurance funds after the merger (KEF *Newsletter*, October 1996). The FKTU claimed the merger would force rises in employees' insurance premiums.

Resource dependency between participants

In the second debate, resource dependency between participants with the same preference for the health insurer system was prominent. Among proponents of the merger, civic groups and opposition parties were closely dependent on each other for resources. The strength of civic groups was mainly derived from their effective capacity to arrange collective action to support particular policies and to mobilise votes in election campaign. Consecutive elections and oppositional dominance of Parliament provided civic groups with a good chance of bringing their resources to the fore to support the argument. At the same time, they needed the backing of opposition parties in pushing forward their proposals to Parliament.

Opposition parties' resources derived mainly from the power to make or amend laws. Opposition parties that held the majority of seats in Parliament played critical roles in changing the health insurer system. Accordingly, civic groups closely interacted with opposition parties in their desire for change. On the contrary, opposition parties' resources in relation to the government were largely attributable to their strong deliberation over government bills in Parliament.

However, the KMA was passive in associating with civic groups, despite the same preference for a single insurer system. Its conservative nature was hard to reconcile with progressive civic groups. Instead, the KMA primarily looked towards lawmakers affiliated to medical doctors as a conduit in putting forward its ideas to Parliament (Kim J.-g., 1992: 68).

Within the opponent bloc, the MHSA unilaterally depended on relevant government departments for support. It needed the assistance from the EPB to secure its budget, and the OP to compete with other departments and to obtain the President's approval. Dr Lee Sang-yong, director general of the MOHW Pension and Health Insurance Bureau, admits the powerlessness of the MHSA:

> The MHSA does not have resources to share with other government departments. The President's political interest is the one and only resource at the disposal of the MHSA. If the President cares about health and welfare matters, the MHSA can easily implement its policies. In relation with the EPB, which controlled public purse strings, the MHSA was always in a weak position, as the EPB did not have any reason to seek the help of the MHSA. In general, the EPB had little interest in MHSA affairs and frequently looked negatively at social welfare. The MHSA always sought to win EPB backing. (Interview on 29 December 2004)

The MHSA and the ruling party showed a high degree of resource dependency in making laws. The ruling party put forward government policies to Parliament. But MHSA resource dependency on other opponents of the merger, such as business interests and the FKTU, did not need to be mobilised during the second debate. Employee health insurers' activities were usually restricted to intermittent support of the MHSA policy towards the merger, albeit their affirmative interaction with the MHSA in blocking the merger (Won, 1990: 61).

Meanwhile, resource dependency between the MHSA and proponents of the merger was not an issue. Opposition parties' cooperation with government departments was uncommon and civic groups were rejected as policy-making partners. Admitting that resource dependency between the MHSA and the KMA was likely to be essential in health policy-making, it was limited during the second debate because their basic views on the merger were completely different.

The President had the greatest resources at his disposal, such as the appointment of high-level officials and the nomination of ruling party candidates, under Korea's strong presidential system. The OP also boasted of its strength in making government policies. It coordinated state affairs on behalf of the President and reviewed departmental reports to the President in advance. Meanwhile, the ruling party officially took part in government policy-making by holding periodic meetings with departments in an attempt to find a single view on policy. Consequently, without ruling party support, the passing of controversial bills was next to impossible.

2) Participants' interaction: laissez-faire

Basic nature of interaction

The pattern of interaction between participants with different perspectives on the merger was generally conflict-based and distrustful. In a transitional period towards democracy, the rules of the game were not firmly established and the government was not yet ready to accept opposition parties or civic groups as decision-making partners. Opponents of the merger closed all channels of dialogue with key proponents. Particularly, the presence of opposition in Parliament accelerated confrontation between governing and opposition camps. Debates pointing out the pros and cons of the merger culminated in March 1989 when President Rho vetoed the agreed merger bill.[17] There was no tradition of mutual trust in Korean politics between participants with different views on any matter.

However, the same bloc members were mostly in unison with each other, despite differences in methods. The relationship between opposition parties and civic groups was generally consensual, as they mutually benefited from cooperation. Opposition parties led the parliamentary decision-making between October 1988 and March 1989, representing civic groups' views. They closely interacted to accomplish a common target, the making of a single insurer system, and passed a merger bill in March 1989. Although the KMA also supported the merger, it largely resorted to informal contacts with the ruling party and the MHSA, instead of actively join-

17 For example, the relationship between the government and self-employed insurers union had been one of conflict since the union had held demonstrations in April 1989. In 1989, the government mobilised all possible means to stamp down on illegal strikes (*Donga Ilbo*, 21 October 1989).

ing in a united front.

Major opponents of the merger also maintained, in general, consensual relations between them. Differences in government departments were settled through several levels of formal or informal meetings. They would agree to produce a government draft. The government and the ruling party also cooperated with each other in order to block the pro-merger offensive in Parliament together.[18] The differences within the governing bloc were easily resolved through the active coordination of the OP or through normal institutional channels. The intervention of minor opponents, such as business interests, the FKTU and employee health insurers, was not dramatic during the debate. At the time, they were supportive of the government's position on the matter even though there was little meaningful connection between them.

Frequency of interaction

Interactions between backers of the merger were, by and large, sporadic and irregular. Even though civic groups and opposition parties closely liaised with each other from October 1988, to drive the merger forward, their interaction was neither formalised nor constant.[19] Their contact with government departments was neither frequent nor institutional, as they were not

18 For instance, in the course of the March 1989 parliamentary debate on the merger, the ruling floor leader Kim Yoon-hwan said to Minister Moon Tae-jun: "The President's interim plebiscite will be held sooner or later, and then the merger bill will be altered once more. So let's agree now to an opposition bill with a little revision." (Monthly *Chosun*, May 2001).

19 Despite civic groups' close interaction with opposition parties and academic circles in promoting the merger, their interaction was less institutionalised and sometimes carried out on a unilateral basis by civic groups, through the illegal occupation of opposition parties' offices.

welcomed as the government's policy partners.

Various organised interests, meanwhile, closely worked together during the debate to propose the merger. Activist farmers and healthcare professionals led the formation of a united front of civic groups (NCHIU, 1999: 955). But the KMA usually linked up with the MHSA and the ruling party, which opposed the merger, instead of interacting with other proponents of the merger.[20] At the time, regular contact with the government was limited to authorised groups like the KMA.

Meetings between the ruling and opposition parties happened frequently and they were successful at arriving at parliamentary decisions, albeit their different views on the merger. Their interaction often occurred through the National Assembly Health and Social Affairs Committee. The Committee held seven subcommittee meetings during the 1988 regular session and six meetings during the extra session from February 1989, in order to discuss proposed merger bills.

Contact between governing bloc members who opposed the merger was frequent and institutional in driving the government view forward. The MHSA and the EPB linked up via formal coordination channels, and the OP also constantly interacted with departments on both formal and informal bases. Contact between the MHSA and the ruling party was much more frequent than between government departments.[21] Their formal

20 As an example, the National Health Policy Deliberation Committee was formed in April 1988, with 35 members selected from the KMA and relevant public officials (NFMI, 1997: 501-3). The KMA also held informal meetings several times with the MHSA and the ruling party to promote its policy on health insurance (KMA *Newsletter*, 17 February 1989).

21 The ruling party-government conferences were held 28 times in 1987 to discuss the health insurer system and the health insurance extension to the rural self-employed (Yu, 1990:

meetings were organised as a vehicle to deal with the growing pressure surrounding the opposition parties' merger bill and the following presidential veto in March 1989. The OP also participated in these meetings.

Mobilised strategies of interaction

The second debate on the merger started with progressive civic groups' large-scale protests in January 1988. Where the government had rejected civic groups as policy-making partners, groups mobilised all means at their disposal to place pressure on the government. Among members, activist farmers' groups joined progressive religious groups to initiate the debate. Before the government introduced concessions in April 1988, by increasing its subsidy to the rural self-employed insurers to 50 percent from the previous 35 percent and making agricultural cooperatives' proxy and instalment payments possible (Kim M.-h., 1999: 55), they staged protests in over ten rural areas demanding the merger of health insurers and an increase in government subsidy to support the self-employed insurers (NCMII *Newsletter*, 16 May 1988). Activist healthcare professional groups like the APH and the KPDS issued press releases backing the merger in February 1988. Forty-eight progressive civic groups including farmers, the urban poor and activist healthcare professionals established the NCMII on 28 June 1988 to propose the merger in unison.[22]

From then on, the NCMII was always at the forefront of supporting the merger. The NCMII asked for the National Medical Security Bill on 8

145).

22 Kim Young-yik, Cho Hong-jun and Kim Yeon-myung played a leading role in setting up the NCMII along with representatives from farmers' groups and progressive pharmacist groups.

October 1988 to propose the merger and urged the government to reaffirm its responsibility on health insurance matters.[23] In February 1989, it broke into the office of the minor opposition NDRP, who was seen to be neutral towards the merger. Before and after the presidential veto in March 1989, it used all possible means, such as the issuance of press releases, demonstrations, signature-seeking campaigns and sending letters to the President, to protest about the use of the veto (KPA *Newsletter*, 5 October 1989).

But the NCMII was voluntarily dissolved in April 1989 to form a tighter and more active organisation, the Medical Security Promotion Committee (MSPC), comprising trade unions and student groups. While the NCMII was a loose coalition of civic groups, the MSPC systemically united five sectors of farmers, activist physicians and pharmacists, the urban poor, students and workers sympathetic to the merger. The MSPC staged sit-in protests and signature-seeking campaigns from May 1989, demanding that the vetoed Bill was brought into law. During the parliamentary session from September 1989, it took to the street to pressurise opposition parties to reconsider (KPA *Newsletter*, 5 October 1989).

Opposition parties actively took part in the debate by taking political initiative. Kim Young-sam's RDP and Kim Dae-jung's PPD, competing for the support of civil society, suggested similar bills in November 1988, in order to propose the merger.[24] In the extra session of 1989, three opposition

23 The NCMII bill included the setting up of a single insurer system, the integration of medical insurance with Medicaid and the introduction of progressive insurance premium system that was dependent on recipients' income level (Kim J.-g., 1992: 68).

24 Opposition party bills underlined the need for the merger to spread insurance risk nationally and to improve income distribution as a major plank of the health insurance program (Records of the 144th National Assembly, 1988).

parties including the minor NDRP agreed to introduce a single bill,[25] and kept their promise by passing the National Medical Insurance Bill on 9 March 1989 (Kim H., 2003: 161).

Also, opposition parties introduced a single bill in the 1989 parliamentary regular session to amend appendix clauses in the vetoed Bill, and agreed to finish this process by the end of 1989.[26] They adopted a strategy of coercing the ruling party instead of bargaining with it. Until then, concessions between the ruling and opposition parties were rare. Dr Lee Byoung-giel, the bureau director of the National Assembly, describes the party politics in Parliament:

> Above everything else, rationality is of primary importance when it comes to a bill, in terms of parliamentary decision-making. But during the strong opposition party system of the late 1980s, opposition parties neglected the ruling party and the government. Although the ruling party won the 1987 presidential election, its leadership was hard to emulate three charismatic opposition leaders (the so-called three Kims). Additionally, opposition parties pressured the governing bloc as a way of regaining popularity lost by the presidential election defeat. (Interview on 10 November 2004)

Between March-December 1989, the self-employed insurers' union

25 Originally the NDRP suggested a bill mixing government opinions and the KMA's views. But it changed policy to support the merger after civic groups' illegal occupation of its office (Wong, 2004: 93).

26 Opposition parties suggested a pilot program to assess a single insurer system at first, instead of reviewing the vetoed Bill. But being confronted with strong protests from self-employed insurers union, they switched positions to seek to revise the appendices of the vetoed Bill, which became the pretext for a presidential veto.

conveyed interests through tough methods such as sit-in strikes. They threatened to stage a signature-seeking campaign in case of a presidential veto against the merger bill. They also intensified protests and strikes from September 1989 and occupied opposition parties' offices, demanding passage of the vetoed Bill (*Hankook Ilbo*, 10 October 1989). They resorted to every demonstration of their strength during the 1989 parliamentary session to promote their interests.

On the medical front, the KMA used both power- and mass-level strategies in an attempt to achieve its goal. It kept communication channels with the MHSA open and lobbied ruling lawmakers as well as proposing its own bill in November 1988. Mrs Chung Soon-im, a legislative researcher in the National Assembly, explains the reality of professional groups' lobbying Parliament:

> Many healthcare professional groups lobby the National Assembly Health and Social Affairs Committee over the making of health policy, through those lawmakers who have occupational links to them. In general, political parties appointed representatives from major professional groups as proportional lawmakers and they were allocated positions on occupation-related standing committees. In case of the Committee, approximately two physicians, one pharmacist and one nurse were allocated seats as proportional representatives and they acted as proxies for their occupational groups in making parliamentary decisions. (Interview on 27 December 2004)

On the other hand, the KMA staged demonstrations in support of its aim in February 1989. It tended to resort to extreme actions, like the return of medical licenses, between 1988 and 1989.

In contrast, major opponents of the merger maintained a cooperative stance helping each other to settle their differences. Government departments held frequent meetings and made use of institutional channels to come to agreements.[27] The ruling party-government conference was an official channel to coordinate opinions before government bills reached Parliament. After the passage of the merger bill in March 1989, they drew on every means possible to prevent the bill from becoming law.[28]

But the government refused to open any channels of dialogue with civic groups and opposition parties. For example, after the passage of the merger bill through Parliament in March 1989, the MHSA distributed literature highlighting the bill's unfairness in imposing varying levels of insurance premiums on company employees and the self-employed (Kim J.-d., 2000: 19). In the face of intensified protests from self-employed insurers' union from October 1989, the government rejected any dialogue and were ready to face confrontations with them.[29]

The ruling party also relied on a strategy of confrontation in blocking the intention of opposition parties in Parliament. It supported the government bill in the 1988 regular session without any negotiation with opposi-

27 The MHSA and the EPB jointly led the Medical Insurance Policy Deliberation Committee, which was built in May 1988 to map out a nationwide medical insurance program (Park J., 1996: 148).

28 The MHSA appealed to the mass media by releasing news items pointing to the problems of a single insurer system and held a news conference opposing the merger bill on 10 March 1989 (NCHIU, 1999: 1101). The MHSA took the initiative in recommending a presidential veto in the State Council on 16 March 1989, and it also worked with the NFMI to issue press releases to daily newspapers.

29 The MHSA confirmed that the merger of health insurers could not be a subject to negotiate with self-employed insurers union and ordered NFMI staff to support the issuance of medical insurance cards in case of strikes (*Chosun Ilbo*, 25 October 1989).

tion parties. Although the ruling party reluctantly agreed to the opposition bill in March 1989, anticipating cooperation from opposition parties in revoking the expected interim presidential plebiscite (Kim H., 2003: 161), it pushed for the presidential veto shortly after the passage of the merger bill and calmed opposition parties by proposing a slow paced merger as an alternative. The ruling party adopted stalling tactics in the 1989 parliamentary session in response to opposition parties' requests to reconsider the vetoed Bill (*Jungang Ilbo*, 23 November 1989).

Minor opponents, such as business interests and employee health insurers, were mostly pro-governmental and they relied on power-level methods, including the issuance of recommendation letters and informal talks with government departments or the ruling party, to gain influence. They usually articulated their views through more institutional channels and in a softer manner.[30] For example, the FKI issued a statement opposing the merger in March 1989 (*Jungang Ilbo*, 15 March 1989). But unusually, the NFMI replied in a radical fashion when the merger bill was enacted in March 1989, as its members had vested interests in maintaining a multiple insurer system. The NFMI released biased information over-emphasising the demerits of a single insurer system and issued press releases attacking the passage of the merger bill in major newspapers on 10 March 1989 (Won, 1990: 61).

The FKTU had been pro-government under the traditional corporatist politics of Korea. It directly contacted the government to promote its interests, but its position on the merger debate was unclear. It simply released a statement in newspapers on 15 March 1989, demanding more careful

30 The FKI held 19 meetings with the government and participated in 21 government-sponsored seminars in 1987 (Park J., 1996: 107).

deliberation on the issue. The FKTU had always been prudent in addressing the issue and preferred the use of more institutional and power-level levers in pushing its opinions on the government (Kam, 1994: 50). Mr Choi Chung-il, a career labour activist from the 1980s, criticises the FKTU's conservative approach:

> The FKTU's independence from the government was very limited in nature, as it relied upon government subsidy for a larger part of its budget. It was not worried about the social impact of government policies. So, its view on the merger fluctuated according to its own self-interest in the issue. Furthermore, trade unions in the 1980s paid attention only to the issues related to improving working condition and the security of labour rights, thereby, neglecting social problems. It was from the 1990s, when progressive trade unions were founded in earnest that Korea's trade unions started to become concerned about politics and social reform. (Interview on 11 February 2005)

5. Policy Outputs

1) Final outputs: vetoed agreement

Although proponents of the merger succeeded in passing a merger bill in March 1989, their merger attempt was intervened by the presidential veto and the end of the parliamentary session in December 1989. Like the first debate, key participants in the second debate continuously changed their minds, irrespective of their own views on the merger.

Among proponents of the merger, civic groups kept policy frameworks consistent. They triggered the second debate by staging protests after February 1988 and then went on to form the NCMII in June 1988. The NCMII chose to propose the merger based on a progressive insurance premium rate derived from income. Opposition parties' policies on the merger were not consistent for the duration of the debate. They were not enthusiastic about proposing the merger until the 1988 parliamentary regular session. The two major opposition parties reluctantly submitted bills which were similar to the NCMII bill but only under duress from the increasing pressure of civic groups (Chung and Cho, 2001: 97). With a change of heart by the NDRP in February 1989 to support the merger, the three opposition parties who enjoyed a parliamentary majority passed the National Medical Insurance Bill based on a single insurer system in March 1989 (Kim S.-y., 2011: 89).

After the presidential veto on 24 March 1989, opposition party policies towards the merger became unclear again. While civic groups insisted that the vetoed Bill should be reconsidered, opposition parties suggested the setting up of a pilot merger scheme (*Chosun Ilbo*, 24 October 1989), although this did not happen owing to strong protests from civic groups to reconsider the vetoed Bill.

Amongst opponents of the merger, the MHSA changed its detailed policy several times within the basic frame of a multiple insurer system. Before the second debate heated up in 1988, the MHSA changed its original policy to enter into negotiation with the EPB and the ruling party. In February 1987 the MHSA agreed with the EPB to extend health insurance coverage to the rural self-employed by the then multiple insurer system. But the MHSA compromised with the ruling party in April 1987, to set a mix of county-sized insurers in small cities with megalopolis-sized insurers in metropolitan cities within the framework of a multiple insurer system

(MHSA *White Paper*, 1989).

With the inauguration of the Rho administration in February 1988, the MHSA tried to change from a county-sized insurer system to a megalopolis-sized insurer scheme on the basis of a multiple insurer system. In March 1988, Minister Kwon Yi-hyok briefed President Rho about the plan to form megalopolis-sized insurers in urban areas and to amalgamate rural self-employed insurers (NFMI, 1997: 498). But in the situation where President Rho had no firm opinion about the type of health insurer system, the ruling party and the EPB moved towards favouring the single insurer system once again. Meanwhile, the MHSA and the OP adhered to the multiple insurer system. In June 1988, they finally agreed to establish megalopolis-sized health insurers in big cities, and to enlarge county-sized insurers in small cities by integrating neighbouring insurers. The State Council endorsed it as a government policy in October 1988 and the MHSA and the ruling party submitted it to Parliament in November 1988 (Shin, 2004: 95).

But during the February 1989 extra session, the ruling party changed its mind and decided to cooperate with opposition parties, as it realised that blocking the opposition bill in Parliament was close to impossible. The National Medical Insurance Bill largely reflected the pro-merger supporters' goals, completely ignoring the government's desire to maintain a multiple insurer system.

Meanwhile, opponents of the merger recommended President Rho to veto the Bill, and Rho agreed. After the presidential veto the ruling party changed its policy to one proposing a pilot scheme to set megalopolis-sized insurers and to introduce a gradual drive towards the merger in order to soften opposition protests. But the ruling party changed its mind again during the 1989 parliamentary session, and then sought simply to improve a multiple insurer system.

2) Reflected interests: ending in a tie

The second merger debate resulted in the frustration of the merger attempt once again by the presidential veto and strong opposition from the governing bloc. During the debate, civic groups and opposition parties believed that they had achieved the merger when the merger bill passed Parliament in March 1989. Civic groups successfully triggered the second debate by staging strong protests in February 1988 and pressured opposition parties into initiating parliamentary discussions on the merger. The two main opposition parties' bills mainly reflected civic groups' demands by including the merger of health insurers, the introduction of a progressive insurance premium rate and a 50 percent government subsidy for self-employed insurance premiums (APH *Newsletter* 8, 1988).

The minor opposition party, the NDRP, initially proposed the bill supporting a multiple insurer system based on megalopolis-sized insurers. But in response to the strong protest of civic groups, it changed position and accepted the merger. The National Medical Insurance Bill, passed in March 1989, completely reflected the proponents' views by introducing a single insurer system along with a progressive insurance premium rate system. The Bill also included such important changes as the establishment of a medical insurance deliberation committee, the integration of Medicaid with medical insurance and the creation of an insurance fee coordinating committee (Lee D. et al., 1992: 349). The former MHSA vice-minister Ju Kyoung-sik explains the parliamentary policy-making process:

> The government suggested setting up megalopolis-sized insurers in urban areas in its bill in the February 1989 parliamentary session. But, opposition parties proposed a bill to fully merge health insurers in terms of both organisation and finance. At the time, opposition parties dominated Parliament. At heart, many ruling lawmakers sympathised with the merger, despite their outward adherence to the government bill. So, the National Medical Insurance Bill, which aimed to set up the National Medical Insurance Corporation (NMIC) and to merge insurance funds within two and half years, was unanimously carried by Parliament. (Park K. et al., 2001: 81)

On the contrary, opponents to the merger did not push their opinions strongly and were too weak to steer parliamentary decision-making. MHSA vice-minister Lee Doo-ho expressed his readiness to consider both forms of the health insurer system when the ruling party brought out the merger again, with the April 1988 general election coming up (Kim J.-d., 2000: 100). So, as a compromise, MHSA minister Kwon briefed President Rho in March 1988 about a plan to mix current county-sized insurers with megalopolis-sized insurers in big cities. The MHSA Medical Insurance Policy Deliberation Committee was in favour of implementing an urban self-employed health insurance programme through a multiple insurer system (NFMI, 1997: 501-3), based on megalopolis-sized insurers in big cities and the integration of small insurers in rural areas. The government reaffirmed the Committee opinion as a policy in June 1988, and submitted it to Parliament in November 1988. But in the course of the parliamentary decision-making process, the MHSA was excluded and the government bill was ignored. Table 4.5 compares the bills suggested by each participant with the National Medical Insurance Bill of March 1989.

Table 4.5 Comparison of proposals behind the National Medical Insurance Bill

	Insurer system	Medicaid and health insurance	Insurance premium	Health insurance treatment hospitals	Decision of medical treatment fees
MHSA and ruling party	Multiple insurers	Separation	- Employee: 3-8 percent of standard monthly salary - Self-employed: based on income and property	Designation by the MHSA	MHSA minister
PPD	Single insurer	Integration	Progressive insurance premium rate based on standard income	Designation by the MHSA	MHSA minister
RDP	Single insurer	Integration	Progressive insurance premium rate within 3-8 percent of income	Designation by the MHSA	MHSA minister
NDRP	Single insurer	Separation	- Employee: 3-8 percent of standard monthly salary - Self-employed: based on income and property	Contraction with individual hospital	Formation of independent committee
NCMII	Single insurer	Integration	Progressive insurance premium rate within 3-8 percent of income	Designation by the MHSA	-
KMA	Single insurer	Integration	- Employee: 3-8 percent of standard monthly salary - Self-employed: based on income and property	Contraction with individual hospital	Formation of independent committee
Final Bill	Single insurer	Integration	Progressive insurance premium rate based on standard income (imposition to property in case of no income)	Designation (Public) Contract (Private)	Formation of committee within the MHSA

The Bill, however, was not implemented due to the presidential veto. Although President Rho asked Parliament to reconsider the Bill, the ruling party blocked discussions on the vetoed Bill by resorting to stalling tactics. Opposition parties' concerns also moved on to political matters and cooperation between opposition parties became impossible due to a three-party merger in February 1990.[31] The proponents' aim to make a single insurer was frustrated and the urban self-employed insurance scheme was set on the county-sized multiple insurer system as planned.

6. Conclusion

The second debate coincided with a transitional period towards democracy and thus, the policy context contributed in creating different properties within institutions and policy networks. 1) The Rho administration's national goal to promote political democracy enabled the power relationship between political organisations to become more balanced and policy networks to open up. 2) Major political events greatly affected policy-making and outputs. The 1987 presidential election, the 1988 general election and the expected mid-term presidential plebiscite were all important events. The emergence of an opposition-dominated Parliament changed the existing power relationship between the President and Parliament, as well as policy networks and outputs. 3) Democratising political leadership changed the power relations between political organisations, and policy networks. 4) The vitalised civil society was also influential. Civic groups initiated the second debate, making policy networks open and variable. The diversified strategies that they employed restructured the policy-making system and greatly influenced resultant policy outputs.

31 The new ruling Democratic Liberal Party controlled 217 seats out of 299 parliamentary seats under the planned three-party merger, including the ruling DJP, oppositional RDP and NDRP, to found a grand conservative alliance, whereas Kim Dae-jung's PPD remained at 70 seats (Kihl, 2005: 89).

Institutional features were completely transformed as the Rho administration was based on the different Constitution to that of its predecessor. 1) Regarding the power relationship between political organisations, Parliament emerged as a key player and important policies were initiated by opposition parties. As a result, policy networks were opened and policy outputs were open to change. 2) The institutional properties of the political system greatly affected participants' power relationship and policy networks. The change in the electoral system towards more competitive ways reformulated the power relationship between political organisations. Increased competition of political leadership opened policy networks and enabled opposition parties to dominate Parliament. 3) While decision-making rules largely remained unchanged, they did not work as intended. The emphasis on informal meetings and prior coordination or consent in drawing up policies excluded outsider groups from participating in decision-making. Parliamentary decision-making was largely influenced by the power relationship between the ruling and opposition parties. Many veto points were ceremonial. 4) Previous policies influenced policy networks and outputs. But, a more decisive factor in explaining the properties of policy networks and outputs was not the inertia of established policies per se, but participants' interests and the power relationship between conflicting participants. In many cases, the concept of path creation rather than path dependency may have been more advantageous in explaining the policy-making dynamics in transitional period of Korea.

The policy network structure was directly influenced by the political context. With the progress towards political democracy, civil society and opposition parties were greatly empowered. In open issue networks many related interests engaged in the debate and the intentional exclusion of particular policy actors from policy networks became impossible. Also, policy target groups like civic groups and trade unions began to earnestly engage in debate.

Interactions between blocs were often conflicting, while members of the same bloc were consensus oriented. However, interaction patterns of civic groups and trade unions tended to be unpredictable and uncompromising. They pressurised the government and political parties through mass-level input methods like street protests and sit-in strikes to achieve their goals, making policy networks unstable. Also, participants were unwilling to stick to the rules of the game. Private actors frequently resorted to illegal ways, while official actors repeatedly changed policies on demand. These patterns of interaction had a big influence on paralysing policy outputs.

A very dynamic process drove through the second debate, which led to the extension of health insurance to the urban self-employed under the multiple insurer system. Although proponents of the merger succeeded in getting a merger bill through Parliament, their merger attempt was frustrated again by the presidential veto. Although opponents' intentions were largely reflected in the end, they also failed to achieve their original goal. The result of the debate was to take no action: from any point of view, the consequence of the second debate was policy paralysis.

Chapter
5

Pushing the First Button

Accomplishment of Partial Merger in the 1990s

1. Introductory Comments

Despite continued efforts to introduce a single insurer system, the second merger attempt also failed. Activists in civil society and the medical profession pushed for the merger once more ahead of the 1992 presidential election, but political circles were unresponsive. The ruling party continued to support the multiple insurer system during the election campaign, and the government tried to solve the financial difficulties of the self-employed insurer scheme and the overloaded insurance premiums of the self-employed through a series of finance adjustment measures (NHIC *White Paper*, 2001: 27).

However, the financial deficit of the self-employed insurers became worse despite the government's increases in financial subsidies (see Table

Table 5.1 Financial status of self-employed insurers in the 1990s

	1991	1992	1993	1994	1995	1996	1997
Number of health insurers with a deficit	1	7	15	33	113	147	183
Number of health insurers with a surplus	265	259	251	233	114	80	44
Contribution (bil. Won) (A)	844.2	963.1	1,067.7	1,181.8	1,324.0	1,576.4	2,023.4
Government subsidy (bil. Won) (B)	586.8	592.4	638.1	692.4	755.3	872.3	995.4
Rate of subsidy to total contributions (%) (B/A)	69.5	61.5	59.8	58.6	57.0	55.3	49.2

Source: NFMI (each year), *Medical Insurance Statistical Yearbook* and NHIC homepage (www.nhic.or.kr).

5.1),[1] eventually sparking a further round of debate on the merger. At the same time, proponents of the merger insisted that a multiple insurer system restricted risk pooling to small-sized insurers, and generated unnecessary managerial inefficiency and financial disparity between different kinds of health insurers.

In February 1994, the government established the Medical Security Reform Committee (MSRC), and civic groups and progressive trade unions joined together to fight the common cause in April. Ever since the MSRC took the decision, in June 1994, to gradually improve the health insurance program based on a multiple insurer system, proponents had begun to propose the merger of health insurers in earnest as a part of healthcare reform.

Despite conflict between proponents and opponents of the merger, a balanced status quo existed between 1994-95. While civic groups and progressive trade unions led the proponent bloc, the Ministry of Health and Welfare (MOHW) led the opponent bloc as before.[2] But, the momentum to change the situation arrived at the April 1996 general election. Civic groups and progressive trade unions put pressure on two main opposition parties to adopt the merger as their election pledges. Under pressure, major opposition parties jointly proposed the introduction of the National Health Insurance Bill, advocating the merger, in November 1996.[3] But, the ruling

1 While employee health insurers accumulated vast sums of insurance funds, the self-employed health insurers were chronically in the red and the government was being forced to subsidise them to cover their deficits every year (Chung and Cho, 2001: 97).

2 The Ministry of Health and Social Affairs was renamed the MOHW in 1994, as a way of restructuring government under the Kim Young-sam administration (MOHW *White Paper*, 1995).

3 The Bill included the merger of health insurers, the absorption of the Medicaid into the health insurance program, the adoption of graded insurance premiums and the extension of benefit packages (NHIC *White Paper*, 2001: 28).

party, persuaded by the MOHW, rejected the Bill (Kim J.-d., 2002: 202).

Approaching the December 1997 presidential election, ruling lawmakers from rural areas began to pressure party leaders to accept the merger as a way to win votes in the election. Unpopular President Kim was ostracized from party membership and the ruling party had split from the government. The ruling party, therefore, had incentives to include the merger plan in its election pledge (*Hankook Ilbo*, 14 December 1997).

On 30 October 1997 the ruling party put forward the National Medical Insurance Bill, which intended to partially merge the self-employed insurers (excluding employee health insurers) with the Korea Medical Insurance Corporation (KMIC),[4] to establish the National Medical Insurance Corporation (NMIC). The Bill aimed to slim down government subsidies by lowering management costs and reduce the burden of self-employed insurance premiums through this partial merger. The ruling party also hoped that the extension of a pension insurance scheme to the urban self-employed might be possible without additional finance, by relocating surplus staff from health insurers to this new pension insurance program (Lee K., 2000b: 63).

With opposition consent, the opposition bill, which was drafted in November 1996, was integrated into the ruling party idea and Parliament passed the partial merger bill on 18 November 1997. It was promulgated on 31 December as the National Medical Insurance Act (NMIA), to be implemented from October 1998. The gist of the NMIA was to partially merge health insurers by setting up the NMIC. But their finances would be separately managed and employee health insurers would stay organisationally

4 The government and private school employees' medical insurance had been managed by a single insurer, the KMIC, from the beginning of 1978 (MHSA *White Paper*, 1979).

and financially separate.

However, the MOHW was excluded from drafting the NMIA through Parliament, as the ruling party was not obliged to consult with it if the President had withdrawn from party membership. Although the MOHW was unhappy about the partial merger, it was obliged to follow a parliamentary decision. Instead, it decided to work closely with the Presidency Undertaking Commission (PUC) on drawing up substitute legislation that promoted the making of megalopolis-sized insurers crossing administrative districts, but retaining the structure of a multiple insurer system (NHIC *White Paper*, 2001: 29). Figure 5.1 details the plan for the partial merger.

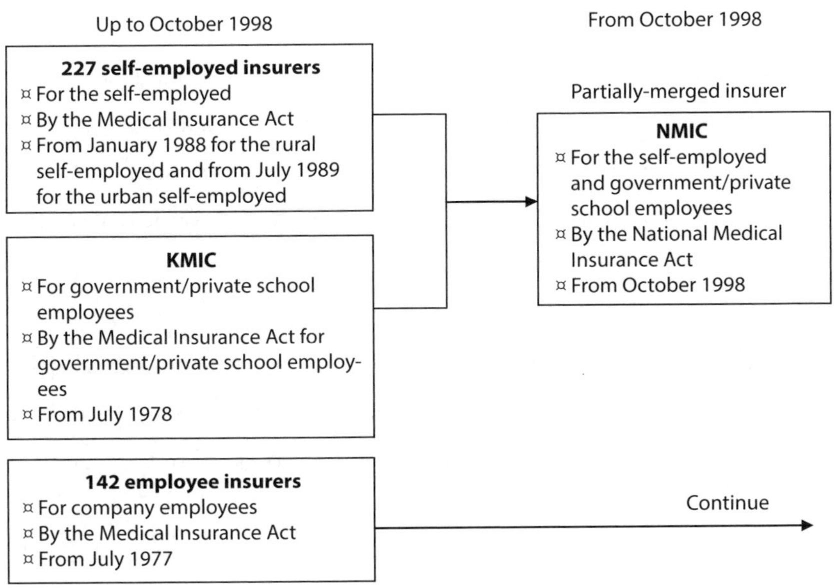

Figure 5.1 The scheme behind the partial merger

2. Policy Context

1) Political context: struggle for the approaching presidential election

Although Kim Young-sam won the 1992 presidential election as a ruling candidate, he called his government the '*Munmin*' (civilian) government so as to distinguish it from previous military regimes and advocated 'the creation of New Korea' as an ultimate governing ideology. To make 'New Korea,' it was necessary to reform the conventional political system. The Kim administration adopted an anti-corruption policy and government restructuring as parts of its reform package (Hong, 2001: 293). Kim's presidential inauguration speech in February 1993 defined 'New Korea' as follows:

> 'New Korea' is a democratic society filled with freedom, maturity and justice and is an affluent community respecting cultural life and human dignity. 'New Korea' is a unified country that a reunited nation lives peacefully... It is 'New Korea' that everyone can joyfully work together and that our descendents can boast of their motherland...

But going into 1995, the Kim administration began to emphasise *segyehwa* (globalisation) and formed the Globalisation Promotion Committee (GPC).[5] In March 1995, Kim explained his plan to globalise the quality of life:

5 The National Welfare Planning Board was established under the GPC to draw up a blueprint on social security (MOHW *White Paper*, 1995: 9).

> The national goal we pursue in the 21st global era is to make Korea a reunified global centre of the world. The global centre means a model state that the world respects and in which each person enjoys an affluent life. To make a rich and comfortable country, we should drive globalisation forward across every aspect of politics, the economy and social life. Social development and the quality of people's lives should also reach this global plateau and become first class. (GPC *White Paper*, 1995: 3)

The government suggested an increase in public assistance and welfare for the elderly, the extension of women's participation in society, the reform of the social security system,[6] and the establishment of social networks, as key policies to increase the quality of life in global standards (MOHW *White Paper*, 1995: 7).

The Kim administration advocated, in 1996, a governing ideology of 'reshaping of history' to escape political deadlock. But President Kim, after becoming entangled in several political corruption scandals, entered a lame-duck phase much earlier in his political life than expected, and was unable to control state affairs. Accordingly, at the end of the Kim administration, the governing ideology did not play any significant role in influencing government policies.

Turning now to political events, there were several elections during the partial merger debate. In an election, to select prefecture governors and local assemblymen, held in June 1995, the ruling Democratic Liberal Party

6 While the government mentioned the reliability of pension and medical insurance provision, the merger of health insurers was not suggested in any detail (MOHW *White Paper*, 1995: 22).

(DLP) registered a humbling defeat,[7] resurrecting retired politician Kim Dae-jung to hold up opposition leadership. The ruling party's defeat in the election forced it to pursue special measures to win back public support and the idea of the merger reappeared. The April 1996 general election was another political event relevant to the debate. While major opposition parties placed the notion of the merger at the heart of their election pledges,[8] the ruling New Korea Party (NKP, the revised name for the DLP after December 1995) insisted on the extension of eligible term and insurance benefits, without any structural changes to the health insurer system.

The December 1997 presidential election marked a turning point in the partial merger debate. According to Kingdon's (2003), it played a 'policy window' role in propelling the merger forward. Although ruling lawmakers from rural areas had publicly backed the merger since late 1996, their desire for change had been continually frustrated by the MOHW during the 1996 parliamentary session. But as the presidential election drew closer, they stepped up their pressure for the merger and the ruling party adopted a policy of backing the partial merger as an election pledge to win votes from the self-employed (Kim, Yang, and Yu, 2013: 84).

Political events, including corruption scandals and the President's defection from the ruling party, were also important in achieving the partial

7 Kim Dae-jung's opposition party won the June 1995 local election by securing 84 mayors/governors and 352 local assemblymen, compared to the ruling party's 70 and 286 respectively (Jee et al., 2001: 429).

8 Of the opposition parties, Kim Dae-jung's the National Congress for New Politics (NCNP) had stuck to the idea of supporting a single insurer system since the 1980s. Although the minor opposition United Liberal Democrats (ULD), a new name of the New Democratic Republican Party (NDRP), was not such a staunch supporter of the merger, it also adopted the merger as an election pledge for the 1996 general election.

merger. The bankruptcy of the Hanbo Corporation in January 1997, with its political connections and the imprisonment of President Kim's younger son, all combined to critically weaken Kim's political leadership and popularity (Buzo, 2002: 182). With the presidential election looming, the ruling party openly asked for Kim's withdrawal and he eventually left the party in November 1997, thus annulling the effectiveness of the ruling party-government conference. The renamed Grand National Party (GNP) supported the partial merger,[9] irrespective of the government's passion for the multiple insurer system.

On the other hand, the Kim administration witnessed burgeoning democratic politics and competitive political leadership. It championed civilian rule as its distinctive character, to be differentiated from its military predecessors (Robinson, 2007: 171). The progress towards an open and democratic politics had become irreversible. While President Kim and his archrival Kim Dae-jung were parochial and authoritative in their personalities, politics was heading towards democracy and openness.

Political leadership was also very competitive at the time. Even though the ruling candidate Kim Young-sam was elected President by a landslide at the direct presidential election in December 1992,[10] the ruling party failed to gain a majority at the 1996 general election obtaining only 139 out of the 299 parliamentary seats (Jang H., 2001: 117). The 1997 presidential election was very competitive, with a narrow margin between major candidates.

9 The NKP was renamed the GNP in November 1997 to wipe out President Kim's unpopular image from the party in preparation for the coming presidential election (Shim, 2004: 443).

10 While opposition candidate Kim Dae-jung scored 33.4 percent and Jeong Ju-young gained 16.1 percent, Kim Young-sam recorded a 41.4 percent polling score (Jee et al., 2001: 416).

Opposition candidate Kim Dae-jung won the election with 40.2 percent of the vote, whilst the ruling candidate Lee Hoi-chang scored 39.7 percent (Buzo, 2002: 183). The peaceful handover of political power for the first time in modern Korean politics proved the competitive and impartial nature of the election.

2) Social context: legitimised civil society

With political democratisation from the late 1980s, political leadership became much more responsive and open, and this translated into increased civil society power. In this respect, the vitality of civil society was intimately intertwined with the political context. President Kim, a career leader of the democratisation movement, provided large numbers of civic group leaders with the opportunity to work in the government.

It was under the Kim administration that politics-oriented civic groups were founded in earnest and became actively involved in political matters. Trade unions were also greatly mobilised and in particular, the emergence of the Korean Confederation of Trade Unions (KCTU), a new militant umbrella union, provided crucial momentum to improve the prospects of organised labour power.[11] Labour strikes in the early 1997 were clear examples of strong labour power.[12]

---

11 Militant labour activists set up the National Representative of Trade Unions in June 1993, to unify emerging progressive trade unions, and the body was renamed the KCTU in November 1995 to be a clear-cut alternative to the then sole umbrella union, the Federation of Korean Trade Unions (FKTU). The KCTU was finally legalised in November 1999 by revised labour-related laws that introduced a multiple unionisation system (Kihl, 2005: 273).

12 When the ruling party unilaterally passed labour laws in December 1996 to a direction of

3. Institutional Features

1) Lame-duck President and ruling party-centric politics

Since the three-party merger to form the giant ruling DLP, in February 1990, the governing bloc had consistently managed state affairs at both governmental and parliamentary levels. As before, the ruling party was not independent of the President who concurrently occupied the party's presidency. Lawmakers were also not free from their affiliated parties.

The landslide victory of the ruling party at the 1992 general election and the 1992 presidential election gave President Kim an unprecedented strong political power base. Despite the constitutional guarantee on Parliament's counter-balancing power, the reality was different. In the midst of nationwide anti-corruption slogans, lawmakers who siphoned off illegal political funds were now in check.

But, towards the end of Kim's presidency, the political landscape was totally transformed. Despite the ruling party's victory at the 1996 general election, Kim's leadership was significantly weakened by the outbreak of a series of corruption scandals (Robinson, 2007: 172). Since 1997, the power balance between the government and Parliament had tilted towards the latter. Presidential contender Lee Hoi-chang and Kim Dae-jung took the political initiative instead of the President. Dr. Lee Sung-kyu, an ex-secretary to President Kim, describes the situation:

---

extending labour flexibility, trade unions staged massive protests in January 1997 to eventually repeal them.

> From the time when presidential candidates are elected, secretaries in the Office of the President line up with prospective candidates to secure their jobs in the next regime. The President also knows the reality of this. But s/he lacks methods to control it. In the latter part of Kim's term, presidential secretaries and government high profiles were divided into three groups according to their preferred prospective candidates, Kim Dae-jung, Lee Hoi-chang and Lee In-je. (Interview on 10 March 2005)

The power relationship between the ruling and opposition parties in Korea was shaped by the context of the President-Parliament relation, as the ruling party was largely reliant upon the President. The ruling party had dominated Parliament since its overwhelming victories in both general and presidential elections in 1992. But, as opposition parties won the 1995 local election and Kim Dae-jung returned from his self-proclaimed political retirement, the power balance between the ruling and opposition parties had swung around and recovered, to a degree. Consequently, the ruling party's polling score dropped to 34.5 percent in the 1996 general election from 38.5 percent in 1992, and it failed to secure a majority with just 139 seats out of 299 seats available (see Table 5.2). Kim Jong-pil's withdrawal from the ruling party, in February 1995, to set up the minor opposition United Liberal Democrats, crucially weakened the ruling party's parliamentary leadership (Shim, 2004: 427).

The power relationship between the President and government departments should also be understood within the changing context of presidential power. The President was able to control government departments through several measures, such as having the authority to promote high-level officials and to superintend departments. At the start of his presidency, the

Table 5.2 Result of the April 1996 general election

	Number of Seats	Proportion of seats (%)	Polling score (%)
Ruling NKP	139 (regional 121+ proportional 18)	46.5	34.5
NCNP	79 (66+13)	19.8	25.3
ULD	50 (41+9)	16.7	16.2
Democratic Party	15 (9+6)	5.0	11.2
Independents and others	16 (16+0)	5.4	12.8
Total	299 (253+46)	100.0	100.0

Sources: adapted from Jee et al. (2001: 434-35) and the National Assembly homepage (www.assembly.go.kr).

President and his staff firmly secured obedience from public officials. But, by the end of term, the President's leadership over departments was greatly emasculated, whereas the ruling party's presidential nominee stood at the centre of the governing bloc.

In terms of the relationship between central and local governments, it was undeniable that local government's power was increasing especially through the introduction of the local autonomy system in the early 1990s. But in reality, central government's power over local government remained largely unchanged. Central government effectively controlled local government through financial subsidies and through official inspection (Kim S.-k., 2001: 223). The power relationship between department high flyers and those lower in rank also remained unaltered. Under the hierarchical administrative system, directors in public organisations secured subordinators' compliance through the monopoly of decision-making and personnel management.

2) Moving quickly towards institutional democracy

The Kim administration was governed by the same set of constitutional rules as Rho's administration. Accordingly, the main institutional properties of the political system were largely unchanged. On the basic governing system, the President influenced Parliament through the ruling party, and picked a parliamentary head among ruling lawmakers. The President was also able to check parliamentary excess through the veto power. The President's dominance over government departments was also stable. The President, as a government head, had the final decision on key state matters and legally controlled public officials through the authority to promote key figures and through using inspection agencies.[13]

The Prime Minister kept an eye on important government issues under presidential instructions. But the reality frequently differed from theory; almost all PMs in Korea refrained from exercising their legal power (Bridges, 2001: 47). During Kim's administration there were five different prime ministers, indicating their fragile status.

Meanwhile, Parliament's ability to counter-balance the President greatly increased. It did so by securing rights to investigate particular state matters, inspect general government offices and impeach the President in case of serious misconduct (Kang, 2004: 394-99).

A multi-party system and the free establishment of political parties were guaranteed by the Constitution. Political parties with over 20 deputies formed parliamentary negotiation bodies, but in practice, it was more common that the ruling party and the two opposition parties had the strongest voice. The so-called 'three Kims' including Kim Young-sam, Kim Dae-jung and Kim Jong-pil had manipulated Korean politics of the 1990s by resort-

13 This is why the Korean strong presidential system is frequently called an 'imperial presidency' (Kim S.-j., 2002: 318).

ing to regional favouritism. Until then, the political party system in Korea had been dependent not on institutions but on political leaders' personal charisma. All major political parties were on a similar conservative ideological spectrum and Korean political parties depended on regional favouritism rather than class interests (Robinson, 2007: 169). Consequently, victory for a socialist party was unlikely.

The Kim administration operated under the same election system as the Rho administration. The President was directly elected to serve a five-year single term and open and fair competition was guaranteed. President Kim won by a large-margin in a free and fair competition. Lawmakers were selected by a single member electorate system. Previously, proportional representatives had been assigned according to the number of seats held in Parliament, but the revised election laws in March 1994 allocated representatives according to the size of votes received in an election for each party. This was an attempt to reduce weighting on bigger political parties (Yoon et al., 2003: 139).

In practice, however, the neutrality and impartiality of an election was not automatically guaranteed in the ways that institutions prescribed. Ministers and bureaucrats usually sided with ruling candidates and secret political funds were channelled to the ruling party candidates. The incumbent President supported the ruling party by providing political money, or by 'raiding the pork barrel.'

3) Stationary rules on decision-making

Despite changes in political institutions with the advancement of democracy, the internal rules of decision-making and conflict resolution in government departments remained more or less unchanged. Established rules by department ordinances constrained decision making and conflict resolution. Decision making power was still concentrated at the top and serious conflicts were mainly resolved by superiors (Cho, 2004: 47). At first glance department decision-making followed the official *ringi* system. But in reality, prior consent (*naerak*) from department chiefs and informal coordination were crucial in sorting out departmental disagreement. As before, government committees in which the participation was only allowed in a handful of recognised interest groups played ceremonial roles, providing occasional advice to those involved in the decision-making process.

Inter-departmental differences were coordinated, at first, via working-level meetings. Vice-ministerial meetings were convened for further discussion, while ministerial conference finally settled differences. In most cases, views of the competent department were largely respected during the inter-departmental coordination. Decisions usually required unanimity to incrementally adjust each department's opinion. The Office of the President (OP) and the OPM also intervened in the process of arriving at important government policies. Although the State Council was the final body to consider government affairs, it was rare that heated discussions took place in this forum (Lee S., 2003: 2).

The ruling party-government conference was important whenever the ruling party enjoyed a parliamentary majority, as government affairs signed off by the conference were predestined to become law. However, during the final years of the Kim administration, the President's control over the ruling party greatly weakened. The issue of merging health insurers was revived by the ruling party as a way of winning votes at the presidential election, without governmental consultation. Normally, the initiative in the governing bloc was passed from the President to the ruling party presidential candidate in the final year of a presidency. The partial merger decision in November 1997 was made by political circles in defiance of the government's opposition in a situation where existing decision making rules were broken down by President Kim's session with the ruling party.

The basic framework of the National Assembly Act, which ruled parliamentary decision-making, remained unaltered during the Kim administration. Draft bills proceeded, at first, to relevant standing committees and bills passed by these committees were then sent on to the Legislation and Judiciary Committee for a legal review. Afterwards, bills were finally endorsed in the plenary session. But in most cases, the plenary session approved bills without any discussion and revision, thereby endowing standing committees with full law making power (Ha, 2003: 27). However, this time, the presidential veto against parliamentary decision was unnecessary, as the ruling party dominated Parliament.

4) Previous policies: escape from the established path

Since the failure of the first merger attempt in the early 1980s, the government and the ruling party had been major opponents of the merger for more than 15 years. The enduring efforts of opposition parties and civic groups to change the current institution of the multiple insurer system had brought nothing but failure. Opponents of the merger, such as the MOHW and employee health insurers, had strong vested interests in maintaining the established system and they effectively mobilised the ruling party to keep the system. The opponents' dominant power until 1996 enabled preservation of the system. It might be argued that the reason why the previous policy tended to persist was heavy reliance not on the inertia of institutions per se but upon related actors' necessity to protect and preserve privileges.

The styles of decision making and conflict resolution also followed established paths. Key opponents of the merger, like the MOHW and the OP, emphasised the risk of any potential merger, thereby, winning over the President and the ruling party to their cause. However, approaching the 1997 presidential election, the political power map within the governing bloc greatly changed. After the President's defection from membership, the ruling party, being freed from government pressure to support a multiple insurer system, began to support the partial merger, as a way of winning votes (Shim, 2004: 447). Dr Kim Yeon-myung, director of the social welfare committee of the People's Solidarity for Participatory Democracy, comments: "The ruling lawmakers from rural areas switched sides and supported the partial merger as a result of pressure from farmers' groups. In every election, farmers' groups intruded into lawmakers' liaison offices asking for support of the merger. Ruling lawmakers were afraid of losing farmers' support at elections, and were thus obliged to propose the merger." (Interview on 19 April 2005)

In this respect, previous policies and decision-making patterns are not permanent. They change according to major actors' political calculations. With the change of the political power map and increased political opportunity, a new policy window opened, breaking away from the previous path. However, change was not the full-scale creation of new institutions but simply an incremental progress. The merger was restricted to partial integration of managing organisations between limited numbers of health insurers (NHIC *White Paper*, 2001: 29). Change agents of current institutions wanted to minimise the risks caused by abrupt institutional change.

4. Policy Networks

Although civic groups had sporadically demanded the merger from the early 1990s, efforts were heightened with the formation of the National Conference for Health Insurance Unification (NCHIU) in April 1994. Since then, civic groups had stood in the vanguard of proposing the merger once more. As was the case of the second debate, a large number of policy actors joined the debate. Parliament was again the major forum for debate. But unlike the second debate, the ruling party changed its position and this time it played a pivotal role in proposing the partial merger from mid-1997 as a way of canvassing for votes. Apart from NCHIU activity, the KCTU and self-employed insurers union, individually, played distinctive roles in proposing the merger. The main opposition NCNP continuously backed the merger.

Meanwhile, opponents of the merger were not so different in character from those of the second debate. While the MOHW stood at the forefront of the opponent bloc, the OP, employee health insurers and business interests supported the MOHW in the debate (Baik, 2010: 243). The President and the mass media were generally opposed to the merger, although they did not promote this view actively. Scholars majoring in healthcare opposed the merger, while social welfare academics advocated it, as before. Table 5.3 divides participants into two blocs.

Table 5.3 Classification of participants during the partial merger debate

	Proponents	Opponents
Official actors	-	MOHW, OP, department committees
Unofficial actors	Ruling party (from 1997), opposition parties, NCHIU, KCTU and self-employed insurers union, social welfare academia	Ruling party (at first), business interests (FKI and KEF), employee health insurers and NFMI, FKTU, mass media, scholars from health and medicine

1) Network structure: party politics in an open network

Nature of participants: number, dominant actors and exclusion

While civic groups demanded the merger from the early 1990s and pressured opposition parties to suggest a merger bill, governing groups blocked the passage of any such bill until 1996. But, with the imminent 1997 presidential election, the ruling party agreed to a plan to partially merge health insurers. In the process of the debate, the number of participants with concerns about the matter multiplied. After 15 years of debate, the issue had finally drawn public attention.

Civic groups were the principal engine behind the push for the merger. The KCTU and self-employed insurers' union also actively got involved in the dispute. Union activists Kim Tae-hyun and Kim Yoo-sun were particularly energetic in proposing the merger. As was true during the second debate, progressive healthcare professionals backed the merger, whereas farmers' groups and the urban poor tended to be inactive (Karl, 1998: 82). Many scholars majoring in social welfare filled the ranks of those supporting the merger theoretically, while some of them directly engaged in civil movement. Kim Young-mo, Lee Gwang-chan, Won Seok-jo and Cha

Heung-bong were particularly in favour of the merger.

Meanwhile, opponents of the merger were stable as before. The governing bloc wished to see the continuation of a multiple insurer system. They had no need to run risk of confusion caused by institutional change, as a nationwide health insurance scheme was already in place after July 1989. For this reason, the ruling party opposed the merger until 1996. Business groups were also negative towards the merger, as their member companies would lose out from the merger. Employee health insurers and the NFMI opposed the merger in order to protect their benefits embedded in a multiple insurer system. The mass media was negative towards the merger too, although not actively so.[14] Scholars, largely majoring in healthcare studies, also sided with the opponent bloc. Among academics, Moon Ok-ryun, Lee Kyu-sik, Kim Byoung-yik, Han Dal-sun and Rho In-cheol strongly opposed the merger.

Until mid-1997, dominant proponents of the merger were opposition parties, civic groups and the KCTU. The major oppositional NCNP and ULD, who had supported the merger from the late 1980s,[15] jointly suggested a merger bill in November 1996. Rep. Lee Seung-jae of the NCNP was the most active proponent of the bill. Under favourable political settings of civilian rule, progressive civic groups and trade unions greatly affected policy-making by voicing their interests. The work of the Citizens' Coalition

14 The mass media were not very interested in the merger at the time, as they were much more concerned about the presidential election and the then economic crisis (Shin, 2004: 140).

15 Kim Dae-jung had been the most ardent supporter of the merger since the 1980s and his party adopted a full and immediate merger as one of its election pledges at both the 1992 and the 1997 presidential elections (Shin, 2004: 138). Kim Jong-pil's ULD also supported the merger in 1996, but its position on the merger was not so inflexible.

for Economic Justice (CCEJ) was particularly noteworthy at the time.[16] For civic groups, the merger issue was a symbolic target for social policy reform. But the decision to partially merge health insurers only became possible once the ruling party switched sides to join those in favour of the merger from mid-1997. It was the ruling party that tipped the scales in favour of the partial merger. Most ruling lawmakers from rural districts advocated the merger, with Hwang Seong-kyun and Moon Jeong-soo as leading figures.

All the while, the MOHW strongly opposed the merger, with the support of the OP and government departments. It upset opposition parties' merger attempts in November 1996 by successfully working alongside the ruling party. Even after the ratification of the National Medical Insurance Act in November 1997, the MOHW did not give up on a multiple insurer system (NFMI, 1997: 666-69). But, other opponents, asides from employee health insurers and the NFMI, were relatively inactive when compared to the second debate, as they tended to side with the populist position, which was beginning to favour the merger.

The vitality of civic groups and trade unions from the late 1980s made the deliberate exclusion of particular actors from policy networks impossible. It was a distinctive feature of Korean society that civic groups formed coalition bodies in order to effectively articulate their interests and they intervened in every important policy-making process in the 1990s (Kim S.-h., 2007: 58-60). The formation of the NCHIU in April 1994 to push for the

16 The CCEJ was established in July 1989 with the goal of achieving economic justice. It focused its efforts, in the early days, on economic issues such as real estate speculation and real name finance transaction, but its concerns extended to almost all important issues in the 1990s (Yoo, 2001: 198).

merger is a model example.[17]

As the 1997 presidential election drew nearer, all relevant policy actors tried to engage in policy networks, because the election was an important political event in which to promote their interests. Between 1996 and 1997, it was impossible to intentionally exclude particular actors opposing government policies, as the major policy-making arena had now become part of Parliament. Parliamentary decision-making, in essence, was more open than the governmental one.

In sum, the policy network structure during the partial merger debate was far closer to an issue network-type in terms of participants' nature, in respect that many policy actors took part in the debate and the exclusion of any particular actors was almost impossible.

Participants' interests in the issue

As before, participants' interests in the merger differed even among the same bloc members. Of the proponents of the merger, civic groups' stated interest in the merger was to reduce the insurance premium burden of the self-employed by establishing a single insurer system (NCHIU, 1999: 12). The promotion of social solidarity through a single insurer system was also important to civic groups. To them, the merger symbolised social reform. But it was undeniable that they were also interested in making use of the issue to solidify the burgeoning civil movement. Dr Kim Yeon-myung, who was the policy director at the NCHIU, explains civic groups' interests in the

17 The NCHIU comprised over 40 activist groups representing the public interest, farmers, trade unions, and health and medical professionals (NCHIU, 1999: 5). Kim Yong-yik, Kim Yeon-myung, Cho Hong-jun and Cho Kyoung-ye played leading roles in setting up and running the NCHIU.

merger:

> For the NCHIU, the merger of health insurers was a symbol of social reform against the evils of the ancient military regimes. The NCHIU believed that a single insurer system represented interests of the old privileged strata, such as bureaucrats, big businessmen and military officials. But candidly speaking, civic groups also had a stake in improving organisational performance through the debate. Civic groups should draw public attention to increase their influence on social issues. In my view, civic groups did not work to pursue only the public interest. (Interview on 19 April 2005)

The stated goal of opposition parties in supporting the merger was similar to that of civic groups. They argued that the merger would promote social solidarity by improving income redistribution and risk pooling (Jang W., 2000: 16). But, in practice, they supported the merger out of political expediency — winning votes in elections, especially from the rural self-employed, a group that had suffered from the heavy burden of insurance premiums. Opposition parties also respected civic groups' opinions and saw them as reliable political supporters.

As far as the ruling party was concerned, lawmakers from rural constituencies preferred a single insurer system, because it was beneficial to their electorate by lowering health insurance premiums. Nevertheless, ruling lawmakers could not but follow the instructions from the President and party leaders who opposed any institutional change. But from 1997, the ruling party freed itself from shackles of the lame-duck President and reversed its position to support the merger, evaluating the merits of a single insurer system in attracting public support (*Hankook Ilbo*, 14 December 1997). Political party, therefore, completely relied upon political gain that stemmed from decisions.

The self-employed insurers' union proposed the merger, expecting that it would lower insurance premiums of the self employed and resolve the financial deficit of self-employed insurers. They also relied on the fact that the merger might alleviate the disparity of insurance benefits between policyholders. The KCTU advocated the merger to consolidate its new organisations through active participation in the debate. It also had an obligation to protect the interests of the affiliated self-employed insurers' union that supported the merger (Shin, 2004: 70). Scholars in the field of social welfare supported the merger because of their concerns about social solidarity, arguing the supremacy of a single insurer system in promoting income redistribution (Kim, Yang, and Yu, 2013: 78).

Among opponents, the MOHW resisted the merger, insisting that a multiple insurer system would be better in minimising the government's financial burden and maximising managerial efficiency through the autonomy of each insurer. But the MOHW had other practical interests in maintaining a multiple insurer system. It could control health insurers more easily by using a divide-and-rule tactic, influencing the management of health insurers under a multiple insurer system. Retired officials would also have a good chance of getting a further role inside these multiple insurers. MOHW officials also worried about the increase in administrative responsibility if the merger proceeded. Kang Chang-koo, a former NCHIU spokesman, considers the reason why MOHW officials opposed the merger:

> Core members of the MOHW had set up a multiple insurer system. They took

great pride in the fact that they had created the institution. Accordingly, they resisted change and sided with the status quo. Besides, a multiple insurer system was easier for them to control than was a bigger organisation. (Interview on 20 December 2004)

Employee health insurers and the NFMI also had vested interests in keeping a multiple insurer system. In the event of a merger, large numbers of staff might lose their jobs and the right to manage insurance funds would be transferred to a unified insurer.[18] Above all, maintaining a multiple insurer system ensured the very existence of their organisation. Business interests preferred a multiple insurer system, as their member companies would lose the right to control insurance funds after the merger.[19] Each company enjoyed financial benefits by individually managing their insurance funds. They also worried about possible increases in employees' insurance premiums after the merger, if it was conducted to compensate the financial deficit of self-employed insurers.

Among trade unions, the FKTU opposed the merger, as its affiliated members would have borne a heavy burden of increased insurance premiums due to the low-level income declaration of the self-employed (Baik, 2010: 244). It thought that the integration of differently contributed insurance funds was intrinsically unfair. At the time, insurance funds of employee insurers were financially healthy, while those of the self-employed insur-

18 It was an open secret that health insurers' directors enjoyed considerable benefits from the deposit of large amounts of insurance funds in commercial banks. (Interview with Dr Chun Chang-bae, a senior researcher of the NHIC, on 9 March 2005)

19 In 1996, the rate of accumulated insurance funds of employee insurers was about 150 percent while that of county-level insurers was just 22.1 percent.

ers were not. Meanwhile, health and medical academia opposed the merger by claiming that a multiple insurer system was more economically efficient. They worried about the possible downward equalisation of health insurance benefits in the event of a merger.

Resource dependency between participants

Resource dependency largely occurred between the same bloc members. Among key proponents until mid-1997, civic groups and the KCTU closely depended on each other to effectively mobilise a large-scale support for the merger. They were the core members of the NCHIU in the partial merger debate. Intimate resource dependence among opposition parties, civic groups and progressive trade unions was also vital at the time. Opposition parties tried to embrace large-scale membership of civic groups and progressive trade unions in order to consolidate their power base. From the standpoint of civic groups and trade unions, opposition party support was essential to see any of their desires transpire into law at a time when the governing bloc was still reluctant to consult with them (Kim Y.-m., 2003: 308-9).

One of the two nationwide umbrella unions, the militant KCTU was on friendly terms with opposition parties and most civic groups. At the time, the government would not accept the KCTU as a legal trade union representative, because it worried about workplace disputes under a system of multiple unions. Meanwhile, the FKTU, the only legally authorised umbrella union, was more docile and sometimes pro-governmental on labour policy. The FKTU needed financial subsidies from the government and in return, the government wanted FKTU support in implementing labour policy. For long, they had maintained a corporatist relationship through both inducement and constraint (Kim, S.-y., 1999: 108).[20]

Major opponents of the merger were the MOHW and the ruling party during the earlier stages of the debate. Other government agencies like the OP and the OPM intermittently took part in the debate. At the time, the MOHW was very dependent on the ruling party, as opposition parties were incessantly proposing the merger in Parliament. In November 1996, the MOHW succeeded in upsetting an oppositional merger attempt by mobilising the support of the ruling party. The MOHW also greatly depended on the resources the OP, the OPM and economy-related departments possessed. But the MOHW was able to call upon their support relatively easily, as they had already agreed to preserve a multiple insurer system.

But from 1997, the political situation began to change. The ruling party wanted to break away and distance itself from the unpopular Kim administration, and changed its mind to accept the merger, anticipating political gains. Therefore, it proposed a partial merger bill in October 1997, despite government opposition (NHIC, 2001: 29). The need to win the election changed the ruling party's policy, and thus, the resource dependency relationship between the ruling party and the government broke down.

Minor opponents of the merger, such as employee health insurers and business interests, could support the MOHW stance in terms of government policies as client groups. But the resource dependency between opponents of the merger became redundant, as the main policy-making arena of the debate was Parliament, and the ruling party began to support the merg-

20 In 1997, the government provided the FKTU with 2,247 million won to subsidise union staff education, labour-day events and overseas training (Ministry of Labour *White Paper*, 1998).

er. Dr Lee Sang-yong, director general of MOHW Pension and Health Insurance Bureau, explains:

> Until the mid-1990s, the MOHW did not really need the cooperation of non-governmental opponents of the merger, as the proponent bloc was just in a minority. But the situation changed fundamentally in 1997. The merger became a grand trend of the time and non-governmental opponents of the merger began to shrink away and follow the rising tide. (Interview on 29 December 2004)

2) Participants' interaction: self-restraint for second best outcome

Basic nature of interaction

Interaction between different blocs was largely conflicting. But the extent of their conflicts was not so serious, when compared to former cases. In the early stages of the Kim administration, civic groups and trade unions were sympathetic to the reformist government, despite their differences towards the merger.

But with the passage of time, the policy orientation of two leading actors of each bloc, the MOHW and civic groups, became irreconcilable. While the MOHW's basic standpoint was to gradually improve the problems of a multiple insurer system, civic groups strongly demanded to set up a single insurer system immediately (NFMI, 1997: 687-89). From mid-1996, civic groups and the KCTU put further pressure on opposition parties to propose the merger, making the relationship between opponents and proponents more confrontational. Being pressured by civic groups, the main opposition NCNP and ULD jointly put forward a merger bill in November 1996. But the combined effort of the ruling party and the MOHW frustrated the merger attempt.

The situation, however, completely changed in 1997. Above all else, the ruling party no longer support the government position. After President Kim left the ruling party, the ruling party-government conference was closed, and the MOHW now faced opposition from political parties including the ruling party.

In this new situation, the MOHW, employee health insurers and the NFMI now propped up the opponent bloc. Relevant departments and the outgoing President were not active in opposing the merger and did not have any power to block the merger (Shin, 2004: 172). Although the MOHW and employee health insurers were unhappy about the merger, they could not help following the decision made by Parliament. Conflicts between political parties and the MOHW were, therefore, settled by the big power imbalance between them, despite their irreconcilable perspectives. Dr Lee Sang-yong of the MOHW details the weakness of the MOHW at the time:

> The one and only source of MOHW power is the political interest of the President and the ruling party when it comes to social welfare. If they stress social welfare, material resources automatically follow. But, President Kim did not pay much attention to social welfare matters, as he had already secured political legitimacy through the free and competitive presidential election. What is worse, the MOHW was completely cut off from the governing power after the President resigned from the ruling party. (Interview on 29 December 2004)

Frequency of interaction

As before, interaction during the debate frequently took place between the same bloc members. While the proponent bloc was mainly led by the NCHIU, its members acted as an affiliate and also an independent actor. The activities of the NCHIU were much more systemic and better organised than those of civic coalitions in the second debate. Well-drilled associations, like the CCEJ and the People's Solidarity for Participatory Democracy (PSPD), drove these activities. As one might have expected, civic groups also repeatedly interacted with progressive trade unions in the drive to achieve the merger.

Interaction between civic groups and opposition parties was also quite frequent. Between 1995 and 1996, they worked together to suggest policies to Parliament (Wong, 2004: 99). Civic groups' intention to merge health insurers was greatly reflected in opposition election campaigns. In 1997, civic groups changed their lobbying target towards the ruling party.[21] Civic groups and trade unions were also active on government committees.[22] From mid-1997, the ruling and opposition parties met frequently to negotiate the merger.

But level of interaction between opponents of the merger was low. While opponents frequently kept in contact until 1996, meetings were sporadic from 1997, as the ruling party-government conference became ineffective after President Kim's secession from the ruling party. Drawing to the end of the presidential term, the OP also failed to pay attention to the issue and was bereft of power to coordinate differences between governing bloc

21 For example, the NCHIU met the ruling party's secretary-general in November 1997 and pressured him to adopt the merger as part of a presidential election pledge (NCHIU, 1999: 21).

22 The KCTU pushed for the merger at the May 1997 public hearing sponsored by the Healthcare Reform Committee (NCHIU, 1999: 512).

members. Relevant departments like the OPM and departments in charge of economic matters were generally passive during the debate, as they were reluctant to cooperate with the MOHW especially where the President was not involved. They were not yet ready to show hostility towards the prospective ruling power. Thus, the MOHW fought a lone battle against multiple proponents of the merger, with a small amount of support from employee health insurers and the NFMI.

Mobilised strategies of interaction

Since its establishment in April 1994, the NCHIU had played a core role in supporting the merger and mobilising all possible means, on behalf of civic groups and progressive trade unions. Until 1996 its strategy was reliant upon the promotion of mass-level arguments as pathway to articulate its interests. Its target of interest input was mainly opposition parties and Parliament. But from 1997, when the ruling party began to support the partial merger, the NCHIU changed its major lobbying target to the ruling party who controlled Parliament. Moreover, differently from the second debate, proponents' strategy became more flexible, as the Kim administration was open to civil pressure. Key NCHIU members, such as major civic groups and the KCTU, were officially invited to be the government's policy partners (Kim S.-y., 1999: 120). Table 5.4 summarises the NCHIU activities during the debate under the Kim administration.

Among NCHIU members, the KCTU's role was crucial in achieving the partial merger. It made use of the issue in consolidating its fledgling organisation, and consecutive elections provided the KCTU with opportunities to boast its membership strength via collective action. Unlike the conservative FKTU, the KCTU demonstrated a clear plan for the merger

Table 5.4 Activities of the NCHIU during the partial merger debate

Year	Activities
1994	Holding seminars, street petitions, protest visits to political parties, and petitions to Parliament etc.
1995	Making use of the June local election, holding seminars, boycotting insurance payments, street petitions, and pressurising local assemblies etc.*
1996	Making use of the April general election (pressure on opposition parties to adopt the merger as an election pledge, lobbying candidates with rural electorates), protest visits to health insurers, and meeting with the President's staff and party leaders etc.
1997	Participation in government committees, switching main interest input channel to the ruling party, putting pressure on presidential candidates to adopt the merger as an election pledge,** and warning the MOHW not to oppose the passed bill etc.

* The Incheon local assembly adopted, in December 1995, a resolution supporting the merger for the first time. The local assemblies of Seoul and Daegu metropolitan cities adopted similar resolutions, in December 1996, urging Parliament to pass the merger bill (NCHIU, 1999: 16-20).

** In consequence, ruling candidate Lee Hoi-chang supported the gradual merger of health insurers, whereas opposition contender Kim Dae-jung advocated the immediate and full merger (*Hankook Ilbo*, 14 December 1997).

Source: adapted from the NCHIU (1999).

and combined the issue with a wage war to address workers' concerns.

In 1995, the KCTU concentrated efforts on drawing workers' attention to health insurance matters.[23] In January 1995, it adopted the merger of health insurers and the extension of insurance benefits as a part of its social reform agenda (KTC, 1999: 205), and formed the Medical Insurance Merger Planning Committee in April 1995 under its jurisdiction, to systemically promote the merger. During 1996-97, the KCTU took advantage of the

23 The KCTU believed that the failure to introduce a single insurer system in the second debate was largely attributable to the inability to ease the worry of an increase in workers' burden by allowing the merger (Lim, 2001: 67).

election phase to push for the merger.

Among KCTU affiliates, the self-employed insurers' union was the most ardent supporter of the merger. They were dissatisfied with their inferior working conditions, when compared to those of employee insurers, and they believed that the merger would reduce their insurance premiums and ease the financial deficit of self-employed insurers (Jang W., 2000: 112). For these reasons, they actively pressured the KCTU and the NCHIU to push for the merger.

Opposition parties had advocated the merger from the beginning.[24] They dedicated themselves to the merger of health insurers and the extension of insurance benefits in their pledges at the 1996 general election. From 1996, they became much more active in advocating the merger, in anticipation of the 1997 presidential election. The NCNP and the ULD jointly suggested the National Health Insurance Bill in November 1996, aiming for a complete merger (Choi S., 2000: 382). In laying down an opposition bill, civic groups lobbied opposition lawmakers, such as Lee Seung-jae, who played a key role in persuading colleagues (Kim J.-d., 2002: 202). But opposition efforts were scuppered by the governing bloc.

In the meantime, the ruling party, who enjoyed a parliamentary majority at the time, led the decision-making process from mid-1997 to partially integrate health insurers. Opposition parties had advocated the full merger at first, but accepted the partial and gradual merger as a second best option. At the time, opposition parties had no need to oppose the partial merg-

24 The main opposition candidate Kim Dae-jung stood for the merger as a presidential election pledge in 1992, while the ruling candidate Kim Young-sam stuck to a multiple insurer system, just proposing improvements in the financial stability of health insurers and the extension of insurance benefits (Public Information Office, 1997: 285).

er because the full merger was believed to follow the partial merger. For this reason, the partial merger was easily agreed upon in November 1997 (NHIC, 2001: 29). According to Kim Yeon-myung, the NCHIU policy director, "civic groups and opposition parties all accepted the partial merger, as the full merger was a coming trend at that time. All relevant actors believed that the partial merger was just a starting point on the path towards the full organisational and financial mergers of health insurers." (Interview on 14 December 2005)

The ruling party proposed a multiple insurer system at the 1992 presidential election (*Donga Ilbo*, 17 December 1992). However, ruling lawmakers differed from party leaders. Lawmakers from rural areas had always had a lingering attachment to a single insurer system, which seemed advantageous to rural residents. As the end of one presidency and the new presidential election drew near, suddenly they had a chance to promote their views through the ruling party's Water and Medical Subcommittee for Rural Residents. The Subcommittee tried to propose its own merger bill in 1996, but failed due to governmental opposition. The President and party leaders still effectively controlled lawmakers.

But from June 1997, when the lame-duck presidency kicked in, the ruling party reconsidered the possibility of a merger again and decided to prepare the ground for a gradual merger plan (Won, 2006: 171). Delegates from rural areas claimed that the merger proposal was included in the party's presidential election pledges. Rep. Hwang Seong-kyun persuaded the ruling candidate Lee Hoi-chang to support the merger, and obtained Lee's consent in August 1997 (Lee K., 2000a: 72).[25] But the ruling party adopted a

25 But during the second debate in the late 1980s, Hwang supported a multiple insurer sys-

method of only partially integrating health insurers instead of going for a complete merger,[26] as it worried about the prospect of conflict between relevant interests if the merger was rushed through too quickly.

The ruling party proposed the National Medical Insurance Bill on 30 October 1997, with the aim of reducing management costs of multiple insurers and lowering the insurance premiums of the self-employed. Rep. Hwang put forward an explanation of the Bill, on 11 November 1997, at the National Assembly Health and Welfare Committee.[27] With opposition party agreement, the Bill absorbed the opposition bill suggested in 1996 and was approved by the Committee on 14 November and by the plenary session of Parliament on 18 November 1997 (NHIC, 2001: 29).

During the partial merger debate, the opponent bloc was led by the MOHW. Until 1996, the key strategy of the MOHW was to persuade the ruling party to obstruct the merger in Parliament, and it succeeded in blocking the merger. The MOHW, in particular, mobilised government committees to support a multiple insurer system on the pretext of minimising administrative confusion that might arise if institutional change was not

tem by saying: "Making megalopolis-sized insurers is more desirable than the merger in preventing the bureaucratisation and rigidity of big organisation." (Records of Health and Social Affairs Committee of the 144th National Assembly of February 1989)

26 The ruling party's merger plan was to gradually introduce a single insurer system within 4-5 years. The first step was an organisational merger between the self-employed insurers and the KMIC for government/private school employees by setting up the National Medical Insurance Corporation (NMIC). The second step was to merge the NMIC with employee insurers by forming the National Health Insurance Corporation (NHIC), and the financial merger would be the final thing to enact.

27 While suggesting the partial merger bill, Rep. Hwang pointed out the failure of a multiple insurer system in solving the issue of medical security for those on low-income and in achieving an equitable burden of health insurance premiums between policyholders (Lee J., 2000: 90).

carefully prepared in advance (Kim et al., 2013: 78).

It was a peculiarity of the partial merger debate that important policies were discussed by diverse types of government committees or task teams,[28] which preferred to improve the current multiple insurer system. Government's policy towards the merger was to graft the merits of a single insurer system onto a multiple insurer system (NHIC, 2001: 28). The Healthcare Reform Committee (HCRC) of the OPM proposed to make bigger health insurers by introducing megalopolis-sized insurers based on a zone of life (MOHW *White Paper*, 1997: 14).[29] But the MOHW opposed this proposal due to the difficulty of establishing a unit of life zone and the possible inconsistencies between administrative districts and life zones. Instead, the MOHW proposed a reinforcement of the finance adjustment program and additional subsidies to the self-employed insurers.

Even after the ruling party's policy change towards the merger from July 1997, the MOHW and government committees defended the multiple insurer system. In November 1997, the HCRC suggested the introduction of a megalopolis-sized insurer system based on metropolitan administrative districts, instead of the previous concept of the life zone, and on the autonomous integration of employee insurers through free market competition. The MOHW tried to persuade lawmakers by extolling the virtues of a mul-

28 Health insurance policies, including the health insurer system, were debated in diverse government committees, such as the Agricultural Development Committee, the Medical Security Reform Committee, the Globalisation Promotion Committee, the Administrative Reform Committee and the HCRC (NFMI, 1997: 639).

29 The HCRC was formed by the OPM in November 1996 to deliberate healthcare reform. But the HCRC, consisted of 30 members from among MOHW officials, medical and pharmaceutical professionals and the medical industry, preferred a multiple insurer system, as most of its members were recruited from opponents to the merger (Lee J., 2000: 73).

tiple insurer system.[30]

But differently from the previous cases, MOHW leadership in opposing the merger started to weaken when the OP began to lose interest in the matter and the general trend was advancing towards supporting the merger. The National Medical Insurance Act (NMIA) was enacted on 18 November 1997 to substitute the then Medical Insurance Act. But the MOHW tried to block the enforcement of the NMIA, instead of recommending the use of a presidential veto, by suggesting a new proposal based on a multiple insurer system (NHIC, 2001: 29). At the government meeting on 24 December 1997, participants decided to advise the State Council to push forward with the creation of megalopolis-sized insurers, based on a multiple insurer system, as a government alternative (PUC, 1998: 283).[31] Thus, the MOHW formally requested that political parties reconsider the partial merger, though the effort amounted to nothing by the promulgation of the NMIA on 31 December 1997.[32]

---

30 The MOHW listed the inequitable burden of insurance premiums between policyholders caused by the low-level income declaration of the self-employed as a serious problem of the merger. Meanwhile, it alleged a multiple insurer system was closer to global trends and to the state's view of enhancing national competence through competition (NFMI, 1997: 666-85).

31 "At the meeting the MOHW insisted on a megalopolis-sized insurer system on the ground that the merger of different kinds of multiple insurers would generate many administrative and legal problems. The recommendation of a presidential veto was also discussed at the time, but participants concluded it might not be desirable, taking into account the parliamentary agreement about the NMIA." (Interview with MOHW Director General Lee Sang-young on 29 December 2004)

32 Refuting the MOHW minister's opposition to the NMIA, the Health and Welfare Committee chairperson said: "The NMIA was unanimously agreed in the National Assembly. Accordingly it is more desirable for the government to follow this parliamentary decision, despite the differences of opinion with the National Assembly, and to sincerely cope with the problems caused in the process of implementation." (Records of Health and Welfare Committee of 185th National Assembly of 1997).

Other relevant departments were inactive in opposing the merger, as the issue was not so urgent to them. In particular, as the presidency was drawing to a close, the OP had lost its power to coordinate the governing bloc. The general atmosphere of governing bloc members, except the MOHW, was not one of resolute opposition to the merger, and government departments passively responded to the issue, simply showing up at government committees. Employee health insurers and the NFMI issued a joint statement detailing the merits of a multiple insurer system after the ruling party's suggestion of a merger bill in November 1997 and made a protest visit to Parliament (Lim, 2001: 60). But they also admitted the inevitability of the merger, as the tide of events flowed against them.

5. Policy Outputs

1) Final outputs: pushing the first button

The final output of the debate under the Kim Young-sam administration was to partially merge health insurers by integrating management systems between 227 self-employed insurers and the KMIC for government/private school employees. But their financial merger and any organisational merger with employee health insurers were excluded from the policy output.

Although the ruling party's desires were largely reflected in the final choice, the policy output was a compromise between the major participants. Some of participants changed their original positions during the course of the debate. Until 1996, main proponents were civic groups, progressive trade unions and opposition parties and they advocated the full merger both organisationally and financially. They also wanted the integration of Medicaid into health insurance program. Their policy goals were clearly expressed in the National Health Insurance Bill of November 1996. But from 1997, the initiative had passed on to the ruling party. Proponents had to prepare for the ruling party's victory in the presidential election, as the ruling candidate Lee Hoi-chang looked to be the most likely winner at the time. For that reason, proponents of the merger accepted the partial merger as the second best outcome that they could achieve.

Up till 1996, the ruling party had stayed in the bloc against the merger and the President had controlled the ruling party. The ruling party-government conference was also effective. The ruling party, accordingly, blocked the passage of the opposition bill in November 1996. However, just after the ruling presidential candidate took office in July 1997, the ruling party altered its stance on the merger and proposed a partial merger bill, hoping that it would appeal to the electorate. Unlike the original proponents of the merger, the ruling party strategised a gradual merger. With agreement from opposition parties and civic groups, the partial merger bill passed into law.

Meanwhile, the MOHW vehemently opposed the merger, even though the detailed assertions supporting its case had changed over time. The MOHW, originally, intended to repair the health insurance program within the framework of a multiple insurer system and formed the MSRC under its jurisdiction to deliberate health insurance policy. The Committee reported in June 1994 on the merits of a single insurer system and how they could be blended into a multiple insurer system. On the other hand, the HCRC recommended the founding of megalopolis-sized insurers in November 1996 based on the mixture of the life zone concept with administrative districts.

The MOHW's final alternative was to propose the setting up of megalopolis-sized insurers based on administrative districts instead of the life zone, and insisted on making an alternative law to the NMIA. The MOHW alleged its alternative would reduce confusion caused by sudden institutional change and make the flexible adjustment of insurance premiums possible. But the MOHW's intention of sticking to a multiple insurer system was frustrated ultimately by the enforcement of the NMIA.

2) Reflected interests: political motivations and semi success

Although a unified single insurer system did not materialise, the debate under the Kim administration opened the door for the full merger. During the process of the debate, original proponents of the full merger also accepted the partial and gradual merger. In this sense, the resultant outputs of the debate largely reflected proponents' assertions and interests. But contrast to previous cases, the major proponent of the partial merger was the ruling party, and without its endorsement the partial merger would have been impossible.

Of the proponents of the merger, civic groups succeeded in demonstrating their capacity to mobilise civil power in policy-making. They employed every possible means to articulate their interests and succeeded in showing a unified front. They effectively made use of political events like elections, and the final result of the debate was also satisfactory to them. Civic groups finally emerged as key policy actors by successfully managing the merger debate.

For trade unions, particularly the progressive KCTU, the debate provided a good chance to demonstrate their large-scale membership and to fortify the unity of the newly emerging, progressive unions. Although the partial merger was not their intended goal, they were satisfied with it. As a result of devoting their energy towards backing the merger, the KCTU emerged as a rival to the FKTU.

Opposition parties also achieved policy goals to a degree. Notably, the main opposition NCNP greatly benefited from its successful advocacy of the merger. During the debate, the NCNP stood at the centre representing the interests of activist groups, and their support was critical in winning the 1997 presidential election (*Donga Ilbo*, 17 December 1997). Unlike the ruling party who had changed policies on the merger, the NCNP had supported the merger consistently. Also, this made the general public perceive the partial merger as a NCNP creation, even though it was actually proposed by the ruling party.

The ruling party changed its policy from 1997 and successfully achieved its goal of the partial and gradual merger. Despite this, the ruling party missed out in the presidential election due to economic failures and rival contestant Lee In-je's betrayal (Shim, 2004: 443).

Opponents to the merger blocked all merger attempts until 1996, through effective cooperation between governing bloc members. But from 1997, the political situation developed unexpectedly. The ruling party broke away from the opponent bloc and other government departments adopted a passive stance towards the merger, as they did not want to contend with a potential President-elect. Staff in the OP clandestinely supported the ruling party's view, not the government, as their jobs largely depended on the in-coming President.

The MOHW stood alone in its opposition to the merger in the midst of turbulent politics of 1997. The opponent bloc practically collapsed as a result of the breakdown of coordinating mechanisms between governing bloc members. The merger of health insurers was becoming an inevitable trend, and it was impossible for the MOHW to stem the tide. Minor opponents such as health insurers and the NFMI were insufficient in maintaining their bloc. In the end, the MOHW's plan to stick by a multiple insurer system was simply overcome.

6. Conclusion

In the partial merger debate, the political context was decisively important in shaping institutions and policy networks as before. 1) The 'globalisation' ideology influenced the debate, being linked with the idea of 'globalisation of the quality of life.' Health insurance program was a means to improve the quality of life to that subscribed by the global standard. 2) Democratising politics and competitive leadership made the governing bloc more responsive and civil society more autonomous. This was again reflected in a balanced power relationship, an open and fluid network structure, and more unstable and augmentative interaction patterns. 3) Political events like the presidential election made a deep impact on the whole process of the debate and on the overall aspects of policy networks. With the 1997 presidential election just around the corner, the ruling party left the governing bloc and brought forward proposals in backing the partial merger. 4) Revitalising civil society and strengthening trade unions more widely opened policy networks and diversified participants' interaction patterns.

The basic institutions were not so different from those during the second debate. But their practical operation fluctuated over time. 1) At least in terms of institutions, the power relationship between political organisations had been balanced since the late 1980s. But the practical power relationship was changeable over time, and the power transfer within the governing bloc from the President to the ruling presidential candidate was crucial in achieving the partial merger. 2) Basic institutional properties of political system were also similar to those of the second debate. During the early stages of the presidency, the President tightly controlled the governing bloc. But, towards the final year of the presidency, the ruling party emerged at the centre of governing system. Even though political party and election institutions were also largely unchanged, the real situation was dynamic. In the situation where the ruling party was an unstable parliamentary majority, minor opposition parties could exercise a casting vote in making policies. 3) The basic decision-making rules were all kept stable by related laws and ordinances. It was particularly noteworthy that many special committees were formed to discuss healthcare reform. But the breakdown of the ruling party-government conference from late-1997 was a crucial factor in enabling the partial merger by shaking up the composition of network membership and interaction patterns. 4) Previous policies began to lose the regulatory power due to the changing political power map. The established institutions saw alterations in the internal power relationship, despite the basic tendency of institutions to persist.

The policy network type during the partial merger was nearer to an issue network in terms of both structure and interaction. A variety of policy actors took part in the open and fluid network, and the intentional exclusion of particular actors became impossible. Of course, the appearance of an issue network type was greatly affected by the policy context, characterised by the progress towards democracy, frequent elections and an active civil society. Network structure was also greatly constrained by the power relationship between political organisations. The dispersion of political power and the change of leading power within the governing bloc pushed Parliament into the main battlefield of debate, and made the roles of political parties and civic groups more crucial.

The basic nature of interaction patterns also changed as the debate evolved. At earlier stages, participants' interactions were unstable and less uniform. But, from mid-1997 when the ruling party changed policy, they became more consultative and conciliatory. Particularly, the impacts of political context, power relationship and network structure on interaction patterns were large. Political democracy enabled civic groups to be a serious policy actor and the power transfer within the governing bloc towards the ruling party forced government departments to accept the partial merger. Finally the network structure, characterised by loosely-knitted open networks and changing dominant actors, generated more compromising interaction patterns, resulting in the incremental merger of health insurers.

The final output of the debate was the partial and gradual merger of health insurers, the result of a compromise between the participants who reshaped their original goals. In shaping these policy outputs the impacts of political context, the power relationship and interaction patterns were remarkable. In reverse, policy outputs could also affect policy networks. For example, the start of the partial merger consolidated the proponent bloc in terms of the future policy network. However, the strong feedback of policy outputs to policy context and institutions was uncommon.

Chapter
6

Unfinished Symphony

Accomplishment of Full Merger in the 2000s

1. Introductory Comments

Opposition candidate Kim Dae-jung, who had always been the most ardent supporter of the single insurer system amongst major politicians of the time, won the December 1997 presidential election. He had proposed the merger of health insurers as one of his election pledges, but even under this new political situation, the MOHW tried to block the implementation of the partial merger agreed in November 1997, making a vain effort to persuade political parties to reconsider the partial merger. After the partial merger bill came into force on 31 December 1997, the MOHW started lobbying the Presidency Undertaking Commission (PUC). The PUC held public hearings to discuss the issue in January 1998, but failed to reach a decision (PUC, 1998: 284).

It was the Korea Tripartite Commission (KTC) that decided to proceed and fully merge health insurers including all managing organisations and insurance funds.[1] The KTC agreed, in February 1998, to pass a full merger bill by the end of 1998, and following this, the PUC selected the full merger of health insurers (henceforth, the full merger) as one of the 100 national policies that the Kim Dae-jung administration (1998-February 2003) would pursue. The MOHW then changed its mind to give working-level support

1 The KTC was formed on 15 January 1998 as a forum to discuss the ways of overcoming the then economic crisis. It comprised the representatives from the government, the ruling and opposition parties, trade unions and business associations (Ha and Yoon, 2004: 63).

to draw a government draft bill (KTC, 1999: 204). In October 1998, the National Medical Insurance Corporation (NMIC) was established to implement the November 1997 decision, partially integrating the management organisations of self-employed insurers and the government/private school employee insurer (Kim J.-d., 2002: 204).

While a government bill to fully merge health insurers passed the State Council on 1 December 1998, the main opposition Grand National Party (GNP) planned to amend the National Medical Insurance Act (NMIA) to absorb Medicaid into the health insurance program.[2] The National Assembly Health and Welfare Committee introduced an alternative called the National Health Insurance Bill, that integrated suggestions from both bills, and it was passed on 23 December 1998. The Bill aimed to set up a single insurer in terms of both organisation and finance, excluding the Medicaid from the proposed health insurance program. But the Legislation and Judiciary Committee suggested separating the finances of self-employed insurers from employee insurers as it was concerned about the possible infringement of private property rights in the event of a compulsory financial merger (Chung and Cho, 2001: 115).

The Legislation and Judiciary Committee, however, failed to reach an agreement due to a boycott of its proposal by the GNP, and the National Assembly Speaker referred the Health and Welfare Committee Bill to a plenary session of Parliament by using his constitutional authority, without the agreement of the Legislation and Judiciary Committee. The plenary session endorsed the Bill as the National Health Insurance Act (NHIA) on

2 The ex-ruling GNP became the main opposition party after being defeated in the December 1997 presidential election (Shim, 2004: 446).

6 January 1999 during the absence of the GNP lawmakers (Lim, 2001: 73). Despite the opposition party's complaint about the ruling party's one-sidedness at the plenary session, the NHIA came into force in February 1999 and paved the way for the full merger.

After the enactment of the NHIA, participants' major worries shifted to the issue of the permanent division of finances between different types of policyholders and the temporary suspension of an organisational merger. While the opposition GNP suggested the permanent separation of employee insurers' finances from those of self-employed insurers, the ruling party planned to just delay the organisational merger for six months and the financial merger for two years.

From mid-1999, attempts to revise the NHIA began in earnest. The MOHW put forward a government draft to Parliament in September 1999, aimed at postponing the organisational merger for six months. Some conservative trade unions, that were negative towards the full merger, launched a petition asking to defer the enforcement of the NHIA. As before, the Health and Welfare Committee put forward another alternative that amalgamated these amended bills, and the revision of the NHIA was endorsed by the plenary session on 7 December 1999. Later, the organisational merger between the NMIC and employee insurers was enforced in June 2000, thus launching a single unified health insurer, the National Health Insurance Corporation (NHIC). But the proposed financial merger was deferred again until June 2003. The brief chronology of the debate to fully merge health insurers is summarised below, and the change in numbers of health insurers is shown in Table 6.1.

Table 6.1 Changes in numbers of health insurance management organisations

<table>
<tr><th></th><th>1989</th><th>1997</th><th>1998</th><th>1999</th><th>2000</th></tr>
<tr><td>Employee insurers</td><td>154</td><td>145</td><td>142</td><td>140</td><td rowspan="3">1</td></tr>
<tr><td>Self-employed insurers</td><td>254</td><td>227</td><td rowspan="2">1</td><td rowspan="2">1</td></tr>
<tr><td>KMIC</td><td>1</td><td>1</td></tr>
<tr><td>Total</td><td>409</td><td>373</td><td>143</td><td>141</td><td>1</td></tr>
</table>

Source: Kim B. (2000: 42).

- **November 1997**: Enactment of the National Medical Insurance Act (partial merger of management organisations of health insurers)
- **October 1998**: Inauguration of the NMIC (by integrating 227 self-employed insurers with the Korea Medical Insurance Corporation for government/ private school employees)
- **January 1999**: Enactment of the NHIA (full organisational and partial financial mergers by December1999 and full financial merger by December 2001)
- **December 1999**: Revision of the NHIA (deferral of the merger: organisational merger by June 2000, partial financial merger by December 2000, and full financial merger by December 2001)
- **July 2000**: Full organisational merger (inauguration of the NHIC as a single insurer by integrating 140 employee insurers with the NMIC)
- **January 2002**: Postponement of scheduled full financial merger until June 2003

2. Policy Context

1) Political context: power alternation and insolvent economy

As a veteran dissident, President Kim had strong ties with the politically excluded strata in Korean society, such as labour and progressive intellectuals (Tat, 2000: 370). Supporters expected him to successfully deal with regional antagonism and economic injustice, and President Kim consequently advocated national reconciliation as its central ideological platform, calling his regime the *Kookmin* (people) government. President Kim stressed, in his inauguration speech of February 1998, the reconciliation between different regions and between economic strata: "I will encourage the people's participation in policy-making. The government will not tolerate any kind of political retaliation, privilege and discrimination."

The Kim administration also aimed for harmony between democracy and the free market economy. As a long-time symbol of Korea's democratisation movement on the one hand, and as a victim of politics-business connections in the other, Kim thought that a combination of democracy and the free market economy could end the economic impasse (Park E., 2000: 366). Thus, the Kim administration pursued economic redistribution, together with neo-liberalism. His inauguration speech emphasised this:

> The most important task with which the government is confronted is to overcome the economic crisis. The government will blend democracy and the free market economy. They are two sides of the same coin and two wheels of wagon. If we split them, we will never succeed. If democracy and the free market economy are developed harmoniously, illegal links between politics and the econo-

my, bureaucracy-led finance, and administrative corruption will disappear.

The debate on the full merger predominantly took place during the first two years (1998-99) of Kim's presidency, and many political events occurred during the time. The 1997 presidential election was critical in making the full merger possible. Major presidential candidates supported the merger as part of their election pledges.[3] Kim Dae-jung advocated the full and immediate merger in response to demands from his major supporters, such as trade unions and civic groups. The result of the presidential election blunted any opposition to the merger from the MOHW, as President-elect Kim had been a strong supporter of the merger (Won, 2006: 171).

The April 2000 general election was another important political event. Originally, the NHIA said that the merger should be implemented from January 2000, but since late-1999 the governing bloc had tried to delay the timing of merger, being concerned about possible political damage in the forthcoming election. They thought a hurried merger might cause a sharp increase in insurance premiums and create managerial confusion (Kim J.-d., 2002: 54). Opposition parties also suggested a deferral of the organisational merger and the permanent separation of insurance funds.

The economic crisis from late-1997 was also important in encouraging the full merger. Cooperation from trade unions was necessary to overcome economic insolvency and the merger was a useful strategy to induce their

3 Of the major presidential contenders at the 1997 election, main opposition candidate Kim Dae-jung supported the full and immediate merger, while the then ruling candidate Lee Hoi-chang promised the gradual merger of health insurers. Minor opposition candidate Lee In-je advocated the setting up of megalopolis-sized insurers based on a multiple insurer system (NCHIU, 1999: 21).

support (Yu, 2000: 147). The Kim Dae-jung and Kim Jong-pil (the so-called DJP) coalition was also a political event that made the enactment and revision of the NHIA possible, by strengthening the power of the governing bloc in Parliament.

Politics had gradually changed to an open and democratic pattern since the large-scale protests of the late 1980s. Democracy and human rights were greatly enhanced during Kim's term of office. But in general, the personalities of old-generation politicians including President Kim were authoritative. They ruled subordinates through personal charisma and induced loyalty through political funds and regional favouritism.

Political leadership selection was also competitive and democratic at the time. Kim recorded a narrow victory at the 1997 presidential election,[4] and the opposition GNP obtained 133 seats of 273 at the 2000 general election and became a leading party, with opposition parties prevailing in Parliament once again (Kim and Kim, 2000: 112).

2) Social context: active civil society

Civic groups and trade unions, along with his hometown residents, had been President Kim's most ardent political supporters for a long time and thus they actively engaged in politics with the Kim administration. The governing bloc also skilfully made use of them to bolster disadvantages deriving from belonging to a parliamentary minority. A distinctive example

4 Kim Dae-jung posted 40.3 percent polling score, whereas the then ruling candidate Lee Hoi-chang scored 38.7 percent and minor opposition candidate Lee In-je won 19.2 percent (www.nec.go.kr).

was the government's tolerance of civic groups' illegal blacklisting campaign, which largely targeted opposition candidates, at the 2000 general election (Kim S.-h., 2000: 92).[5]

Powerful civic groups, such as the Citizens' Coalition for Economic Justice (CCEJ) and the People's Solidarity for Participatory Democracy (PSPD), engaged in all important political and social issues and strongly influenced government policy-making. Other progressive-minded activist groups in the fields of environment, healthcare and medicine, and agriculture were also busy articulating their interests and the merger issue provided an opportunity to engage in debate and were also officially invited as the government's policy partners.

The increasing power of trade unions was worthy of close attention. From the beginning, the Kim administration was a pro-labour government (Koo, 2007: 86), as Kim Dae-jung made a policy coalition with trade unions during his election campaign. The economic crisis forced the government to accept them as partners. In particular, the militant Korean Confederation of Trade Unions (KCTU) was legalised by the introduction of a multiple unionisation system in November 1999 and played a pivotal role in proposing the full merger. Meanwhile, the Federation of Korean Trade Unions (FKTU) led the opponent bloc against the merger.

5 At the time, civic groups formed the Citizens' Alliance for General Election aiming to obtain a clean election and it blacklisted disqualified candidates. The CAGE claimed that 70 percent of blacklisted candidates in the Seoul-Kyonggi regions were defeated and two-thirds of all blacklisted candidates lost in the general election (*Korea Herald*, 14 April 2000).

3. Institutional Features

1) Skilfully manipulated power

Kim Dae-jung only just won the presidential election thanks to the so-called DJP coalition. But his political power base was not solid, as the opposition GNP was in a parliamentary majority and the economically privileged electorate was unsympathetic to his politics. Ironically, the chance to consolidate his political power came from the economic crisis. People believed that supporting the Kim government would overcome economic difficulties.

In the earlier part of his presidency, President Kim and Prime Minister Kim Jong-pil skilfully manipulated ruling lawmakers using their charisma and by effectively managing civil society in policy-making. The founding of the KTC in January 1998, under the government's leadership, was also helpful in strengthening the political power of the Kim administration (Yu, 2000: 148). The opposition GNP, despite its numerical weight in Parliament, was suffering from a leadership struggle shortly after the 1997 defeat and Lee Hoi-chang's resignation from party presidency. Later, Lee took control of the party presidency once more, in August 1998, and managed to strengthen the GNP's influence on state affairs. The GNP remained a leading party, despite its failure to win a parliamentary majority at the 2000 general election (see Table 6.2).

In the meantime, President Kim's attempt to shape government affairs and manage the ruling party was greatly undermined after the 2000 general election, as he missed his chance to nominate ruling candidates as party chairman, under the five-year single term presidency. Parliament developed

Table 6.2 The result of the 2000 general election

	Number of seats	Proportion of seats (%)	Polling score (%)
Ruling MDP *	115 (regional 96+ proportional 19)	42.3	35.9
GNP	133 (112+21)	48.9	39.0
ULD	17 (12+5)	6.2	9.8
Independent and others	7 (7+0)	2.6	15.3
Total	272 (227+45)	100.0	100.0

Note: * MDP (Millennium Democratic Party, renamed from the NCNP in January 2000).
Source: adapted from the National Assembly homepage (www.assembly.go.kr).

counterbalancing powers against the government again. To make matters worse, trade unions tried to secede from the KTC, blaming the government's bias in its dealings with the KTC.

Regarding the power relationship between the ruling and opposition parties, the major ruling party and the minor ruling ULD were in the minority from the beginning. But despite being under represented, they matched opposition parties through the support of the government at the early stages of the presidency. After the change in political power, the Kim administration used several special measures, like the investigation of opposition political funds, to consolidate its power base. Political retaliation from the winner of the election had long been a tradition in Korean politics.

The President's dominance over government departments was guaranteed both officially and in practice. The President was the government's official head and could demand obedience from departments through constraints and inducements. Generally, the President's domination over government departments and bureaucrats was absolute in his earlier term of office.[6] But, it was worth noting that the OPM also exercised unprece-

6 President Kim tightened control over government departments in the early part of his

dented power in the situation where Prime Minister Kim Jong-pil shared governing power as a co-founder of the DJP coalition government.

The dominance of central government over local government and the privileges of the upper strata in public organisations had been constant. Even under the local autonomy system from the early 1990s, local governments' obedience was secured through specific legislations. Subordinates' obedience to high-ranking figures in the government bureaucracy had been a virtue under the authoritative organisational culture (Han, 1999: 106). Decision-making power was concentrated in the upper strata and internal communication was usually downward.

2) Towards democratic institutions

Institutions in the Kim administration remained largely unchanged, as the government operated under the same Constitution and through similarly related laws. Institutions have a basic tendency to persist, despite changes in politics. But, under the basic governing system, a new tripartite system emerged as a core institution to overcome the economic crisis (Koo, 2007: 86). At least until 1998, the KTC was the most influential decision maker in important state affairs. The Kim administration also tried to transform the governing system by accepting civil society into the circle as a key political ally.[7]

term by presiding, at firsthand, at the State Council and at the Economic Policy Coordination Conference, which were, in the past, chaired by the Prime Minister (Yang, 2003: 277).

7 The most distinctive example of civil society's inclusion into the governing system was its interference in the 2000 election to veto particular candidates. Civic groups classified 134 lawmakers as unsuitable candidates, mainly targeting the opposition GNP. 67 GNP lawmakers were on the list, while 35 MDP and 30 ULD lawmakers were included respectively (Monthly *Shin Donga*, March 2000).

The powerful President also remained at the centre of governance, and the ordinances prescribing hierarchical order between government departments remained unchanged. Although the institutions prescribing the Prime Minister's role and function were unchanged, his/her practical power greatly increased.[8] The first half of the Kim administration exhibited new characteristics — those of coalition government — under the presidential system.[9]

Multi-party and unicameral systems remained untouched. The freedom to organise political parties (except the communist party) was constitutionally guaranteed and the internal democracy of political parties was enshrined in law. But as before, the reality differed from theoretically structured institutions. The political party system consisted of a two-party system, one a strong ruling party and another rival opposition party. Minor opposition parties were hidden from public eye. Although the United Liberal Democrats (ULD) was a coalition partner, it was left out of a negotiation body as it only won 17 seats at the 2000 general election (Shim, 2004: 471).

Political parties resorted to regional favouritism, making their party platforms similar. The threat from communist North Korea and the state's long-time control over the people skewed public opinion to the right.[10]

---

8 Kim Jong-pil and his followers occupied the premiership and some ministries for almost the whole period of the Kim administration. The department ministers, including the MOHW that were allotted to Kim Jong-pil's party, were more loyal to their private boss Kim than to the President.

9 The nominal pretext of the coalition was Kim Dae-jung's promise to introduce the cabinet system during his presidency. But President Kim did not keep the promise and Kim Jong-pil officially broke away from the coalition in August 2001, blaming President Kim's betrayal (Shim, 2004: 478).

10 The attempt of the progressive Democratic Labour Party (DLP) to be a parliamentary member miserably failed by recording only 1.2 percent polling score and no seats at the

Within this narrow ideological spectrum, would-be politicians depended on regional political bosses to be lawmakers. Internally, political bosses maintained an effective dictatorship by distributing political funds and handpicking electoral candidates. So, deputies could not act as independent players.

The election system also remained unchanged. The President was directly elected and his/her term in office was restricted to a five-year single term, turning the President into a 'lame-duck' after only a few years at the helm (Kwon Y., 2003: 908). The parliamentary election system had been based on a single electorate system since 1987, enabling a particular party to dominate a particular region.[11]

The proportional representation system changed only marginally. When the ruling MDP proposed holding two ballots for candidates and political parties, the GNP and the semi-ruling ULD opposed the proposal by reaffirming their support for the existing single ballot system and the allocation of proportional seats by votes obtained nationally (Tat, 2000: 378).

3) Makeshift decision-making system

Rules regulating department decision-making and conflict resolution were ingrained in the system and therefore had a tendency to last. The *ringi* system was a key department decision-making mechanism as before. It was originally intended to encourage participation in department decision-making.

2000 general election.

11 At the 2000 election Kim Dae-jung's MDP gained over 95 percent of the seats in Cholla province, while the GNP was dominant in Kyoung-sang province (Kim and Kim, 2000: 113).

Table 6.3 The committees prescribed in the NHIA

Committee	Function	Composition
Health Insurance Review and Coordination Committee	Reviews important matters on health insurance policy like the establishment of benefits criterion	Representatives from insurers, policyholders, employers, healthcare sector, and public interests
NHIC Finance Steering Committee	Reviews important matters on health insurance finance like insurance premiums	Representatives from employees, the local self-employed, and public interests

Source: abstracted from the NHIA.

But in practice, documents were drafted under a superior's guidance making the drafting process an *ex post facto* formalisation (Cho, 2004: 48). Under a hierarchical organisational climate, decision-making power was concentrated in the hands of managerial supervisors, and the *ringi* system merely created complicated 'red tape.' Conflict within departments was also largely resolved by superiors (Kim M.-h., 1999: 18).

There were also several committees advising or reviewing department decision-making. Table 6.3 selects the committees prescribed in the NHIA and related ordinances. Especially, task force-type government committees played important roles during the debate. For example, the Medical Insurance Integration Planning Board (MIIPB) was important in setting up a detailed governmental draft.[12]

Formal rules on inter-department decision-making were also fairly solid. Diverse channels of communication and coordination operated to settle

12 The MIIPB was formed on 23 March 1998, comprising 31 members that were drawn from relevant officials, academia, civic groups and policyholders, to specify the merger plan. It consisted of three subdivisions taking charge of management system, insurance premiums and financial stability, and medical treatment fees, respectively (MIIPB, 1998: 209).

inter-department differences.[13] In theory, the OP and budget departments should have taken the initiative. But in most cases, institutions did not work as prescribed. The degree of a department's influence relied not upon formal hierarchy but upon a minister's personal power (Lee S., 2003: 12). Kim Jong-pil's premiership strengthened the OPM's authority in making government decisions. While previous Prime Ministers were satisfied with ceremonial and advisory roles, Kim Jong-pil exercised power in the way it was formally prescribed, as he was a coalition partner.

The State Council was the final deliberating body on state affairs as before. Although the role of the State Council was strengthened a little under the Kim administration, old habits remained, operating on a ceremonial basis as before. Prior consent by the President and informal agreements between relevant departments were much more important in making policies.

With an oppositional majority in Parliament, the government-ruling party conference was a key place to draw up government drafts. There were many conferences ranging from working-level meetings to top-level gatherings presided by the PM. Conference attendees were usually relevant departments, such as the OPM, the OP and the ruling party. In the initial stages of the presidency, the OP took the initiative and the relevant department usually consulted in advance on the issues. The so-called DJP weekly meeting, or other top-level talks, coordinated key state affairs.[14]

Parliamentary decision-making rules were well defined by the National

13 Main functions of ministerial conferences were to share responsibility and exchange information. Conferences were divided into regular and provisional ones, and working-level meetings, composed of high-ranking officials, were held before arranging ministerial conferences (Lee S., 2003: 10-16).

14 The State Affairs Conference was formed in September 1998 to coordinate differences between the allied governing parties (Yang, 2003: 278).

Assembly Act. Unwritten conventions were also respected. A unicameral system from the 1960s made parliamentary legislation simple. Both lawmakers and the government could propose bills, and these bills were then reviewed in order by relevant standing committees and the plenary session. Discussion and coordination always came in advance by majority rule.[15] In many cases, standing committees agreed upon a single alternative. While discussions at standing committees were substantial and argumentative, reviews at the plenary session were often token and simply ceremonial.

But practically, the distribution of power in Parliament between the ruling and opposition parties was much more important than parliamentary rules per se, because these rules could easily be distorted by power imbalances. In the event that opposition parties dominated Parliament, government bills were largely revised or rejected in its parliamentary review.

4) Previous policies: a newly constructed road

The decision to gradually introduce a single insurer system was made in November 1997, and Kim Dae-jung's victory in the presidential election forced opponents of the merger to abandon their hopes for a multiple insurer system. The political elite believed that the merger would win the support of the public and thus the MOHW had no choice but to prepare a detailed government policy for the merger.

---

15 Differently from law, standing committee decisions were unanimous in most cases. Rep. Jeong Ui-hwa explains the reality: "During my three years' experience as representative, discussions at standing committee level were usually ceremonial. In the course of three years, I have never seen a standing committee take a vote on the decisions made by sub-committees…" (Records of Health and Welfare Committee of the 208th National Assembly of September 1999)

Even though the technicalities of decision-making were not that different from in earlier debates, the established pattern of policy-making also changed, along with fundamental shifts in the socio-political context and power relations. Civil society was formally admitted into the decision-making process, and new institutions like the KTC were built. A new path of policy-making had been created.

But adherents to the previous policy still cherished the multiple insurer system and they sought to delay the merger for as long as possible. Established policies resisted against institutional change once again, to prevent possible chaos from a rushed merger. But a complete U-turn to previous path and policies was no longer an option for them. In November 1997, a decision was taken to proceed with the partial merger, thus, creating a new system of health insurer. Consequently, the debate moved away from arguments about the type of health insurer system towards how the actual merger would occur. Mr Chung Kil-oh, the executive director of FKTU policy bureau and a core opponent to the merger, confirms this fact:

> The FKTU also accepted the irreversibility of any decision about the merger. The problem was more that the government marched onwards the merger without enough detailed consideration of the preconditions required for the merger. The basic policy of the FKTU was not so different to that of the progressive KCTU. The FKTU just had a different approach with regard to the methods of the merger and the level of political struggle involved. (Interview on 21 December 2004)

Briefly, the emergence of a new institution, i.e. the partial merger, disrupted the established multiple insurer system and operated as a new path constraining the creation of future institutions, i.e. the full merger. Changed power relations played a 'policy window' role in creating a new institution (Kwon S., 2003: 85). So, even though the established path and previous policies constrained the creation of a new path and policies, they are not unmalleable. Instead, they were reformed with the change in political context and power shifts. As before, the renewed path or policies acted as a regulator of changes through the process of consolidation.

4. Policy Networks

The Kim Dae-jung administration practically accomplished the full merger by enacting the National Health Insurance Act. When the NHIA was set up in 1998, proponents of the merger, including civic groups and progressive trade unions, were supported by the new governing elite, and thus dominated policy networks. The drive towards the full merger became more than just a general trend (NHIC, 2001: 29). Opponents also recognised that the tide had turned against them and argued about the timing and procedure of the merger.

But in the process of revising the NHIA in 1999, the opponent bloc, led by relatively conservative trade unions, made a strong counterattack. Now, the conflict between trade unions of different political orientations became one of the distinctive features of the full merger debate. Some conservative groups and business associations also sided with the opponent bloc. Even though MOHW officials did not oppose the merger openly, they hoped to retain a multiple insurer system. Notably, the governing bloc changed its policy and sought to delay the timing of the merger in preparation for the

Table 6.4 Participants' changing positions during the debate

		Proposing the merger	Opposing or postponing the merger
1998	Official actors	OP, OPM and other government departments	MOHW officials (not openly)
	Unofficial actors	Ruling party, opposition parties, NCHIU (civic groups, KCTU, self-employed insurers union etc.)	FKTU and employee insurers union, business interests (FKI, KEF) etc.
1999	Official actors	-	OP, OPM, MOHW and other government departments
	Unofficial actors	NCHIU (civic groups, KCTU, self-employed insurers union etc.)	FKTU and employee insurers union, business interests (FKI, KEF) etc.

forthcoming general election in April 2000. Table 6.4 shows the participants' fluctuating positions during the process of making and revising the NHIA between 1998 and 1999.

1) Network structure: free and open to all with no ticket required

Nature of participants: number, dominant actors and exclusion

Almost all interested actors were involved in the full merger debate, making policy networks open and fluid. As before, network participants made up two conflicting blocs. But unlike before, from the beginning the progressive governing bloc was one of the most ardent proponents of the merger. Progressive trade unions and civic groups were active in supporting the merger, and government actors and political parties intervened in policy-making as before. To them, the debate was symbolic, as it provided a forum through which to demonstrate their commitment to reform (Kwon S., 2003: 86). And in this way, the debate in the Kim administration turned into an ideological struggle between the progressive and conservative blocs.

Meanwhile, the relatively conservative FKTU and employee insurers union led the opponent bloc, forming a united front — the National Conference for Social Insurance Reform (NCSIR) — in May 1999.[16] Business interests, employee health insurers and their association, the National Federation of Medical Insurance,[17] were also in the opponent bloc, albeit their weakened power under the new progressive regime.

Dominant actors in policy networks repeatedly changed as the debate evolved. Until the enactment of the NHIA in January 1999, the proponent bloc, composed of the ruling party, the OP,[18] civic groups and the KCTU, dominated policy networks. They saw the merger as necessary to gain the support of trade unions in restructuring the labour market (Baek, 2001: 167). Potential opponents like the FKTU and business interests also tacitly agreed with the merger under pressure of economic insolvency. The opposition GNP had already endorsed the merger by adopting it as a presidential election pledge in 1997. Among the GNP deputies, Hwang Seong-kyun and Kim Hong-sin were strong pro-merger enthusiasts.

At the revision stage of the NHIA, the proponent bloc began to show of differences with regard to the possible postponement of the merger.

16 The NCSIR opposed the merger for the following reasons: The ultimate goal of health insurance is not income redistribution but risk pooling; the merger is inconsistent with social justice by overpricing workers' insurance premiums; the merger would add to the government's financial burden and makes timely raising of insurance premiums more difficult; and the financial merger violates the constitutionally held guarantee of property rights (NCSIR, 1999: 5-6).

17 The NFMI's opposition to the merger was led by Yoon Seong-tae, Han Oh-seok and Baik Moon-gyu and others (Interview with Chun Chang-bae on 9 March 2005).

18 The presidential chief secretaries on health and welfare matters were Kim Yoo-bae and Cho Gyu-hyang.

The governing bloc became more pragmatic and insisted on six months' breathing space before proceeding with the organisational merger and a two year deferral of the financial merger. On the other side of the fence, idealists such as civic groups and the KCTU insisted that the full merger should be immediately introduced, blaming the governing bloc's retreat for any delay (NCHIU *Newsletter*, 20 December 1999). But from 1999, the governing bloc, seeking deferral of the merger, took control.

The intentional exclusion of particular policy actors was structurally impossible at the time. Moreover, the Kim administration actively encouraged the participation of civic groups and trade unions in policy-making to reinforce its fragile power base. For example, the KCTU was legalised as an umbrella trade union in November 1999, along with the existing FKTU. According to Yishai's (1992) classification, the policy network during the full merger debate was closer to that of an issue network because of the impossibility of intentional exclusion. Only pro-government actors, like employee health insurers, were reluctant to openly agree with opponents for fear of government's potential retaliation.

Participants' interests in the issue

Participants' real interests were differed even amongst the same bloc. There was also a discrepancy between real and stated interests of participants. Among proponents of the merger, governing bloc members supported the merger as a way of achieving social justice, as MOHW Minister Cha Heung-bong mentioned in an interview with the Monthly *Chosun* of May 2001:

> Any policy has both merits and demerits. The merger of health insurers is no

> different. I stand in the vanguard of the merger, as I believe that it has more merits than demerits. The merit of a single insurer system is to achieve a relatively equitable burden of health insurance premiums between the different strata of policyholders. The merger has, therefore, a meaning in institutionalising the mutual assistance between the people...

The merger was also not only a ruling party pledge at the 1997 presidential election,[19] but also a symbolic policy that allowed the new governing elite to demonstrate their reformative image. Despite MOHW officials' preference for a multiple insurer system, they too followed the general trend espoused by the ruling elite.

But the practical reasons for supporting the merger were quite complicated. The governing bloc backed the merger to win votes in rural areas. On the flip side, it sought to delay the merger to avoid administrative chaos and losing votes ahead of the 2000 general election. The governing bloc also wanted political support from civil society for backing the merger. Additionally, the merger was an intermediary by which militant trade unions that supported the merger could be persuaded to back much needed economic reform measures in the KTC (Kang, 2003: 249).

Civic groups supported a single insurer system because it would promote income redistribution by resolving self-employed insurers' financial deficit. To them, the merger was also a key symbolic issue of healthcare reform, along with the separation of drug prescribing and dispensing. Besides moral justification, civic groups had a practical interest in backing the

19 Kim Dae-jung pledged that one trillion wons of insurance funds saved by the merger would be diverted to the education budget.

merger. They were more able to influence government policy-making and solidify their organisational unity by keeping the merger at the forefront of the policy agenda. The merger provided them with a good pretext to build a coalition between progressive civic groups.

The militant KCTU stressed the positive role of a single insurer system in promoting the relative equity of insurance premiums between company employees and the self-employed and in reducing the financial deficit of self-employed insurers. The merger also gave KCTU a good chance of strengthening its emerging organisation against the rival FKTU. Another practical reason was that the self-employed insurers' union, the FKTU's affiliate, strongly advocated the merger, as outlined by the vice chairperson (Kim Hoi-seon) and policy adviser (Kwak Tae-hyung) of the NHIC employee insurers union:

> Self-employed insurers union put up solidarity and equity as an excuse for their support of the merger. But the most urgent reason why they advocated the merger was in their own selfish interests to improve the personnel management system of self-employed insurers. At that time, there was a big wage gap between self-employed insurers and employee ones. They also had problems in the system of promotion because more than 5,000 staff entered offices at a time when self-employed insurers were established between 1988 and 1989. They hoped to improve wages and promotion system as a result of the merger. (Interview on 21 December 2004)

To farmers' groups, the merger would lower insurance premiums and extend insurance benefits for farmers. They would also benefit by sharing the accumulated funds of employee insurers.

The opposition GNP's standpoint was ambivalent. It did not oppose the merger per se, and practically led the decision towards the partial merger in November 1997. It also agreed to the full merger in 1998, despite its abstention from parliamentary voting in January 1999.[20] But the GNP position changed in 1999, to one proposing suspension of the organisational merger and of repealing the financial merger. In changing its policy, the GNP stressed that the financial merger would worsen inequities between policyholders because of incomplete income declarations of the self-employed. In fact, the conservative GNP realised its key power base was in the middle class — in groups like employers and employees in big companies — and the merger was disadvantageous to them.

During the full merger debate, the FKTU and employee insurers' union became key opponents of the merger, replacing the MOHW. The FKTU originally agreed to the merger in the KTC, but completely changed its policy to oppose the merger, after the admission of the employee insurers' union as an affiliate to the organisation in July 1997 (Lee K., 2000a: 73). It opposed the merger as it would deepen income disparity between policyholders while the government's financial burden would increase. They also worried that the merger might cause the inefficient use of insurance finance (*Hankyoreh Shinmun*, 3 August 1998). The NCSIR's press release on 13 June 1999 shows the opposition of trade unions to the merger:

The imbalance in insurance premiums and reverse income distribution be-

20 While the GNP abstained from voting in protest at the intervention of the National Intelligence Service in parliamentary matters, it did not oppose the merger per se, as the gradual merger was its party platform during the presidential election campaign (NCHIU, 1999: 21).

> tween workers and the self-employed will be widened if health insurers are forcibly merged without close monitoring of the declared income of the self-employed and without the increase of government subsidy. The government should recognise that the principles of social insurance, including income redistribution and equitable insurance premiums, might collapse if the merger is forced through.

But their real interest lay in the possible increase of employees' insurance premiums from the merger. They worried about the low levels of income declaration by the self-employed as it would cause a sharp increase in employees' insurance premiums (FKTU, 1999: 389).[21] They also worried about the possible financial loss for employee insurers when surplus funds were amalgamated with deficits. The merger was feared to damage the stable management of personnel, too.[22]

Business associations' main reasons for opposing the merger were twofold. The first was a possible increase in employers' insurance premiums as a result of the merger, because they shared insurance costs with employees. They worried that the merger would mean an increase in employers' burden

21 Where farmers' income declaration rate was no more than 57 percent and that of the urban self-employed was only 25 percent, the merger would cause an increase in employees' insurance premiums. Thus, the FKTU insisted that insurance funds should be managed separately until the income declaration rate of the self-employed reached 80 percent (*Chosun Ilbo*, 13 September 1998).

22 Unlike the self-employed insurers' union, employee insurers' union enjoyed job stability under a multiple insurer system. If the merger went ahead staff would be reduced and the survivors would work and rotate across local areas, worsening their quality of life. Accordingly, its critics said: "The FKTU and employee insurers union are opposing the merger to protect its affiliate and union members' job security." (Interview with Kang Chang-ku of the KCTU on 20 December 2004)

to compensate for the financial deficit of self-employed insurers. Then there was the fear of losing the right to manage accumulated insurance funds. Until then, employee insurers had banked over 2.5 trillion won in funds and enjoyed a host of benefits like extra influence at commercial banks, being one of the largest depositors. (Interview with Dr Chun Chang-bae of the NHIC on 21 October 2004)

We know that most MOHW officials were negative to the merger, albeit surreptitiously in many cases. Officials thought that a rushed merger would bankrupt some insurance funds and force up the need for government subsidy. The former MOHW senior official Kim Jong-dae (2002: 105) argued:

> I warned the Minister several times that the abrupt merger would cause bankruptcy among insurance funds, but he ignored my advice. Minister Cha Heung-bong unilaterally ordered the merger in June 1999 and I distributed pamphlets to make public aware of its predictable problems. Mr Cha relieved me of my post for that reason...

They also worried about possible confusion if computer systems and organisations were too hurriedly integrated. There was also interest in maintaining a multiple insurer system, as it was good security for retired officials and offered the MOHW easy control over health insurers by using the divide-and-rule method.

Resource dependency between participants

Resource dependency between participants was complicated in the full merger debate. The government depended on the ruling party to pass reformist policies in Parliament, whereas the ruling party benefited from policies that government implemented. Ruling lawmakers were also greatly dependent on the President who handpicked them as ruling candidates and distributed political money in his/her role as party chairperson (Chung, 2003: 25). What is more, any revolt against political bosses, including President Kim, invariably led to defeat in elections, particularly where voting was heavily influenced by regional favouritism. But, the relationship between the President and departments was unilateral. The President exercised power through the right to appoint high-level officials. During the early part of term in office, the President's control over departments was particularly strong (Yang, 2003: 277).

Ruling party-MOHW dependence was also inevitable. The MOHW needed the ruling party's assistance to pass laws, as opposition parties were usually hostile to government policies. Meanwhile, the ruling party needed the MOHW's help in gathering votes. It was conventional that the government publicised programs deemed to be advantageous to the ruling party, whenever there were elections ahead.

Resource dependency between the ruling and opposition parties was also high at the time, as the latter was a parliamentary leader. But in fact, their cooperation was difficult to achieve given that the 2000 general election was only just around the corner. A tradition of mutual concession and cooperation between them was not established yet under the zero-sum game politics of the time.

The most distinctive feature of the Kim administration was its dependency on civil society. From the beginning, the Kim administration was pro-labour and populist government (Kim S.-j., 2002: 313). At the 1997 presidential election, civic groups and trade unions supported Kim Dae-jung for his progressive and pro-labour colour. After being elected President, Kim adequately made use of his supporters to bolster his flimsy power base and resurrect the ailing economy. According to civil movement activist Dr Kim Yeon-myung:

> The Kim Dae-jung administration, as a minority government, positively accepted trade unions and civic groups as friendly supporters. Through cooperation with progressive trade unions and civic groups, the Kim administration tried to weaken the power of major newspapers, which were critical to the government, and to recruit new political elite from civil society. (Interview on 19 April 2005)

Civic groups and trade unions also sought cooperation from the governing bloc. As government policy partners, they maximised their influence on policy-making, making organisational enlargement possible. But resource exchange with opposition parties remained low, as they had branded the main opposition GNP as elitist and reactionary.

From 1999, the governing bloc changed its position and tried to postpone the implementation of the agreed merger. Its decision to do so was driven by a massive petition organised by the FKTU and employee insurers union, between July-August 1999.[23] The governing bloc, then, came under pressure just before a general election in which it aimed to win a parliamentary majority, as President Kim argued in the State Council in October 1999:

23 The FKTU argued that over 5 million people signed in protest over the merger and submitted the petition to the National Assembly in September 1999.

> The government wished to begin the merger. But it became difficult because the opponent bloc received a petition signed by more than five million people. The Kookmin government is a democratic government that respects the will of the people. (Health Solidarity, 2001: 155)

For the FKTU, governing bloc support was imperative in maintaining its privileged status as a representative umbrella union in the face of growing power of the progressive KCTU.[24]

Although the resource dependency between the governing bloc and employee insurers union was not major, the former needed cooperation from the latter to implement the merger.[25] Employee insurers union wanted to effectively articulate their interests by setting up stable communication channels with the governing bloc.

Opposition parties needed a coalition with conservative social groups to win seats at elections. To the conservative GNP, support from the FKTU and affiliate unions was vital to secure a majority at the 2000 general election. The GNP also sought to gain political influence by counterbalancing the weight of activist civic groups and progressive trade unions through cooperation with the FKTU and conservative groups in blocking the merger. The FKTU also needed ties with opposition parties, who occupied a larger parliamentary fraction, if it was to effectively articulate its views in terms of

24 In 1997, the KCTU comprised 1,144 unions and 523,748 members, while the FKTU consisted of 4,223 unions and 1,021,133 members. But their influences on state affairs were similar, as the KCTU consisted of big companies and was more cohesive (Gil, 2000: 249-51).

25 For example, employee insurers union obstructed the enforcement of the merger by rejecting the submission of relevant materials in 1999 (Health Solidarity's press interview on 8 November 1999).

labour policy.

Finally, the MOHW tried to put off the merger, by making use of the governing elites' concerns about suddenly destabilising a system. But its desire to force a suspension of the merger timetable greatly depended on the decisions of the ruling party and the President. The ruling party and the President also needed bureaucrats' support in carrying out policies. In this way, governing bloc members were dependent on each other in seeking to force a suspension of the merger, although not in equal degree.

2) Participants' interaction: die-hard battle between mortal enemies

Basic nature of interaction

In the first round of the debate up to January 1999, the proponent bloc was dominant, successfully enacting the NHIA, its members working in cooperation with each other. Although MOHW officials were leaning against the merger, they could not openly oppose it. Civic groups and progressive trade unions were very friendly to the governing bloc, as they had a common interest in restructuring the established social and political system. Even opposition parties were also not overly hostile to the merger. The country was suffering from an unprecedented economic crisis and this forced the opposition GNP to cooperate with the new governing bloc (Buzo, 2002: 184).

But the FKTU, who became a key opponent from 1999, changed its policy to openly oppose the merger, despite its prior agreement to the merger in the KTC (KTC, 1999: 204). After employee insurers' union became a member in June 1998, the FKTU began to oppose the merger under the pretext of lower income declaration of the self-employed (Health Solidarity,

2001: 152).[26] The FKTU opposed the merger strongly and caused fierce conflict with pro-merger supporters. While Chung Kil-oh and Lee Dong-ho led the FKTU, Kim Hoi-seon and Bae Jeong-kwon also took responsibilities as the employee insurers' union opposed the merger.

Civic groups and progressive trade unions also toughened their stance in attacking opponents of the merger. In early 1998, MOHW officials who had advocated a multiple insurer system for a long time were constantly attacked and civic groups pressured President Kim not to appoint anti-merger bureaucrats in high-ranking posts (NCHIU, 1999: 529-34). From late-1998, they concentrated on fighting the FKTU and employee insurers' union for their ambivalence and selfishness.

Entering the second round of the debate from January 1999, conflicts between network participants grew. The governing bloc changed policy and now sought to postpone the merger, but civic groups and the KCTU accused it of reneging (NCHIU *Newsletter*, 20 December 1999). The opposition GNP was also criticised as it tried to postpone the organisational merger and repeal any financial merger. The NCHIU statement released on 12 July 1999 said:

> In December 1998 opposition chairman Lee Hoi-chang said: "The full merger is my conviction and the GNP's official opinion, and the GNP will cooperate with the passing of legislation to introduce the merger." But the GNP changed its mind suddenly. Unless the GNP overturns its breach of promise, the NCHIU will publicise the name of lawmakers who voted to suspend the

26 The FKTU issued a statement, on 23 October 1998, requesting the withdrawal of a full merger bill suggested to the National Assembly (FKTU, 1999: 576).

merger and will see them defeated at the next general election… (NMIC, 1999: 184-85)

The relationship between the ruling and opposition parties remained unstable, and it now became increasingly ideological. While progressive trade unions and civic groups supported the governing bloc, the opponent bloc was composed of the GNP, the FKTU and conservative social groups.[27] Although the NCHIU and the KCTU were unhappy with the government's change of policy, they refrained from directly attacking the governing bloc.

However, the fiercest conflict occurred between trade unions at different ends of the political spectrum. The conflict between two labour groups from 1999 was a distinctive feature of this debate. Minor participants like progressive healthcare professionals and farmers' groups also attacked opponents, largely targeting opposition parties and the FKTU. Policy actors were divided into two blocs, those concerned with the suspension of merger timing and those arguing a full and immediate merger.

27 The FKTU was originally pro-Kim Dae-jung and formed a policy coalition during the presidential campaign. But after the election, it began to blame Kim's pro-business policy and inclination in favour of the KCTU, and officially ended its policy coalition in December 1999 (FKTU, 2000). Chung Kil-oh of the executive director of FKTU Policy Bureau released details of the relationship between President Kim and the FKTU: "The FKTU preferred Kim Dae-jung as second best and set up a policy coalition during the 1997 presidential election campaign. But after his inauguration as President, Kim advocated unrealistic market-oriented economic policies. The FKTU opposed the neo-liberalist restructuring of the labour market, and broke away from the policy coalition with the Kim administration." (Interview on 21 December 2004)

Frequency of interaction

During the first round of the debate, interaction between proponents of the merger was very frequent. Governing bloc members stayed closely in contact through formal institutional channels. The Presidency Undertaking Commission provided the MOHW with a channel to secretly persuade the new governing elite to discard the gradual merger plan. The KTC played a key role in drawing up macro economic and social policies, providing policy actors with a mechanism through which to interact. The decision to push forward with a full merger bill by December 1998 was made in the KTC after a series of 27 meetings (Kim Y.-j., 1998: 867). From March 1998, when the MIIPB was formed in the MOHW, participants including civic groups and healthcare professionals intimately worked together. The MIIPB held 12 general meetings, 23 division meetings and 8 round-table talks to thrash out a detailed merger plan (MOHW *White Paper*, 1998: 14).

Besides these official routes, there were various unofficial interaction channels between proponents of the merger. Civic groups and the KCTU articulated interests through personal ties with the governing elite and the issuance of recommendation papers. Progressive civic groups were particularly well placed to support the setting up of the NCHIU on 11 April 1994, comprising 72 activist groups representing workers, farmers, civil activists, consumer and healthcare, with the aim of proposing the full merger (NMIC, 1999: 129).[28] Among these groups, while the PSPD, CCEZ and KCTU were key members of the NCHIU, such figures as Kim Yong-yik, Kim Yeon-myung, Cho Hong-jun, Lee Tae-soo, Yang Bong-min, Huh

28 The NCHIU was replaced by the Health Solidarity, in July 1999, to better cope with the plans to delay the merger and to extend the target of activities.

Young-koo and Cho Kyoung-eh led the NCHIU during the full merger debate.

However, opponents to the merger did not actively work together to stop the merger, as they also accepted that the merger was likely to happen. They did not form a coalition yet. Rather, the FKTU participated in the KTC and endorsed the introduction of the merger.

From the second round of the debate from 1999, the frequency and direction of interaction between participants became more complex. Governing bloc members frequently discussed matters through both formal and informal channels as before, in delaying the merger. Meanwhile, civic groups and the KCTU did not depend on formal channels so much, as their policy goal began to split away from that of the governing bloc. They, instead, expressed their opinions through the issuance of press releases. The interaction between progressive civic groups proposing the merger and conservative groups opposing the merger largely unfolded through a barrage of deliberately provoking press releases.

The FKTU and some conservative groups opposing the merger also joined to form the NCSIR on 10 May 1999. However, unlike the NCHIU, which was made up of 72 different civic groups, NCSIR members consisted of the FKTU and just six other minor conservative groups. The degree of unity and the displays of interaction between them were much lower than those of the NCHIU. The following interview extracts compare the NCHIU and the NCSIR:

> While the NCHIU comprised of almost all core members of civil society, the NCSIR just brought no more than small and medium-sized company workers into the coalition. The NCSIR lacked cohesion and spontaneity. The influence

> of the NCHIU was huge when compared to that of the NCSIR, because the size and cohesion of the former overwhelmed the latter… (Interview with Kang Chang-koo of the NCHIU on 20 December 2004)

> We admit the limitation of the NCSIR. The NCSIR's key members were not trade unions but workplace councils, which were reluctant to strongly oppose government policy. Under the black-and-white logic of criticising the opponents to the merger as reactionaries, NCSIR members began to retreat… (Interview with Chung Kil-oh of the FKTU on 21 December 2004)

In general, formal interactions between participants decreased during the second round in inverse proportion to the growing differences on the postponement of the merger. Instead, core members with different views on the merger reacted in a negative manner by issuing damaging press releases that criticised each other.

Mobilised strategies of interaction

The full merger debate under the Kim administration was divided into two rounds. The first round from December 1997 resulted in the successful enactment of the NHIA in January 1999. Opponents were passive about trying to block the merger attempt as many felt that the country was heading for a single insurer system. But in the second round in 1999, potential problems from rushing into an unprepared merger became apparent.[29] So, with

29 An example was the low-level income declaration of the self-employed. The merger without solving this problem would ruin any idea of income redistribution between company employees and the self-employed (Kim H., 2003: 55).

the 2000 general election drawing ever near, the governing bloc decided to delay the timetable of the merger, splitting the proponent bloc. Civic groups and the KCTU demanded the full and immediate implementation of the agreed merger plan.[30] Original proponents remained in agreement over the need to press on to achieve the full merger, although they disagreed over technical differences and the timing of the merger.

Under the Kim administration, traditional opponents of the merger also did not oppose the merger per se, because the partial merger was already accepted by 1997. Their key strategy had now become one of seeking to postpone the organisational merger for as long as possible and to push for the permanent separation of insurance funds. They tried to split the notion of the financial issue from the organisational merger, instead of just accepting the merger per se. The FKTU and employee insurers union led the opponent bloc. The basic policy of the opposition GNP was now also to oppose any form of financial merger. While most MOHW officials approved of the merger following the tide, opponents like Kim Jong-dae criticised the merger vehemently. Business interests and health insurers were not so active in opposing the merger.

For the duration of the debate, major participants used a variety of strategies to articulate their interests. For civic groups and progressive trade unions, the merger was a model example of social reform. Although civic groups and trade unions sometimes acted individually, they usually promoted the merger in unison. As a main proponent of the merger, the NCHIU

30 A statement issued by the Health Solidarity on 11 October 1999 argued: "The government's intention to suspend the merger in preparation for the 2000 general election symbolises the failure of the government's welfare reform, and we will fight to achieve the full merger to the last."

mobilised diverse strategies ranging from institutional participation in government committees to lobbying and demonstration. Specifically the NCHIU:

- Sat on both the formal department committees prescribed in health insurance-related laws and on the temporary government committees like the MIIPB.
- Met high-flyers in the government and political parties to put their case for the merger. For example, the NCHIU held meetings with the National Assembly Speaker in October 1999 and the MOHW minister in December 1999.
- Issued statements urging the merger. In a press release from December 1997, the NCHIU urged the government to promulgate the National Medical Insurance Act, worrying about a possible abrogation of the Act. From late-1998, press releases strongly blamed the FKTU for stalling the merger on the one hand, but on the other, they praised the passage of the NHIA.
- Put pressure on the government by intervening in staff appointment matters and asking for tighter inspection on the management of employee insurers. For instance, press releases called on MOHW officials who had blocked the merger to be fired,[31] and requested the dismissal of corrupt MOHW officials (NCHIU, 1999: 567-69).[32] The NCHIU

31 In particular, the blame focused on the dismissal of Yoon Sung-tae who had been a key opponent of the merger since the 1980s (NCHIU, 1999: 529-69).

32 The NCHIU attacked some MOHW officials as corrupt mafia: "MOHW officials like Kim Jong-dae and Song Jae-sung achieved personal gains by maintaining a multiple insurer system. They put a priority on maintaining their jobs at the sacrifice of the public interest." (NCHIU, 1999: 687)

also demanded that the government investigate the misappropriation of employee insurers' finances (NMIC, 1999: 77). In contrast, it welcomed the new MOHW minister in May 1999 in the following fashion:

> The NCHIU sincerely welcomes Mr Cha Heung-bong's appointment as the new MOHW minister. Mr Cha has fought for welfare reform for a long time and has the conviction and knowledge to put reform into practice. He is a representative reformist in healthcare, who was forcibly removed from public office in the early 1980s by Chun Doo-hwan's military regime. He has led practical policies in medical insurance integration on behalf of this government ... (Press release on 25 may 1999)

- Sponsored public debates, held demonstrations and staged sit-in strikes to urge the enforcement or to protest the suspension of the merger.[33]
- Pressurised political parties. The NCHIU met with opposition leader Lee Hoi-chang, in December 1998, to push the passage of the NHIA, and visited political leaders in September 1999 to protest about their betrayal (NCHIU, 1999: 626-28). In July 1999, it pressured political parties to carry out their merger promise by threatening them with the withdrawal of support at the forthcoming election (NMIC, 1999: 184-88).
- Attacked conservative trade unions opposing the merger. In Novem-

33 The NCHIU held a public seminar in January 1998 on 'the basic orientation of medical security under the Kim government', which included details about plans to merge health insurers. In December 1998, it staged large-scale protests in favour of the merger, and went on sit-in demonstrations from late 1999, urging the immediate enforcement of the merger (NMIC, 1999: 238).

ber 1998, the NCHIU demanded an exhaustive inspection of employee insurers union activities, in particular, investigation into any misuse of insurance funds. It accused the FKTU, in November 1999, for its inflating the number of petition signatures opposing the merger (Won, 2006: 173).[34]

Separately from NCHIU activities, each civic group and trade union engaged in diverse activities to advocate the merger. Activist healthcare professionals, farmers' groups and public interest groups issued press releases. Particularly, the KCTU and self-employed insurers union actively took part in the entire debate, employing every possible means to promote the full merger. Kim Yoo-seon and Kang Chang-koo were particularly active in developing these policies.

The government also wanted the merger, despite its tilt towards a strategy of suspension from 1999. The government's work on the merger dated back to the inauguration of the PUC in December 1997. The PUC initially reviewed the health insurer system without prejudice,[35] but finally recommended that President-elect Kim Dae-jung pursue the full merger.[36]

---

34 The NCHIU alleged the real number of signatures was just 26.4 percent of that publicised. Cho Hong-Jun, a director of NCHIU Medical Insurance Committee, said in newspaper interview: "The legitimacy of suspending the merger went away by manipulating signature-seeking campaign. The government should reprimand persons who decided to put off the merger and should repeal the decision. The government must build an executive committee for the merger in which civic groups participate…" (*Kyounghyang Shinmun*, 23 November 1999).

35 At first the PUC Social and Cultural Subcommittee concluded the merger should be deliberately reviewed after the inauguration of the new government,instead of a hurried decision (PUC, 1998: 358).

36 Among the PUC's 100 national agendas, the merger was listed as the 72nd agenda, mentioning the merger bill should be introduced by December 1998 to upgrade social security

Although participants failed to agree on the technicalities of the merger,[37] the KTC decided to amend relevant laws until 1998 so as to introduce a single insurer system. The government then incorporated progressive civic groups and other interests into the policy-making system by establishing new committees.

But from 1999, the government decided to postpone the agreed timetable for political reasons,[38] as it was worried about the negative impact of the merger in the coming election, especially the possible increase in insurance premiums and administrative chaos caused by rushing the merger through too quickly. This time, the MOHW played an important role in pushing for the suspension.[39]

The ruling party's strategy towards the merger was identical to that

---

and improve national health (PUC, 1998: 107-8).

37 The KTC Social Security Subcommittee discussed a possible increase in workers' insurance premiums if the merger went ahead, and the Steering Committee also reviewed this matter but failed to reach an agreement (KTC, 1999: 53-57).

38 Minister Cha denied any political considerations in suspending the merger: "The suspension of the merger has nothing to do with the general election. A report on computer systems and possible citizen's complaints was critical to the decision to delay the merger. After receiving the report, I consulted with the OP and asked for the ruling party-government conference. On 7 October 1999, I explained the necessity for suspension to the ruling party and the ULD." (*Jungang Ilbo*, 18 October 1999). Rep. Kim Myoung-sup also said in Parliament: "We intend to put off the merger of the management organisations for six months, because the smooth implementation of the merger will be difficult in face of the FKTU's strong opposition. A sufficient time is needed to prepare the imposition of a new level of insurance premiums and to amend relevant ordinances." (Records of the 208th National Assembly of October 1999)

39 The MOHW ministers during the full merger debate were Joo Yang-ja (March 1998-April 1998), Kim Mo-im (May 1998-May 1999) and Cha Heung-bong (May 1999-August 2000), and they were relatively positive towards the merger. Among MOHW officials, Lee Sang-yong and Yang seong-il were active in proposing the merger. (Interview with Dr Chun Chang-bae on 9 March 2005)

of the government.[40] In the first round, it incorporated progressive social groups into the decision-making process in order to bolster its vulnerable power base. But, with the 2000 general election ahead, the ruling party changed its policy and suggested making a revision to the NHIA in July 1999, in order to delay the merger. But, albeit the difference on the timing of the merger between the ruling party and the NCHIU, they greatly relied upon each other politically (Hong, 2001: 86).

After the inauguration of the Kim administration, leading opponents of the merger changed from being the MOHW to the FKTU and employee insurers union, as government departments could not block the new governing elite who pushed forward with the merger as a symbolic reformist policy. In the first half of the debate, the FKTU also participated in government policy-making. It took part in the KTC, the MIIPB and other government committees in order to articulate its interests in health insurance policy (Kim Y.-j., 1998: 867). But the FKTU altered its views towards the merger when the employee insurers' union became affiliated in June 1998. It began to impose conditions for acceptance of the merger,[41] and refused to agree to the detailed content of the merger. From late-1998, the FKTU and employee insurers' union used diverse strategies to oppose the merger. These included:

40 Among ruling lawmakers, Lee Seong-jae, Lee Hae-chan and Park Sang-cheon were devoted supporters of the merger.

41 In July 1998, the FKTU suggested two conditions in agreeing to the merger: two categories of insurance premium system should be maintained until the level of income declaration of the self-employed reached 80 percent; three kinds of insurance funds should be preserved until government subsidies to self-employed insurers reached 50 percent (FKTU, 1999: 389).

- Production of official statements opposing the merger;[42]
- Using public opinion to pressurise the governing bloc;[43]
- Presentation of a petition to Parliament;[44]
- Staging demonstrations, general strikes and signature-seeking campaign;[45]
- Blocking the implementation of the merger;[46]
- Making use of litigation as a strategy;[47]
- Formation of a united front (NCSIR).

Between July and August 1999, the NCSIR staged a large-scale petition campaign to discourage the payment of insurance premiums, and submitted a petition signed by 5.1 million persons to Parliament in Sep-

42 For example, they sent letters urging to raise the income declaration rate of the self-employed and opposing the government's merger proposal to the MOHW in September 1998 (FKTU, 1999: 105).

43 They published newspaper advertisements in August 1998, attacking the merger (FKTU, 1999: 576).

44 The FKTU sent a petition to Parliament in December 1998, requesting the suspension of the NHIA (Lee J., 2000: 118).

45 The FKTU staged protests after September 1998 to block the NHIA legislation. In particular, employee insurers union went on strikes, in February 1999, to protest about the enforcement of the merger and to ask for a separation of insurance funds in the event of the merger (Lim, 2001: 80).

46 Employee insurers' union ordered its members, in February 1999, not to cooperate with the government and recalled staff who were working on the government task team to prepare the ground for the merger. Additionally, it refused to submit related documents in September 1999 (Health Solidarity *Newsletter*, 8 November 1999).

47 Employee insurers union took the NHIA to the Constitutional Court in May 1999, on the ground that the Act violated the constitutionally guaranteed right of equality (*Jungang Ilbo*, 29 May 1999). In September 1999, it filed a suit against the government on the grounds of arbitrary reduction of advance notice of government legislation (Lee J., 2000: 120).

tember 1999.[48] From September 1999, the NCSIR focused its activities on lobbying the government and Parliament, using mass-level strategies such as petitions against the merger and survey research that supported its case.[49] Also, the NCSIR staged protests and published newspaper advertisements encouraging policyholders to refuse to pay their insurance premiums (NEIU, 2000: 41-4). The following is a press release issued by the NCSIR on 9 October 1999, demanding the suspension of the merger:

> Deferring the merger just for six months is to cheat the people and to recognise the government's policy failure. We urge the government to postpone the merger for at least two years and to draw up a rational alternative to the health insurance program. The government should positively seek a national consensus on the merger. In particular, we strongly urge the resignation of MOHW minister Cha, who has caused the failure of government policy and inflicted intolerable pains on the general public.

Now, looking at other proponents of the multiple insurer system, business groups took part in government committees and issued press releases opposing the merger. But in the early stages of the new regime, they did not strongly criticise the merger attempt. Thus, they agreed to the introduction of a single insurer system in the KTC. Their top concern was not on social insurance but on economic matters as they viewed the country to be in seri-

48 The Health Solidarity alleged that a number of signatures were bogus and they should be investigated. The NCSIR later publicly apologised for exaggerating its estimates (*Hankyoreh Shimun*, 8 November 1999).

49 For instance, the NCSIR published the findings of a survey in September 1999, showing that there was a 72.5 percent negative response to the merger amongst 850 people surveyed (NCSIR, 1999: 172-74).

ous economic difficulty, and they sought to cooperate with political leaders in order to survive. For these reasons, even after 1999 when the debate was intensified, business interests were not overly hostile.

The MOHW had been a key opponent of the merger until 1997. Even after the passage of a partial merger bill in November 1997, it had still tried to frustrate the merger by delaying the implementation of the agreed policy.[50] Among MOHW officials, Kim Jong-dae, Song Jae-sung and Choi Sun-jeong were leading opponents of the merger (Interview with Dr Chun Chang-bae on 9 March 2005). Nevertheless, the MOHW had to support the approach of the new governing bloc and formed the MIIPB to study specific methods of carrying out the merger (NMIC, 1999: 110). Dr Chun Chang-bae, who is a research fellow of the NHIC and worked in the MIIPB at the time, comments on the work of the MIIPB:

> Although the MIIPB was founded under the auspices of the MOHW, progressive trade unions were its key players. The MOHW was excluded from the core decision-making of the MIIPB. Trade unions recommended many of the board members and sought to exclude MOHW officials who still favoured a multiple insurer system. Trade unions opened a hot line to the OP to directly compromise important MIIPB work on the matter. (Interview on 9 March 2005)

But from 1999, pro-merger high-flying officials joined the ranks of senior staff at the MOHW and key opponents like Kim Jong-dae were re-

50 In the November 1997 report, the MOHW pointed out the foreseeable problems of the merger and suggested a megalopolis-sized insurer system as an alternative (MOHW *White Paper*, 1997).

moved. Though the MOHW took part in planning for a suspension of the merger in late-1999, it did not oppose the full merger per se anymore.[51]

The opposition GNP did not resist the merger either, and at least until 1998 was one of the strongest proponents in guiding the merger plans forward. At the parliamentary session in December 1998, the GNP agreed to legislate the NHIA to propose the full merger, although the proposed parliamentary timetable was not fulfilled due to the GNP's reluctance to change its position on the other issue.[52]

But from 1999, the GNP altered its stance and promoted a policy that sought to defer the organisational merger and repeal the financial merger. The GNP was now insistent in promoting its own bill with the ruling party in Parliament. Chung Ui-hwa, Shim Jae-cheol and Lee Won-hyung were at the forefront of those opposing the merger. The GNP blamed the procedural defect in the passage of the NHIA at the plenary session of January 1999,[53] and instead put forward its revised bill in February 1999, suggesting the permanent separation of insurance funds (Lim, 2001: 73). Later, in July 1999, the GNP put forward a fresh bill in which it alleged to delay the organisational merger for two years and to separate insurance funds perma-

51 With the appointment of Cha Heung-bong as MOHW minister, in May 1999, and the consequent resignation of Kim Jong-dae, the atmosphere inside the MOHW changed and the merger was much influenced by public opinion.

52 The GNP boycotted the National Assembly Legislation and Judiciary Committee, accusing its rival of spying on its activities in Parliament through the National Intelligence Service.

53 It was a parliamentary convention that bills were suggested at a plenary session after passing all the checks and winning consent at the Legislation and Judiciary Committee on legal matters. But the National Health Insurance Bill was referred to the plenary session by the National Assembly Speaker's authority without the Committee's agreement, because of the GNP's absence.

nently. In December 1999, however, it agreed to revise the NHIA to defer the organisational merger for just six months and the financial merger for one year.

5. Policy Outputs

1) Final outputs: realistic compromises but still broken promises

Although the merger of insurance funds was delayed until June 2003, the debate under the Kim Dae-jung administration concluded with the complete organisational merger to establish a single unified insurer from July 2000. During the debate, detailed government policies on the merger changed several times, but the principle of setting up a single insurer system was preserved. The final outputs of the full merger debate were (NMIC, 1999: 12):

- The partial organisational merger between self-employed insurers and the KMIC, from October 1998, by making the NMIC;
- The completion of the organisational merger comprising all kinds of health insurers by June 2000, under the NHIC;
- The deferral of the full financial merger to December 2001 (but, enforced from July 2003 in reality).

Meanwhile, policy content had fluctuated many times in making the unified insurer, due to pressure group efforts and the governing bloc's internal needs. The NMIA of November 1997 only laid down the partial organisational merger, excluding the financial merger.[54] Opponents, like the MOHW, tried to frustrate the enforcement of the NMIA (PUC, 1998: 283). But the KTC decided to push forward with the full merger and the MOHW had no choice but to follow.

The National Assembly Health and Welfare Committee passed the NHIA on 23 December 1998 and the January 1999 plenary session endorsed it without any amendments. In passing the NHIA, the government bill proposed in December 1998 largely remained intact. A key component of the NHIA was the completion of the organisational merger by absorbing employee health insurers into the NMIC and the achievement of the financial merger between employee health insurers and government/private school employees by December 1999. The full financial merger, including the insurance funds of self-employed insurers, would be achieved by December 2001. Health insurance premiums would be imposed by a single criterion based on income, irrespective of policyholders' jobs.

But in June 1999, the main opposition GNP decided to push for the revision of the NHIA to separate insurance funds permanently and put off the organisational merger for two years. The ruling party also proposed the revision to the NHIA in July 1999, indicating its wish to see a postponement of the organisational merger for six months and the financial merger for two years. The current insurance premium system would be maintained, taking into account current low income declaration rates among the self-employed.

54 The second stage, which the ruling GNP planned, was to fully merge the organisations of all health insurers and to partially merge the insurance funds between employee insurers and the KMIC, whereas the final stage was to complete the financial merger within 3-4 years (Chun and Kim, 2009: 144-45).

On 26 November 1999, the ruling and opposition parties agreed to revise the NHIA to delay the organisational merger between employee health insurers and the NMIC for six months, to start from July 2000. The partial financial merger between employee health insurers and the KMIC was postponed for one year to be accomplished by December 2000. But the full financial merger, including self-employed insurers, would be achieved by December 2001 as scheduled. The current dual insurance premium system based on both the wage for employees and the total income for the self-employed would be preserved.[55] Table 6.5 compares the original NHIA of January 1999 with the revised version of December 1999.

The NHIA was revised even before it came into being. The low level of income declaration rate of the self-employed and a fear of possible confusion among policyholders in the event of the hurried merger were alleged reasons

Table 6.5 Major differences between the original NHIA and the revised one

	Original NHIA	Revised NHIA
Organisational merger	• Full organisational merger by December 1999 by setting up the NHIC	• Postponement of full organisational merger for six months (until June 2000)
Financial merger	• Partial financial merger between all sorts of employee insurance funds by December 1999 • Full financial merger comprising self-employed insurance funds by December 2001	• Postponement of partial financial merger for one year (until December 2000) • Full financial merger including self-employed insurance funds by December 2001
Insurance premium imposition system	• Single criterion based on Policyholders' income	• Maintenance of the current dual criteria for employees and the self-employed

55 In this case, the self-employed's insurance premiums would be imposed by level of income, and the rate of employees' insurance premiums could be differently decided between company employees and employees in public organisations (NMIC, 1999: 13).

to revise the NHIA (Health Solidarity, 2001: 149). But the real reasons were political for both the governing bloc and opposition parties. The governing bloc worried about possible complaints from policyholders, derived from administrative inconvenience and increased insurance premiums by the merger, with the 2000 general election ahead. Meanwhile, opposition parties had to respond to the demands of the FKTU and employee insurers' union. Rep. Kim Hong-sin of the opposition GNP criticised the suspension:

> It is a strategic decision taken because of the coming election to suspend the organisational merger for six months and the financial merger for two years. Civic groups and the mass media are all blaming the revised bill. In particular, I'd like to say opposition colleagues that I cannot understand the reason why the opposition GNP shares the same strategic calculation as the ruling party… (Records of Health and Welfare Committee of the 208th National Assembly of 1999)

2) Reflected interests: reluctant compromise at crossroads

The aim to fully merge health insurers was eventually achieved under the Kim administration, in a sense that the NHIA was enacted and a single, unified insurer was established in July 2000. The result of the first round debate, between December 1997 and January 1999, was to prepare the ground for a single insurer system from January 2000. In drawing up the decision, key proponents, including the governing bloc, civic groups and progressive trade unions, took the initiative and achieved their goal by successfully enacting the NHIA in January 1999. Although the MOHW was a reluctant partner, it could not resist the political will of the new governing elite. In 1998 when the economic crisis was at its peak, restructuring society and the economy was top priority, so the opposition GNP and conservative trade unions were forced to agree to the merger. Furthermore, to the Kim administration who claimed to be a reformist government, the merger was important symbolically.

However, as the political and economic situation changed in 1999, the degree of conflict between the government and trade unions, irrespective of their ideological spectrums, deepened in the process of restructuring the labour market. With the economy recovering, trade unions began to withdraw their support for the Kim administration. The opposition GNP and the FKTU began to demand the suspension of the organisational and financial mergers. The governing bloc also decided to delay the implementation of the merger due to 'insufficient administrative preparation.' But differently from opponents of the merger, the governing bloc strongly adhered to the full merger, organisationally and financially. Meanwhile, civic groups and progressive trade unions demanded the full and immediate merger of health insurers in line with what had been decided in January 1999.

The revised NHIA in December 1999 largely reflected the preference of the governing bloc. As the governing bloc had wished, the organisational merger was postponed for just six months. The financial merger was delayed by one year, to be enforced from January 2001. Although opposition parties and the FKTU succeeded in delaying the timing of the merger, they failed to achieve their ultimate aim of permanently separating financial funds. Neither civic groups nor the KCTU succeeded entirely. Accordingly, the interests of the governing bloc were largely met during the revision of the NHIA, whilst the interests of other participants were only partly achieved, irrespective of their views towards the merger.

6. Conclusion

The full merger debate lasted two years from December 1997 to December 1999, when the NHIA revision was finalised. The debate was initiated by the new governing elite, keeping its promise to carry out their presidential election pledge. Civic groups and progressive trade unions pressurised the governing elite to push forward the merger. The economic crisis was another reason behind the merger. But the process of the debate was not simple; many policy actors got involved, all with different interests and motivations. Major proponents of the merger changed their views to postpone the agreed timetable. The fierce dispute between trade unions in different ideological spectrums was an exceptional feature.

As with previous case studies, the primary emphasis could be laid on the heavy impact of policy context on charactering institutions, policy networks and policy outputs. Democratised politics and consecutive elections widely opened policy networks and diversified interaction patterns. Revitalised civil society enabled civic groups and trade unions to mobilise every possible means of interest input. 1) Among governing ideologies, the emphasis on national integration gave an impetus to initiate the full merger debate as a means of promoting social solidarity between different economic strata. 2) Political events, such as the 1997 presidential election, the emergence of a new political and administrative leadership and the 2000 general election, were greatly influential on policy networks and resultant outputs. 3) Competitive and responsive political leadership opened up policy networks more widely. The tight results of the elections forced the governing bloc to compromise with opposition parties in Parliament. 4) With the increasing power of civil society, civic groups and trade unions led the entire process of the debate, which made policy networks more open and varied.

While the general appearance of institutional features had hardly changed, the practical operation of institutions and the power relationship became more democratised and balanced with the ongoing progress of political openness. 1) The concentration of administrative power in the President's hands during the early term of presidency halted departments' objection to the merger, and the balanced power between the ruling and opposition parties made their interaction more compromising. 2) The emergence of the KTC as a new institution played a crucial role in deciding the full merger and affected policy networks. The formation of a coalition government was another important institutional factor that affected policy-making patterns. 3) Previous policy on the merger functioned as the established path, constraining policy networks and outputs. The decision of November 1997, to partially merge health insurers, limited the options available.

The overall feature of network structure during the full merger debate reflected an issue network type. Many policy actors freely entered into open networks and the intentional exclusion of particular actors was absolutely impossible. Although the same bloc members had similar interests in the merger, they did not always match. Resource dependency also developed in various ways. This issue network-type structure diversified interaction patterns and made policy outputs unpredictable.

Major players mobilised all possible interaction strategies during the debate. While the first round of the debate was more mild and consultative, the second half of the debate from 1999 was turbulent. Civic groups and trade unions became more militant, relying on mass-level methods of interest input. Again, these styles of interaction patterns had a profound effect on policy outputs, which changed dramatically and were adjusted to delay the timing of the merger. Interaction patterns also affected the network structure by constraining the degree of resource dependency and participants' cohesiveness. In this respect, the relationship between network structure and interaction is not unilateral, but reciprocal.

The final output was to delay the scheduled merger. During the first round of the debate, participants were unanimous in introducing a single insurer system. But in reality, it was impossible to implement the agreement with just one year's preparation. The governing bloc, therefore, decided to postpone and other participants, except civic groups and progressive trade unions, agreed. Also, the output fed back into the system, constraining interaction patterns during the period of remaining debates until the financial merger was finally enforced in 2003.

Chapter
7

Successful Health Insurance Reform or Reluctant Compromise?

Comparison

1. Comparing the Four Case Studies

Debates on the merger of health insurers have spanned 20 years from the early 1980s, and have been one of the most turbulent and long-standing in the field of Korea's health policy. In essence, participants fought over different perspectives on the health insurer system. During the two decades, Korea's political landscape has been radically reshaped as the country has moved from a dictatorial system to a democratic one, making the policy-making process very dynamic. Civil society has been re-energised with the steady march of democratisation since the mid 1980s. Many relevant interests have tirelessly taken part in the entire process, fighting to achieve their policy goals.

Since the mid 1980s, the issue has become a symbolic social reform agenda for a more equitable society, bringing together various civic groups and trade unions. The issue turned into one of struggle between reformist activists and vested interests. Participants split into two conflicting blocs, and the intensity and duration of their conflict has been long and painful.

During this time, policy context and institutions experienced dynamic changes, generating fluctuations in policy networks and outputs. The final output of the debates was to gradually accomplish the merger in incremental stages: partial organisational merger; full organisational merger; partial financial merger; and full financial merger. Figure 7.1 draws together the gradual change towards the full merger of health insurers. Meanwhile, the

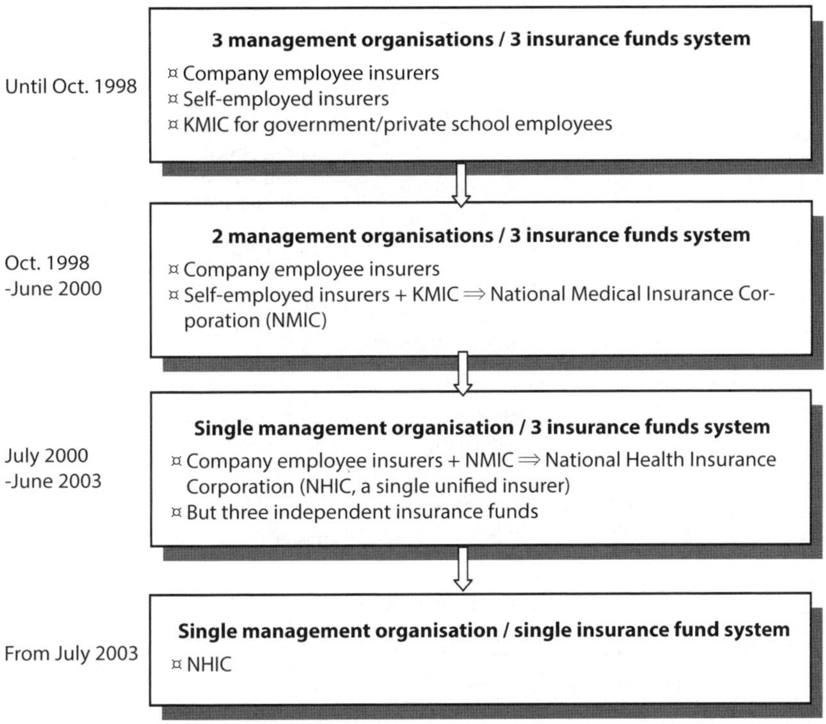

Figure 7.1 The changing pattern of health insurer systems in Korea

debates were divided into four distinctive stages in terms of political regimes and the discernible effort to make or revise relevant laws. Table 7.1 distinguishes each stage of the debate.

Table 7.1 Distinctive characters of each debate

	First debate (1980-82)	Second debate (1988-89)	Partial merger (1996-97)	Full merger (1997-2003)
Initiators and triggering motives	- MHSA minister - Plan to extend health insurance to the self-employed	- Farmers' groups and activist healthcare professionals - Farmers' overloaded burden of insurance premiums	- A few lawmakers of the ruling and opposition parties - Serious deficit among self-employed insurers and the coming presidential election	- Governing bloc, progressive civic groups and trade unions - Inequity between policyholders and the economic crisis
Key proponents of the merger	MHSA and the ruling party	Farmers' groups and opposition parties	The ruling and opposition parties, civic groups	Governing bloc, progressive civic groups and trade unions
Key opponents of the merger	Bureaucrats in the Office of the President (OP)	MHSA and the ruling party	MOHW and relevant departments	FKTU, employee insurers union, opposition GNP
Major conflicting parties	Bureaucrats in the MHSA and the OP	Civic groups vs. MHSA	Civic groups and political parties vs. MOHW	Civic groups and KCTU vs. FKTU
Regimes and politics	- Authoritative politics - Strong governing bloc and weak opposition parties	- A transition towards democracy - Opposition dominance of Parliament	- Democratising politics - Presidential lame duck	- Democratised politics - DJP coalition government
Parliamentary leader	Ruling party	Opposition parties	Ruling party	Both
Settlement of the issue	By the President's instruction	By presidential veto and three-party merger	By making the National Medical Insurance Act	By making and revising the National Health Insurance Act
Policy network type	Closer to policy community	Closer to issue network	Closer to issue network	Closer to issue network
Resultant outputs	Frustration of the merger attempt	Presidential veto and frustration of the merger attempt	Decision to partially merge management organisations	Decision to fully merge management organisations and finances
Distinctive impacts	Departure of the ensuing debates, purge of MHSA officials	Empowered civic groups' putting the issue as a symbol of health reform	Beginning of incremental merger	Substantial completion of the merger
Others	Early days of presidency	Early days of presidency	Final term of presidency and lame duck	Early days of presidency and economic crisis

2. Policy Context: Political Turbulence and Vitalised Civil Society

1) Political context: from authoritarianism to democracy

Each government had distinctive governing ideologies and set its own framework in managing state affairs. But mostly, the influence of governing ideologies on institutions and policy networks has been limited because they have been nothing more than a stated slogan of a political regime which was not necessarily applied in practice.

Also, there have been many political events, which have played the role of a 'policy window,' setting off fresh rounds of the debates on the issue. In particular, presidential and parliamentary elections have been the catalyst on several occasions. In the first debate, the 1980 military coup froze society, concentrated power in the hands of the President and the OP, and caused the extreme change in politico-administrative leadership. The new MHSA minister initiated the first debate unexpectedly, placing the merger issue onto the political agenda. Moreover, the military coup also needed paternalistic social policy to underpin its illegal rebellion, and healthcare reform was considered to be one way to achieve this.

While elections were ceremonial in authoritarian politics, they became more influential on policy-making and outputs as Korea moved towards democracy in the late 1980s. Elections had a strong impact on increasing the number of network participants and their interactions. In the second debate, the extension of the health insurance program to cover the rural self-employed was introduced in advance of the 1987 presidential election. The 1988 general election also forced the governing bloc to appease farmers by increasing government subsidies to self-employed insurers. A scheduled presidential midterm plebiscite made the ruling party agree to a merger bill in March 1989.

The 1997 presidential election was a decisive factor leading to the partial merger, by excluding government departments from any significant participation in the debate and empowering the ruling party. When the debate was drawing to a close, the switch in power at the 1997 presidential election was a critical driving force behind keeping the partial merger on track as scheduled. The 2000 general election changed policy content by providing the governing bloc with an excuse to delay the scheduled merger.

Intertwined politics and leadership competition have also been an important determinant in terms of institutions and policy networks. Authoritarian political leadership during the Chun administration generated a power imbalance between political organisations and therefore limited the merger debate to only within the governing bloc, thus generating closed policy networks. After the late 1980s, politics dramatically changed to be more democratic and open, decisively influencing policy-making and policy outputs.

Transitional politics on the road to democracy under the Rho and the Kim Young-sam administrations and democratised politics under the Kim Dae-jung administration all empowered civil society, strengthened opposition parties and encouraged power balance. Consequently, policy networks became open and fluid, making the debates more turbulent and policy outputs unpredictable. Parliament replaced the government as the main arena of debate. So, in most respects the dynamics of policy-making and outputs then became closely interrelated with the type of politics and political leadership. Table 7.2 compares the political context of the four case studies.

Table 7.2 Comparison of political context over time

	Characteristics of political context
First debate	**Governing ideology:** just and welfare society, economic stabilisation
	Political events: military coup (May 1980), plebiscite (Oct. 1980), dissolution of Parliament (Oct. 1980), presidential election (Feb. 1981), general election (March 1981), emergence of new regime and MHSA minister
	Politics and political leadership style: closed politics, authoritative and non-competitive political leadership, indirectly-elected President
Second debate	**Governing ideology:** political democratisation, national reconciliation and creation of advanced motherland
	Political events: presidential election (Dec. 1987), emergence of new regime (Feb.1988), general election (April 1988), opposition parties' dominance, President's mid-term plebiscite, three-party merger (Feb. 1990)
	Politics and political leadership style: transitional politics towards democracy, competitive political leadership, oppositional majority, directly-elected President
Partial merger debate	**Governing ideology:** creation of new Korea, civilian rule, globalisation, reformative change
	Political events: general election (April 1996), local elections (June 1996), presidential election (Dec. 1997), President's withdrawal from ruling party membership, President's lame-duck
	Politics and political leadership style: democratising politics, competitive leadership, directly-elected President
Full merger debate	**Governing ideology:** societal unity, harmony of democracy and market economy, economic distributional justice
	Political events: presidential election (Dec. 1997), general election (April 2000), economic crisis (from Nov. 1997), DJP coalition, political power alternation
	Politics and political leadership style: democratised politics, power alternation, competitive political leadership, directly-elected president

2) Social context: from forced silence to an autonomous civil society

Social and political contexts are interrelated. The activities of civic groups and trade unions tend to be more energised in an open and democratised political arena. Also, a vitalised civil society was influential in making institutions more democratised and policy networks more open and fluid. In Korea, the vitality of civil society has been directly proportional to the progress in political democracy. Since the 1987 popular protests, various civic groups and trade unions have actively engaged in state affairs, widely opening up policy networks.

In detail, the formation of activist civic groups and the labour movement were tightly controlled during the first debate of the early 1980s, producing undemocratic institutions and closed policy networks. But since mid-1987, civil society energised itself on the back of democratic change, and civil power revolutionised institutions and policy networks during the consecutive debates on the merger. A variety of politics-oriented civic groups were formed and trade unions were vigorous in promoting labour interests. Since the second debate, which occurred in the midst of transitional democracy, civic groups and trade unions have been key players in policy networks, greatly affecting policy outputs. They formed a series of united fronts to push for the merger in unison (see Figure 7.2). Oppositional dominance of Parliament provided these groups with a very good chance of success in terms of promoting their causes.

During the Kim Young-sam administration, from February 1993, civic group leaders were officially invited into government posts and the government made use of civic groups as neutral arbitrators in the settling of controversial state affairs.[1] The Korean Confederation of Trade Unions (KCTU), a progressive peak trade union, formally participated in government committees along with the privileged Federation of Korean Trade Unions (FKTU). Trade unions, emboldened by their access to power, sought to repeal the labour-related laws passed in December 1996.

1 A good example was the CCEJ's successful arbitration in the conflict between pharmacists and herbal doctors surrounding the prescription of herb medicine in the early 1990s.

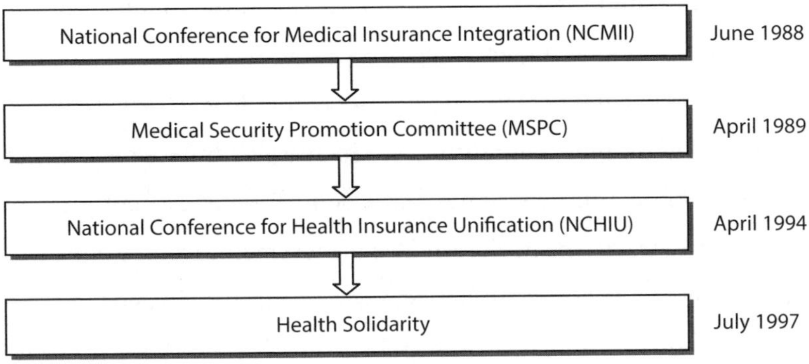

Figure 7.2 The united fronts formed by civic groups proposing the merger

Furthermore, the Kim Dae-jung administration, inaugurated in February 1998, worked more closely with civil society as a way of strengthening its relatively weak power base. From that point onwards, the enormously empowered civil society has intervened on all important matters, including the debate on the merger. Even OP staff in the Rho Moo-hyun administration (2003-2007), the most pro-civil society government in Korean history, complains about the excessive levels of power and influence wielded by civic groups:

> Civic groups should be changed now… I cannot understand the fact that civic groups have to evaluate all the things that the government does… If civic groups want to act like this, they should transform themselves into a political party… The role of civic groups in advanced countries is to serve the people and society. But civic groups in Korea are over-politicised… (*Donga Ilbo*, 12 March 2005)

Trade unions, regardless of their political propensities, were officially invited to participate in government committees and the militant KCTU was legally authorised as a competing association from November 1999, thereby opening up a multiple unionisation system in Korea (Kihl, 2005: 273). But distinctively, despite the indisputable increase of trade union power during the 1990s, membership rates and labour disputes did not proportionally increase. Traditionally, Korean labour movements were led by small numbers of oligarchic leaders in big companies, and largely depended on extreme methods like hunger strikes and sit-ins, which did not need the mass mobilisation of union members. Labour Minister Kim Dae-hwan of the Rho Moo-hyun administration diagnoses the cause of Korean trade union militancy in an interview with a UK newspaper:

> ... Labour militancy is a reaction against the suppression of workers before democracy was introduced in 1987. Back in the 1960s and 70s the Korean government was focused on development of the economy. Labour was not dealt with as an important issue. Then, during democratisation, trade unions tried to increase their rights in a somewhat extreme way. Seventeen years later, we still see volatility. The principle of dialogue and compromise requires trust between labour and management but that has been lacking (*Financial Times,* 23 August 2004).

3. Institutional Features: Towards Balanced and Democratic Political Institutions

Institutional features have been largely affected by the policy context, particularly through the political context. The power relationship between political organisations has constrained other institutional variables, like decision-making rules. Institutions have also greatly regulated policy networks, exerting a strong pull on participants' interactions and affecting resultant policy outputs.

1) Power relations between political organisations: towards balance

Power relations between political organisations intimately interact with the policy context. As political scientists (Lipson et al., 1995; Hill, 2014) claim, political power tends to concentrate in the hands of the executive in closed and non-competitive political systems, while political power in open and competitive political systems is likely to spread much wider. Also, when elections are approaching — such as presidential and parliamentary elections in this instance — power relations tend to become more balanced. Power relations also regulate the practical operation of other institutional features like decision-making rules and policy networks.

As the first debate arose shortly after the 1980 military coup, the power imbalance between political institutions was severe. Political power was concentrated almost exclusively in the hands of the President and small numbers of the governing elite. Particularly, the President and his staff monopolised decision-making power, subordinating the ruling party and government departments. Opposition parties, the mass media and civil society were under the state's tight control.

However, massive civil protests from June 1987 balanced power relations between political organisations. The President's power in policy-making was greatly weakened. During the second debate, opposition parties came to dominate parliamentary decision-making, pushing aside the ruling party. Civic groups and trade unions were now completely out of government control. But some presidential powers remained, and the President was still very much at the heart of government decision-making through the use of veto power over bills.

In earlier terms of his presidency, President Kim Young-sam and a handful of governing elite had strong influence over Korean politics. But from mid-1995, when opposition leader Kim Dae-jung returned from his self-proclaimed political retirement, opposition parties were reanimated and they brought Parliament back to the centre of political affairs. The ruling party also failed to win a majority at the 1996 general election. The power balances between the ruling and opposition parties and between the President and Parliament were thus restored. From 1997 President Kim entered the final term of his presidency, as a lame-duck President. This seriously weakened the OP's control over state affairs. Accordingly, political parties dominated the partial merger debate and most of the resultant outputs mainly reflected the compromise between them.

Although Kim Dae-jung's power base was not consolidated from the beginning, the precarious economy and effeminate opposition leadership

Table 7.3 Changing power relations during the debates

	Power relationships between political organisations
First debate	Government > Parliament, President > government departments and ruling party, ruling party > opposition parties
Second debate	Government ≤ Parliament, President ≥ government departments and ruling party, ruling party < opposition parties
Partial merger debate	Government < Parliament, President = government departments and ruling party, ruling party = opposition parties
Full merger debate	Government ≥ Parliament, President > government departments and ruling party, ruling party = opposition parties

enabled him to have influence within state affairs. From 1999, revitalised opposition leadership and opposition parties' numerical majority balanced the power relations between the ruling and opposition parties and between the government and Parliament. But the power hierarchy between government agencies remained unchanged. Table 7.3 illustrates the change of power relations between the state's political organisations.

2) Democratising political institutions

In the Chun administration, the Constitution officially endowed the President with the right to control Parliament and all government departments. Under the strong presidential system, the ruling party-dominant Parliament was unable to effectively check presidential power. Key opposition politicians were banned from political life. Civic groups and trade unions were put out of business. The roles of the PM and the State Council became mostly ceremonial.

However, the governing system greatly changed as a result of the 1987 popular protests and the subsequent Constitutional revision. The Constitutional amendments of October 1987 aimed at diffusing political power, and thus the governing system operated checks and balances (see Table 7.4). In particular, Parliament's right to check the government was greatly strengthened, by allowing Parliament to inspect government offices, while the President's right to disband Parliament was dissolved. But the President could check Parliament by use of veto power against parliamentary decision. The influence of civic groups and trade unions on state affairs also greatly increased with the progress of democracy.

The basic governing system under the Kim Young-sam administration

Table 7.4 Comparison between the Constitutions of 1980 and 1987

	The 1980 Constitution	The 1987 Constitution
President	• Head of the state and the executive • Seven-year single term • Indirect election by electoral college • Proclaim a state of emergency • Proclaim a martial law • Dissolve Parliament • Address at Parliament and demand an extra session • Request the reconsideration of the bill • Appoint PM and other cabinet members	• Head of the state and the executive • Five-year single term • Direct presidential election • Take minimum necessary financial and economic actions • Proclaim martial law • Address Parliament and demand an extra session • Request the reconsideration of the bill • Appoint PM and other cabinet members
Parliament	• Restriction of total opening days (within 150 days) • Restriction of agendas and opening days in case of the President-requesting session • Investigate specific matters of state affairs • Resolve the dismissal of PM and cabinet members • Pass a motion for the impeachment of the President, PM and cabinet members	• No restriction on total opening days • Inspect general state affairs • Investigate specific matters of state affairs • Recommend the dismissal of PM and cabinet members • Pass a motion for the impeachment of the President, PM and cabinet members

Source: adapted from the Constitutions of 1980 and 1987.

remained unchanged, as it was regulated by the same 1987 Constitution. Under this system all relevant laws ensured balances between governing bodies, and constrained the operation of political organisations. But the key difference was the Kim administration's favourable outlook on civil society.

The Kim Dae-jung administration's basic governing system was also identical to that of its predecessor due to its unchanged Constitution and related laws. So, institutions had a basic tendency to be stable. But new institutions like the KTC and the Presidency Undertaking Commission (PUC) were born and the Kim administration formed a coalition with ultra-rightist Kim Jong-pil.

The basic institution on the political party system has not undergone any serious change through the entire period of the debates, despite the revision of the Constitution and related laws. The Constitution has constantly guaranteed the free establishment of political parties and a multiparty system. Laws protected the autonomy and internal democracy of political parties. The following characterise the reality of Korea's party system during 20 years of the debate.

The structure of Korea's political parties has been that of one ruling party with one or two opposition parties, irrespective of the stated multiparty system. The degree of state control over opposition parties and the relative power between the ruling and opposition parties have wavered over time. In the early 1980s, military coup leaders restructured the system to one ruling party and two disrupted opposition parties. But the 1985 general election saw the emergence of a strong opposition party, and the nationwide popular protests in 1987 totally changed the political map. It was impossible for the government to control opposition parties and opposition leaders seized the political initiative. The 1988 general election then produced another result, the system of a weak ruling party and three strong opposition parties, and this transformation decisively influenced policy networks and outputs in the second debate.

Although the three-party merger in February 1990 produced the one dominant ruling party and weak opposition parties system once again, the electorate rectified this political imbalance in favour of the ruling party at the 1992 and 1996 general elections by voting for opposition candidates in ever greater numbers. In general terms, the power relationship between the ruling and opposition parties became more balanced in the Kim Young-sam and Kim Dae-jung administrations.

Second, major political parties all pursued the same conservative political ideology and their party platforms were essentially all shadows of the same colour. They tried to satisfy every strata of the population. Amidst the intimidation from communist neighbours, progressive or socialist parties had failed to take root in Korean politics. The progressive Democratic Labour Party, for the first time, joined Parliament after the 2004 general election.

Third, despite progress towards political democracy, regional favouritism and party oligarchy still remained. This in turn damaged the internal democracy of political parties. Charismatic political leaders, such as the so-called three Kims, secured loyalty by resorting to plutocracy and using their influence over the nomination of parliamentary candidates. They arbitrarily renamed or dissolved political parties, whenever they felt the need to do so.[2]

Finally, although the practical relationship between the government and the ruling party within the governing bloc has fluctuated over time, the dominance of the former over the latter has been more familiar. During the first and second debates in the 1980s, the government dominated state affairs. Exceptionally, the ruling party overwhelmed government departments and lame-duck President in the partial merger debate, which occurred in the final year of presidency. The government, however, restored its control over the ruling party during the full merger debate.

The revised election system, which came into being because of Constitutional amendments in 1980 and 1987, directly interacted with the po-

2 The average life span of Korea's political parties is just 3.2 years in contrast to the UK Conservative Party's 173 years and the Labour Party's 99 years, largely due to 'boss politics' and abrupt political changes in Korea. The record for longevity is 17.6 years, set during the 1960-70s by the Democratic Republican Party (*Donga Ilbo*, 26 February 2005).

litical context and the power relations. It has also affected policy networks by constraining interaction patterns, because the election system could alter politicians' strategies on how to deal with other network participants. For example, a more competitive election system may compel the government and political parties to become more responsive to demands of organised interests (Heywood, 2002: 241-43).

The election system under the Chun administration was completely in favour of the governing bloc. The President was indirectly elected through an electoral college, without any competition. Parliament adopted a unicameral system and recruited lawmakers in two ways. Elections in local constituencies adopted the medium electorate system to guarantee the winning of ruling candidates. The proportional representation system was also greatly favourable to the ruling party.

Under the Rho administration, the election system became more competitive thanks to the change in the Constitution and relevant laws, in 1987. The President was directly elected and his/her term was shortened to five years. The parliamentary election system changed to a single-member electorate system, opening up competition, and even though the proportional representation system was favourable to the ruling party as before, much of its unfairness was corrected. Through the new election system, the 1987 presidential election was highly competitive and the 1988 general election resulted in opposition dominance in Parliament.

Ruling candidate Kim Young-sam won the 1992 presidential election by a large margin. The presidential electoral system and the length of the President's term in office remained unchanged. A unicameral system and the two-tier selection of lawmakers were also preserved. But the proportional representation system was improved so as to better reflect the views

Table 7.5 Change of election systems since the 1980s

	Chun administration	Rho administration	Kim Young-sam administration	Kim Dae-jung administration
Presidential election	Indirect election	Direct election	Direct election	Direct election
President's office term	Seven-year single term	Five-year single term	Five-year single term	Five-year single term
Parliamentary election system	Medium elector-ate system	Single-mem-ber electorate system	Single-mem-ber electorate system	Single-mem-ber electorate system
Proportional representation system	Two thirds to a leading party and one third to other parties	Distribution in line with seats won in regional districts	Distribution in line with polling score won in regional districts	Distribution in line with polling score won in regional districts

Source: adapted from Yoon Hyoung-sup et al. (2003) and Lee and Kim (1996).

of opposition or small-sized parties. Political neutrality of public servants was reinforced. And, as a result, the ruling party failed to win a majority at the 1996 general election.

The Kim Dae-jung administration's parliamentary and presidential election systems were also basically unchanged.[3] Government intervention in elections and plutocracy were continuously diminishing. This time civic groups actively intervened in the election process in a partisan fashion, helping the ruling party, because they believed it to be more pro-civil society. Table 7.5 summarises the change of election systems during the debates on the merger.

3 But in July 2001, the Constitutional Court judged the proportional representation system, which distributed seats by the rate of polling score in regional districts as unconstitutional as it violated the idea of equal and direct elections prescribed in the Constitution. Following the decision, eligible electorate cast two ballots, one for a constituent delegate and another for a proportional representative, from the April 2004 general election (http://www.nec.go.kr).

3) Decision-making rules: the discrepancy between institutions and their practical operation

Rules on decision-making and conflict resolution have been well defined and stable, despite the change in policy context. As Meyer and Rowan (2012) argue, culturally embedded rules tended to persist, and competent actors also were reluctant to change rules in a situation where they could flexibly adapt rules for their own benefits.

At a department level, the *ringi* system has formally regulated internal decision-making and conflict resolution. Despite heavy administration, it has contributed to stabilising decision-making and ensuring communication channels within departments. There were also several levels of formal meetings, to settle intra-department differences.

Working, vice-ministerial and ministerial level meetings have contributed to making inter-department decisions. The OP and the PM have coordinated 'bigger picture' matters of national importance. The ruling party has also intervened in politically sensitive issues. Until the 1980s, intelligence agencies and public security departments also played important roles in coordinating inter-department differences. The State Council has been the final decision-maker of government policies.

Ruling party-government conferences have been held before final government decisions. The conference was divided into several levels according to participants' status, ranging from working-level to ministerial-level. In the meantime, the role of opposition parties in making laws has greatly increased since the mid 1980s. But government meetings with opposition parties were mainly a farce. In the debates, serious dialogues between them did not exist. Exceptionally, important political issues were settled by face-to-face meetings between the President, as a ruling party chairperson, and presidents from main opposition parties.

Decision-making and conflict resolution in Parliament have followed the lines laid down by the National Assembly Act. Despite superficial changes in some detail, basic decision-making procedures have remained largely untouched. The most important decision-maker in Parliament has been a standing committee and its subcommittees. During merger debates, practical decisions were made by the Health and Welfare Committee. Standing committee bills were sent to the Legislation and Judiciary Committee to be reviewed for legal mistakes in terms of definition, words or phrases. Rep. Joo Sung-young explains the role of the Legislation and Judiciary Committee in parliamentary decision-making:

> More than 90 percent of the Legislation and Judiciary Committee members are composed of legal professionals. The Committee mainly reviews the system, words and phrases of proposed bills, as standing committee members are usually deficient of knowledge on legal matters. The contradiction to other existing laws and possible unconstitutionality of clauses are also checked. The Committee does not review suggested bills from a policy point of view. The decision at the Committee mostly follows a unanimity rule. It is very seldom case that the Committee is forced to come to a vote. (Interview on 19 March 2005)

The plenary session finally endorses the bills by majority rule usually without discussion, and the passed bills are then sent to the government to promulgate within 15 days. Although the President can demand parliamentary reconsideration, the bills are automatically effectuated by two-thirds of lawmakers' decision.

However, reality, once again, does not match the theory. The practical operation of institutions has fluctuated with the change of political context and power relationship, differently constraining policy networks and outputs. Politically powerful actors decide whether or not to observe current game rules, in a situation where they can easily manipulate the rules. Korea's new political elite, who were unwilling to endorse the performance of the previous regime, tended to deny the existing political rules. Naturally, they distorted these rules and set up new rules and institutions at their convenience. In this regard, as Lowndes and Roberts (2013) argue, rules are not established by accident but reformulated to reflect political reality. Policy actors have discretion in interpreting rules, which are often abstract and discrepant from reality.

At the departmental level, the Minister's will and superiors' instructions were largely reflected in decision-making, regardless of any existing rules. Prior consent from superiors or informal coordination was more important in making decision than formal meetings. Department committees were also mainly ceremonial as they lacked decision-making powers.

The opinion of the competent department was largely respected at inter-departmental level. While the OP was influential in handling government affairs, the roles of the OPM and the State Council were generally ceremonial under a strong presidential system. Likewise, prior consent and informal coordination remained more crucial than formal procedures. However, in relation to the merger debates, the Kim Young-sam administration did set up several government committees in which organised interests participated. The Kim Dae-jung administration, in effect a coalition government, empowered the Prime Minister and built new coordination systems that helped to narrow the two coalition parties' differences.

The ruling party-government relationship was largely shaped by the political context and practical power situation. Informal meetings and prior coordination were also highly respected. In essence, the government dominated the ruling party-government conference during the first debate, while the conference was led by concerted efforts in the second debate. During the partial merger debate, the ruling party was more influential at the conference, eventually dissolving the conference after President Kim Young-sam left the ruling party. The Kim Dae-jung administration set up the Council for State Affairs to coordinate coalition members. The President-PM weekly meeting was a top-level dialogue platform.

Parliamentary decision-making depended on the number of seats held by the political parties (see Table 7.6). The ruling party dominated Parliament during the first debate, while opposition parties took the initiative in the second debate. Although the ruling party was dominant in the partial merger debate, it refrained from self-indulgence. Opposition parties did not run Parliament in the full merger debate, despite their majority status, in earlier times of the President's term in office.

Table 7.6 Composition of Parliament during the debates

National Assembly (Election year)	Number of seats (proportion of seats, %)		Polling score (%)	
	Ruling party	Opposition and others	Ruling party	Opposition and others
11th (March 1980)	151 (54.7)	125 (45.3)	35.6	64.4
12th (Feb. 1985)	148 (53.6)	128 (46.4)	35.2	64.8
13th (April 1988)	125 (41.8)	174 (58.2)	34.0	66.0
14th (March 1992)	149 (49.8)	150 (50.2)	38.5	61.5
15th (April 1996)	139 (46.5)	160 (53.5)	46.5	53.5
16th (April 2000)	132 (48.3)	133 (51.7)	45.7	54.3

Source: abstracted from the National Assembly homepage (www.assembly.go.kr).

It was rare for the plenary session to oppose any standing committee bills, which had already been brokered between the ruling and opposition parties. Key affairs were decided at meetings between floor leaders or party policy directors, while particularly important matters were settled by party presidents. During two decades of debate, the presidential veto was exercised just once (in the second debate), as it was of great political burden to the President.

4) Previous policies: incremental changes

Historical institutionalism insists that current policies are reliant upon previously established policies and the path upon which they lie. In the merger debates, previous policies and decisions taken about the health insurer system have played a part in shaping policy networks, particularly in terms of network membership and interaction patterns. Under this influence, policies tended to gradually change and the decision-making style was inclined to follow the established path.

In detail, Korea had adopted a multiple insurer system from the beginning, in line with the Japanese system. While the multiple insurer system exhibited weaknesses from the 1980s, the government coped with them by enlarging the size of health insurers. Until then, there were few players and they commonly shared a vested interest in maintaining the established system. The opponents of the merger frustrated the first merger attempt in the early 1980s.

The second debate was triggered by the extension of health insurance coverage to the self-employed. Opposition parties and civic groups proposed the merger to promote social solidarity and reduce the insurance premiums of the self-employed. But opponents of the merger simply proposed megalopolis-sized insurers within the framework of the insurer system. So, those in favour of the established policy responded to the merger attempt by partly repairing the existing system, thereby frustrating the merger attempt once more.

Previous policies and embedded interests surrounding the health insurer system partially remained even in the Kim Young-sam administration. But a new political opportunity in the 1997 presidential election demanded change. A critical moment was the ruling party's change of mind to accept the partial merger. Ruling lawmakers who saw the benefits of backing the merger in the coming election began to support the merger. So in this case, the established institution was not a fixed entity but malleable, dependent more on the change of context and involved interests. But the institution responded to the pressure by minimising the scope of change. The final output of the debate resulted in only a partial and incremental change of the established institution.

The partial merger decision in 1997 was a starting point in the advance towards the full merger. The power switch of the 1997 presidential election

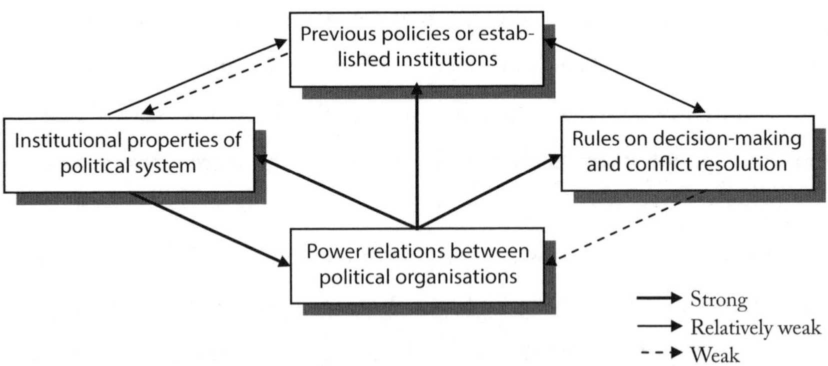

Figure 7.3 Interactive relationship between the variables of institutional features

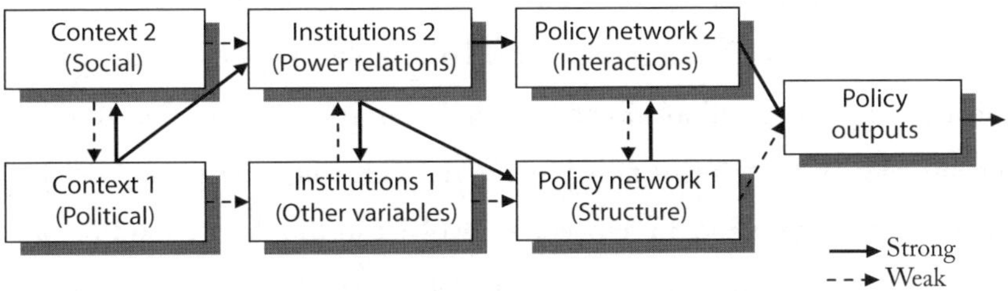

Figure 7.4 Strength of relationship between the analytical components

opened a policy window and thus, allowed for a tide of support behind the full merger. The power switch also meant a change in the power relations between principal policy actors. The MOHW were forced to follow decisions made by the new governing elite, and civic groups and trade unions became core policy actors. But, unfortunately, a little more time was needed to completely destroy the remaining vested interests. Vested interests in a multiple insurer system still resisted institutional change from 1999, by seeking to suspend the agreed merger schedule. Figure 7.3 maps the route of interaction between the variables composing institutional features and Figure 7.4 overviews the position of institutional features in relation with other components.

4. Policy Networks: Towards Open and Fluid Issue Networks

For the duration of ensuing debates, policy networks have been greatly affected by both the policy context and institutional features, individually or in combination. In particular, the political context and the power relation between main political organisations have been highly significant in shaping policy networks. During the first debate, authoritarian politics and an unbalanced power relationship had a defining impact on both the structure and interaction patterns of policy networks. But since the second debate, a large number of actors have become involved in the debates and private actors like civic groups have initiated the debates. The following are illustrative descriptions of policy networks for the 20 years covering the debates:

- The general type of policy networks has changed from that of closed policy networks to open issue networks since the late 1980s, doubling network players.
- The political context and the power relations between political organisations, among institutional features, have had a big impact on shaping policy networks.
- The merger agenda has changed from that of a simple health policy issue to a symbol of social reform since the late 1980s, thereby greatly increasing network participants and interactions.
- While participants have been divided into two blocs, their motivations for or against the merger have been remarkably different, even within the same bloc. Moreover, the fierce conflict between participants has frequently resulted in policy paralysis and sometimes produced hasty policy outputs.
- Of the unofficial policy actors, civic groups and trade unions have actively taken part in the debates since the second debate while the mass media and professional interest groups have shown just limited interest.
- Excluding the first debate, the major debating arena was Parliament rather than the government. Thus, political parties have played key

roles and the larger part of interest group inputs have been directed at Parliament.

- Since the second debate, civic groups have shown consistency in proposing the merger, while the governing bloc has changed policies several times.

1) Network structure: doubling the number of network participants

Nature of participants

The number of major participants greatly increased after the second debate. During the first debate, key participants were limited to the governing bloc including the OP, the MHSA and the ruling party. The President functioned, not as a simple participant, but as a final judge. Minor participants like business groups and opposition parties played limited roles while civic groups and trade unions were inactive at the time. But since the second debate, participants have doubled as the general trend towards democracy continued. The main debating arena moved to Parliament, and opposition parties led the debate. Activist civic groups, including farmers' groups, progressive health professionals, and trade unions — particularly self-employed insurers' union — occupied key positions in policy networks.

Under the Kim Young-sam administration, the issue stirred every relevant policy actor so it opened policy networks more widely. The Kim Dae-jung administration also invited all interested parties to participate in the debate. During the 20 years of debates, numerous policy actors have become involved and the issue has turned into a symbolic reformist policy attracting attention from almost all of the progressive civic groups and trade unions. Figure 7.5 compares key participants, describing their relative importance in policy networks.

Dominant actors have changed over time. In the first debate the OP

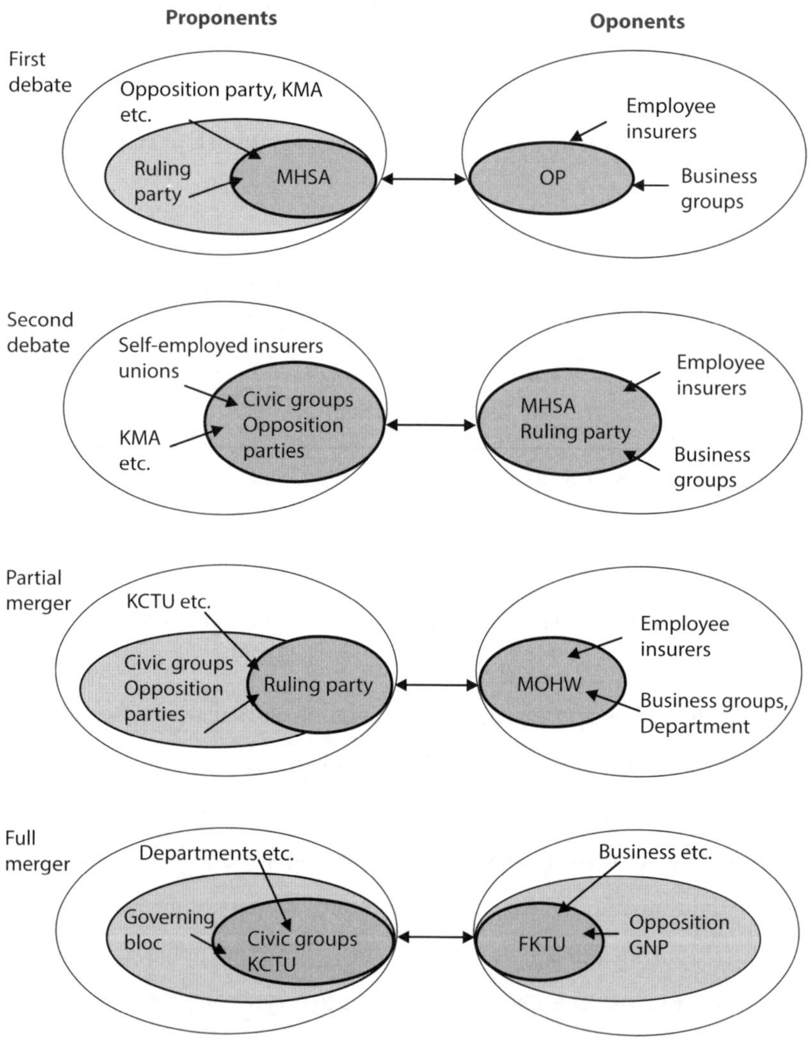

Figure 7.5 Participants and their roles in the debates

led the opponent bloc, whereas the proponent bloc was led by the MHSA, particularly the minister, and the ruling party. But the MHSA gave up the fight in the face of the OP's strong opposition, leaving just the ruling party alone in the proponent bloc. In this regard, the conflict in the first debate mainly occurred between governing bloc members, especially between bureaucrats with different views on the merger. Until then, the proponent bloc was not firmly established, and it was unimaginable that opposition parties or civil society could have taken the lead in the closed political circumstance.

In contrast, the proponent bloc led by civic groups and opposition parties managed the second debate. The MHSA, the OP and the ruling party made up the opponent bloc to the merger. Self-employed insurers union, entering the debate late, then emerged as a new leading proponent, staging tough protests to advocate the merger.

During the partial merger debate, civic groups and opposition parties ruled the proponent bloc until 1996, while the MOHW and the OP ran the opponent bloc. The ruling party passively followed government opinion, and the President seemed largely indifferent on the issue. But with the presidential election drawing nearer, the ruling party became a core proponent after 1997. The emasculated government had to accept the decision compromised by political parties. So the large power gap between the two blocs resulted in the decision to partially merge health insurers.

The composition of leading participants in the full merger debate also fluctuated over time. Until 1998, when the National Health Insurance Act was introduced, the new reformist governing elite, progressive civic groups and trade unions were the dominant proponents of the merger, while opponent bloc membership was unclear. The MOHW was excluded from key actors. But from 1999, the governing bloc decided to campaign for postponing the

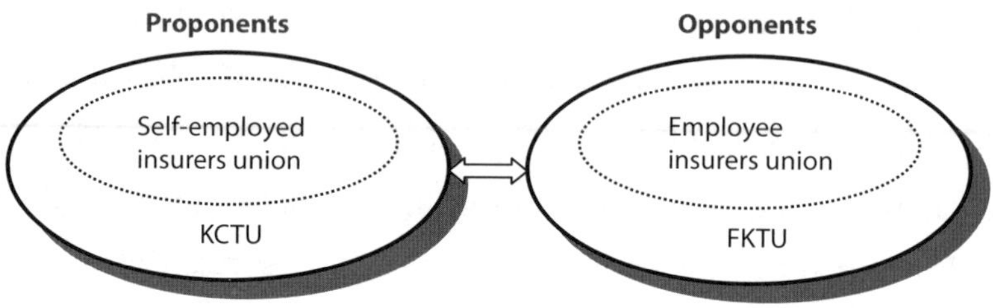

Figure 7.6 Labour-labour conflict in the full merger debate

timing of the merger, breaking up the proponent bloc. On the flip side, opposition parties and conservative trade unions began to clearly oppose the merger. Particularly, trade unions with different policy orientations were key conflicting actors during the second round of the debate (see Figure 7.6).

The intentional exclusion of distasteful policy actors was possible in an authoritative political system, like the Chun administration. But it is too great a leap in argument to say that some policy actors were deliberately excluded from policy networks, despite the small numbers of participants in the first debate. Until that point, the merger issue was not politically serious for the governing bloc. Many potential interests simply did not realise the seriousness of the issue during earlier debates, and civil society was still undeveloped after the turmoil of the military coup.

In fact, it was after the second debate that the intentional exclusion of particular actors became impossible with the rapid progress of democracy. Various civic groups formed a united front to articulate their interests in the merger, and the emergence of progressive peak trade unions made the labour movement much more militant. Opposition parties were freed from state oppression. And, while the Rho administration kept activist civic groups and trade unions at arm's length, the Kim Young-sam administration sporadically brought them inside policy-making circles. The Kim Dae-jung administration went further and tried to incorporate them to check the influence of established conservative groups. Thus, it would be fair to say that all relevant interests were able to enter or leave policy networks freely.

Participants' interests in the issue

While participants in the debates formed two blocs in accordance with their partisan interests in the merger, membership within and of the blocs have fluctuated over time and both their stated and actual interested have changed.

Nonetheless, the fundamental logic behind those proposing or opposing the merger has been consistent over time. Proponents claimed the merger would be better to achieve social justice and minimise management costs. In contrast, opponents listed the merits of a multiple insurer system in maintaining labour-business cooperation and efficiently managing self-governing insurance funds. Participants, therefore, took diametrically opposing positions on the causes and effects of the same phenomenon. Figure 7.7 shows how differently they understood the same phenomenon and Table 7.7 contrasts different views on the single insurer system.

Opponents and proponents of the merger had their own logic under these fundamental differences, rebutting the other party's arguments. But in practice, participants' stated reasons backing their allegations differed from their real ones, although the interests of major participants have remained constant. Table 7.8 and Figure 7.8 summarise changes in each bloc's stated allegations and the real interests of each participant respectively.

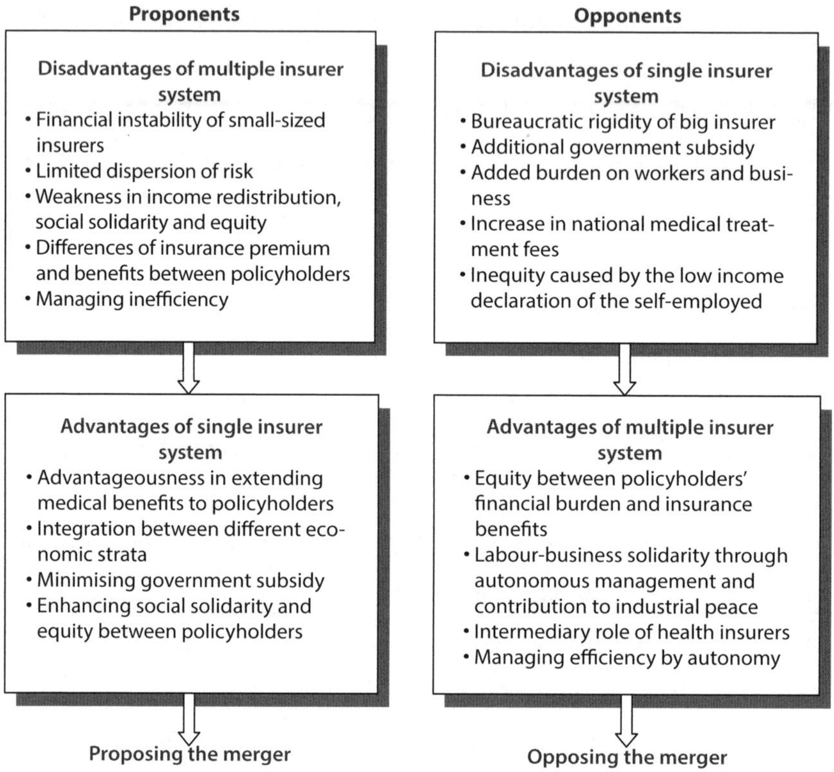

Figure 7.7 Two conflicting views on the health insurer system

Table 7.7 Different interpretations on the merits of a single insurer system

	Proponents	Opponents
Economic efficiency	Increase in managerial efficiency by making a big unified insurer	Inefficiency caused by bureaucratic rigidity and ownership deficiency
Distributional justice	Fulfilment of social equity between different strata by imposing the same criterion of insurance premiums	Aggravation of income redistribution by the low-level income declaration of the self-employed
Government's additional burden	No additional government burden in extending health insurance program by transferring the accumulated insurance funds of employee insurers	Inevitability of additional government subsidies to self-employed insurers

Table 7.8 Formal reasons for proposing or opposing the merger

	Proponents	Opponents
First Debate	For the extension of health insurance program without additional government funding	Direct confrontation between the government and policyholders and the inevitability of the government's additional budget burden
Second Debate	Farmers' high insurance premiums and the preparation for the extension of health insurance to the urban self-employed	Infringement of the constitutional right of property and possible additional government funding
Partial Merger	Increasing budget deficits amongst self-employed insurers and rural residents' demand for the merger	Managing inefficiency
Full Merger	Presidential election pledge and mutual concessions at the tripartite commission, social solidarity between different economic strata	Cancellation of financial merger by reason of possible inequity between different types of policyholders and the impossibility to develop the same criterion of insurance premiums

Resource dependency between participants

During the first debate, resource dependency largely occurred among governing bloc members. The MHSA needed help from other departments to agree on government decisions. The dependency between the MHSA and the OP was necessary to make government policies, but their hostile opinions frustrated the merger attempt proposed by the MHSA, in a situation where the MHSA unilaterally depended on the OP for support. The resource dependency between government departments and the ruling party was also crucial in terms of legitimising policy. Their dependency was relevant during the earlier rounds of the first debate, but it became irrelevant from 1981, when the MHSA disregarded the issue. Other minor participants were also dependent on each other and the government, under the closed political system of the time.

Opposition parties seized the initiative during the second debate and

- **MOHW officials**: easy control over multiple insurers, reappointment of retired officials to health insurers, other personal benefits etc.
- **OP**: Minimisation of the burden on the President's sovereign power, direct confrontation with policyholders
- **Ruling party**: reappointment of party bureaucrats to health insurers, keeping pace with the government
- **Established trade union (FKTU)**: response to demands from affiliated employee insurers union, concerns about the increase in employees' insurance premiums
- **Employee insurers union**: increase of employees' insurance premiums, transfer of accumulated insurance funds to a unified insurer, staff's occupational instability, disadvantage in personnel management
- **Employee health insurers**: occupational instability of directors and officials, benefits from the control of insurance funds
- **Business interests**: increase in insurance premiums for workers and employers, outflow of accumulated insurance funds, loss of control on insurance funds

Opposing the merger

⇕

Proposing the merger

- **OP**: carrying out election pledges, compromise with progressive civic groups and trade unions (in the full merger debate)
- **Ruling party**: winning votes from the self-employed, support from civic groups and implementation of election pledges (in the partial and full merger debates)
- **Opposition parties**: winning votes from the self-employed, taking the political initiative, getting support from civic groups and trade unions
- **Civic groups**: symbolic event for internal unity, realisation of organisational goals like distributive justice, reduction of insurance premiums for farmers and the urban poor, strengthening organisation and civil movement, influence on policy-making
- **Progressive trade union (KCTU)**: opportunity to strengthen organisation, response to demands from affiliated self-employed insurers union, competition with the FKTU
- **Self-employed insurers' union**: transferring established insurance funds, benefits in salary and promotion, increase of job security and financial stability
- **Korea Medical Association**: merits in collecting medical treatment fees

Figure 7.8 **Practical interests of each participant in the merger**

they depended upon civic groups and trade unions for political support. The government and ruling party also acknowledged the necessity to cooperate with civic groups and trade unions, but were reluctant to accept them as official policy partners. Practical inter-dependence between the ruling and opposition parties was also not that meaningful during the second debate, when opposition parties dominated Parliament. Even then, opposition leaders had not admitted the legitimacy of the military-based governing bloc. But the MHSA greatly depended on the resources of the President and the OP as before, in opposing the merger bill.

The partial merger debate coincided with the 1997 presidential election just around the corner. Political parties, irrespective of their status, depended on civic groups and trade unions to win votes in the election. The ruling party and government departments, meanwhile, showed a heavy dependency until 1996 to block the merger attempt of civic groups and opposition parties. But from 1997, the ruling party wanted to secede from the unpopular government, and the lame-duck President could not hold the ruling party within the governing bloc. So, in the new situation where a partial merger bill was brought forward by ruling lawmakers, the ruling and opposition parties no longer relied upon the government to enact the bill.

The full merger debate occurred during the earlier term of presidency and governing bloc members cooperated with each other to support reformist policies. Although MOHW officials were still reluctant to back the merger, they were obliged to follow instructions from new governing elites, as they were unilaterally dependent on them. The resource dependency of the governing bloc on civic groups and trade unions was also urgent to bolster its fragile power base and to overcome the economic crisis. Civic groups depended on the governing bloc, too, in order to achieve their goals. The ruling and opposition parties' inter-dependence was necessary, as the debate unfolded largely in Parliament. Opposition parties and conservative trade unions relied upon each other for support in the forthcoming general election.

2) Participants' interaction: from simple to diverse and mass-level patterns of interaction

Basic nature of interaction

Participants' interaction patterns are directly affected by the policy network structure (Marsh et al., 2001: 10). Participants in the merger debates were divided into two confronting blocs and their basic interaction pattern was one of conflict, despite changes in levels of conflict over time. Members of the same bloc were not always consensual, as their real interests were not identical. In the first debate, conflict largely occurred between bureaucrats with different views on the merger. Key staff in the OP were temporarily dispatched from the MHSA and their conflict with MHSA officials was caused not only by different policy preferences but also by their bureaucratic power game. The relationship between proponents, particularly between the MHSA and the ruling party, was also not so consensual from 1982, as the MHSA gave up proposing the merger.

The second debate occurred in a period of political transition towards democracy. Participants mobilised every possible means to articulate their interests. While the same bloc members were cooperative with each other, the relationship between different blocs was largely hostile. Although the interaction between opposition parties and civic groups had still not matured, they were basically consensual. But interaction patterns between the ruling and opposition parties and between the government and civic groups were principally confrontational, because they all failed to accept each other as respectable partners. The government also distrusted trade unions.

While the two blocs in the partial merger debate were confrontational until 1996, the degree of conflict decreased over time. Major proponents including civic groups and progressive trade unions accepted the legitimacy of the Kim Young-sam government. Despite their different views on the merger, the government and civil society maintained a friendly relationship during the earlier part of Kim's presidency. Ruling and opposition parties' conflicts were also greatly lessened during this period. In particular, the ruling party switched sides and supported the partial merger from 1997, negating any residual conflicts among key actors.

Participants maintained a consensual stance during the first round of the full merger debate, despite their different views on the issue. Particularly, key proponents including the governing bloc and civic groups showed strong cohesiveness due to mutual need. The opponent bloc was also put in a position where it had little choice but to follow the general trend of accepting the merger due to the prevailing economic crisis. Thus, the National Health Insurance Act was enacted in January 1999 without any serious conflict between key participants. But in 1999, when the suspension of the merger began to be discussed, arguments were sparked once again. Antipathy between trade unions with different political orientations was remarkable, along with their intention to take the initiative and leadership of the labour movement. The relationship inside the original proponent bloc also became increasingly confrontational as civic groups pressurised the government to honour its promises.

Frequency of interaction

The first debate developed within the governing bloc, and as a result, major players largely interacted through formal routes. But their frequent interaction was not helpful in settling differences, as they pursued contrasting policy aims. The ruling and opposition parties were also obliged to frequently interact in Parliament, and the MHSA busily debated with political parties during parliamentary discussions. Meanwhile, talks between the government and organised interests were uncommon, and no meaningful coalition was formed even between the same bloc members at the beginning of the debates.

Civic groups and opposition parties took the initiative in proposing the merger during the second debate, but their interaction was not institutionalised and infrequent. On the other hand, talks between the ruling and opposition parties took place in Parliament. Governing actors' interactions were well coordinated to effectively cope with the merger attempt. But the formal and frequent interaction between the governing bloc and civic groups were ad hoc, because the legitimacy or legality of civic groups was still not fully recognised institutionally.

During the partial merger debate, contact between opposition parties and civic groups was frequent owing to some similar policies. Interaction among civic groups became well organised during the 1990s as they set up united fronts to push for the merger. As for the opponent, the government and the ruling party frequently interacted through institutional channels to block any merger attempt. But this all changed in mid-1997, when the ruling party swapped sides to back the partial merger.

Governing bloc members frequently interacted during the full merger debate, in several ways. But their interaction with civic groups and trade unions was infrequent, despite common aims. After 1999, the pattern of formal contact between proponents broke down, as erstwhile partners disagreed about the timing of the merger. Meanwhile, civic groups and progressive trade unions did not pay any attention to contacting opposition parties who had different political views from them. Of the opponents, the FKTU and employee insurers union were united but opposition parties did not meet with them frequently.

Mobilised strategies of interaction

The first debate was led by the governing actors and formal institutions (e.g. inter-departmental conferences) were the major arenas of discussion. Governing actors did not have to resort to radical strategies to achieve their goals. Instead, they depended on various formal and informal meetings to push their opinions. Minor participants, including business associations and health insurers, also largely employed power-level strategies to articulate their interests via informal meetings with government departments. At that time, it was almost impossible for private actors to mobilise mass-level strategies, e.g. massive protests in the shadow of a dictatorial regime. As mentioned before, activist civic groups were not yet permitted, and all trade unions were under tight control.

Of the major participants, the MHSA persuaded the President and other departments of the necessity and merits of a single insurer system, and it mainly used institutional channels like the ruling party-government conference to advertise its message. The MHSA wanted to avoid direct confrontation with the OP. The ruling party also mostly relied upon formal channels to propose the merger and persuaded the President to listen to its case. It pressurised the MHSA into proposing a merger bill instead of directly facing up to the OP itself.

While the OP also interacted with the MHSA and the ruling party through official meetings to win the argument, it largely depended on persuading the President. Minor participants such as trade unions, the KMA and business interests mainly employed power-level strategies of interest articulation, including the publication of letters of support and the participation in government committees.

During the second debate, activist civic groups launched radical mass-level strategies to achieve policy goals. They formed a united front in June 1988 and employed every possible means to back the merger. Self-employed insurers' union adopted radical methods such as illegal sit-in strikes. Vitalised civil society and the oppositional dominance within politics enabled civic groups and trade unions to use a range of strategies to promote their interests.

Governing bloc members interacted through institutional channels as before, but they still did not recognise the legality of civic groups and adopted a confrontational stance towards opposition parties. Opposition parties, who were in a parliamentary majority, compelled the governing bloc to accept the merger, refusing to compromise. Accordingly, the governing bloc resorted to a presidential veto to combat oppositional one-sidedness.

It was noteworthy that the KMA mobilised both power and mass-level strategies to promote its interests. It participated in government committees and held informal meetings with departments on the one hand, and on the other, returned medical licenses in protest at the government's health policy. Sometimes, even pro-government bodies, such as business interests, mobilised mass-level methods, like the issuance of press releases in a politically transitional period.

During the partial merger debate, civic groups played a key role in proposing the merger as before, but their activities softened because the

Kim Young-sam administration was quite friendly towards them. They were invited onto government committees intermittently. Unlike previous cases, the progressive KCTU was also less antagonistic towards the government. Civic groups and trade unions did not have to resort to mass-level strategies as major political parties were committed to introducing a single insurer system. Their main target of interest input was the political party, as Parliament took the political initiative during the final year of Kim's presidency.

Although the ruling party scuppered opposition parties' attempt to introduce the merger in 1996, it changed its mind in 1997 and supported the gradual merger due to the forthcoming presidential election. So, the ruling party cooperated with opposition parties and put forward legislation — a partial merger bill — in November 1997 with lawmakers playing a pivotal role. And, this demonstrated that small numbers of key policy advocates could exert a profound influence in changing the established policy.

From the list of opponents, the MOHW and the OP relied upon a strategy of seeking to persuade the ruling party and other departments of their cases, and formed task teams to improve the multiple insurer system. The MOHW continuously put forward alternatives that would block any possible merger and won over political parties by outlining benefits of a multiple insurer system. Government departments had no choice but to use institutions such as formal meetings.

During the full merger debate, the governing bloc officially allied with civic groups and the KCTU. Accordingly, civic groups and trade unions did not resort to mass-level activities until 1998. The KTC's decision to introduce the full merger was a symbolic event that illustrated a growing institutional consensus between the new governing elite, business and labour. But entering 1999, when the governing bloc decided to postpone the timing of the merger, civic groups and progressive trade unions mobilised all possible mass-level activities to achieve a full and immediate merger. In effect, after 1999 they left their power-level strategies behind and launched protests at the government's decision to delay the merger.

The governing bloc tried to incorporate civil society into the policy-making process, by establishing new institutions like the KTC. The new power bloc in the OP and the ruling party led the debate in the governing camp while the MOHW was excluded from key decision-making. But when entering the second round of this final debate in 1999, the governing bloc's alliance with civic groups and trade unions sharply decreased as a result of its policy change to now delay the merger.

Among opponents of the merger, the main opposition GNP was cooperative in pushing forward with the merger bill in 1998, to keep its presidential election pledge. But after confirming the opposition of its traditional supporters to the merger, the GNP changed sides and decided to fight to suspend the organisational merger and cancel the financial merger. However, the GNP largely stayed within institutional routes in terms of its activities, although it antagonised the ruling party in Parliament.

The FKTU formed a policy coalition with Kim Dae-jung at the 1997 presidential election. It took part in several government committees and agreed to the merger at the KTC. But from the late 1998, the FKTU began to employ radical mass-level input methods, such as street petitions, litigation and non-compliance, to frustrate the merger. Minor opponents, including employee health insurers and business interests, were passive in articulating their interests, as they accepted that most were now in favour of the merger. They just participated in government committees and intermittently issued press releases.

To sum up, public actors, such as government departments and political parties, have largely relied upon the established institutional patterns of activities, irrespective of their opinions on the merger. Although during the first and second debates they were in confrontation with each other, their activities largely followed the defined way of conflict resolution. Meanwhile, with regard to private actors, the activities of civic groups and trade unions fluctuated according to the political context and development of the debates. They used every means at their disposal to promote their interests after the second debate, thereby taking advantage of the completely transformed political system. The government had lost control of them. But during the partial merger debate and the first round of the full merger debate, their activities decreased as they were politically recognised.

5. Policy Outputs: Frequent Policy Paralysis

1) Final outputs and changes in policy content

Policy outputs result from interactions between the preceding components of the analytical framework. In the case studies, while the direct impact of interaction patterns on the policy outputs as final choices has been remarkable, interaction patterns have also been regulated by contextual, institutional and structural constraints. But the relative influence of these precedent components on policy outputs has been inconsistent. Policy outputs affect policy outcomes through enforcement and have adversely impacted upon the precedent components in feedback.

The output of the first debate was to extend health insurance coverage to the self-employed by the then multiple insurer system. The OP's strong opposition and President Chun's final instruction to halt the debate frustrated the first merger attempt. During the debate, the MHSA, an initiator of the debate, changed its detailed proposals several times and eventually discarded the merger plan. Although the ruling party strongly insisted on the merger, it could not survive opposition attacks from the powerful OP under the settings that the MHSA withdrew the support to the merger. Meanwhile, the OP held fast to its faith in a multiple insurer system during the entire period of the debate and succeeded in persuading the President to oppose the merger.

The second debate was triggered by a sharp increase in the insurance premiums of rural residents who were incorporated into the health insurance program from January 1988. With the progress of socio-political democracy, civic groups led by activist farmers and healthcare professionals united to propose the merger. They filed pressure on opposition parties who seized the political initiative at the time, and it seemed that they had achieved the merger by compelling opposition parties to pass the National Medical Insurance Bill in March 1989. However, the final output was distorted by President Rho's veto and the second merger attempt resulted in more frustration.

During the debate civic groups stayed consistently faithful to the merger, despite small changes in terms of the health insurance premium system. But other major participants changed their policies several times as the situation unfolded. Two major opposition parties held their original promises on the merger until March 1989. But from then on, their policies on the merger were inconsistent, belatedly returning to support the original merger plan. The minor opposition party completely changed its policy due to civic groups' sit-in protests in February 1989 and moved to support the merger. Ruling party policy was also unstable. It opposed the merger at first, in line with government departments, but then it worked to pass the merger bill in March 1989. After the presidential veto, it swung back the other way, and completely turned against the proponent bloc again. Although the MHSA and the OP consistently opposed the merger, how they intended to do so in policy terms also changed frequently.

The partial merger debate ended with the successful enactment of the National Medical Insurance Act in November 1997, which pursued a partial organisational merger. Although it was an incomplete merger, excluding the organisational merger with employee health insurers and the financial merger, the debate proved to be the first step towards the full merger. Since then, proponents of the merger have led all of the policy networks.

Major participants changed policies several times. Civic groups and opposition parties, who supported the full merger both organisationally and financially, accepted the ruling party's gradual merger plan as a compromise. In contrast, the ruling party reneged in 1997, with the presidential election just around the corner. It opposed the merger until 1996, keeping pace with the government, but then it began to support the gradual merger from 1997 as a way of winning votes. Of the opponents, the MOHW tried to deflate the issue by proposing the enlargement of the size of health insurers on the basis of a multiple insurer system. But the MOHW and other departments failed to keep a multiple insurer system, as the ruling party broke away from the governing bloc.

The full merger debate consisted of two discernible rounds and policy outputs were different in each. While the first round set the timetable for a relatively speedy full merger by passing the National Health Insurance Act (NHIA) in January 1999, the second round ended in December 1999 with a revision of the Act which postponed the planned merger. The original policy outputs of January 1999 were to complete the organisational merger and to partially merge insurance funds by December 1999 and to finalise the financial merger by December 2001. But under the revision of the Act, dates for final outputs changed to achieving the organisational merger by June 2000, the partial financial merger by December 2000, and the full financial merger by December 2001. The health insurance premium system also changed from the income-based single imposition system to the dual imposition one based on income and salary.

With regard to the change of policy content, civic groups and the KCTU kept their original policy goal of aiming to fully merge health insurers, while the other major participants changed their opinions dramatically as the second round of the debate began. Originally, the new governing elite took the initiative in proposing the merger and their views remained unchanged. But ahead of the 2000 general election, they changed the schedule to postpone the timing of enforcement, worrying about any possible confusion the unprepared merger might cause. Even opponents of the merger, such as the FKTU and opposition parties, agreed to the merger in 1998. But they reversed their positions from 1999 to oppose the full merger and back the idea of separating insurance funds. In the final phase, major opponents adopted a strategy of postponing the organisational merger and blocking the financial merger permanently. Figure 7.9 compares the policy outputs in each case study.

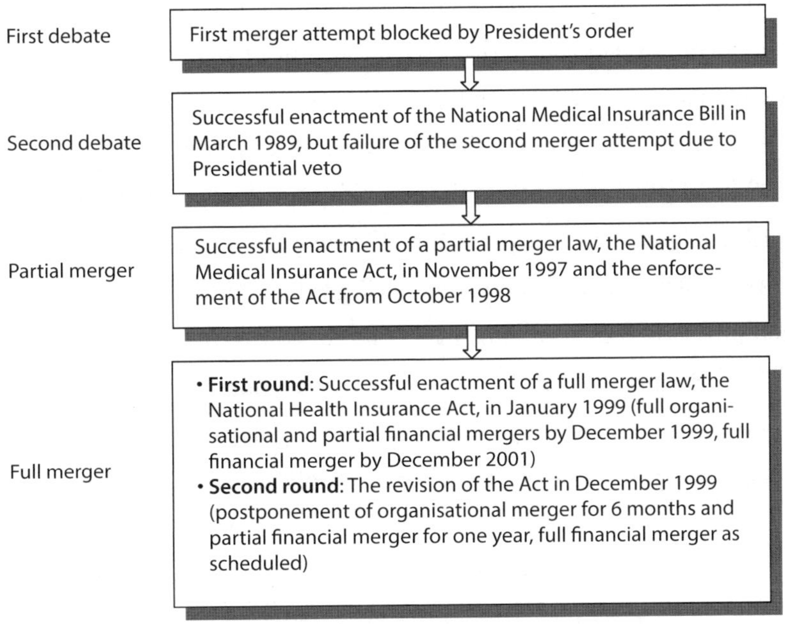

Figure 7.9 Comparison of the final outputs of the debates

2) Reflected interests

Reflected interests have varied over time. During the first debate the OP's interests came out on top, while those of proponents such as the MHSA and the ruling party were neglected. Using the debate as an opportunity, the MOHW rewrote its policy to become the most ardent supporter of the merger. During the earlier rounds of the second debate, civic groups and opposition parties had their interests properly reflected as the merger bill was passed in March 1989. However, the ruling party and the government were able to block the merger attempt by calling on the presidential veto and from then on, refused to compromise with the proponent bloc.

Up to 1996, the government and the ruling party successfully blocked any merger attempt by either civic groups or opposition parties. But the ruling party changed its mind from mid-1997 and put forward a gradual merger plan. The National Medical Insurance Act (NMIA) of November 1997 mainly reflected the ruling party's view, completely neglecting the wishes of government departments. The views of original proponents of the merger, such as opposition parties, civic groups and the KCTU, were partly reflected as part of a parliamentary compromise.

At the first half of the full merger debate, the interests of major proponents, including the governing bloc, civic groups and the KCTU, were largely reflected in the NHIA of January 1999.

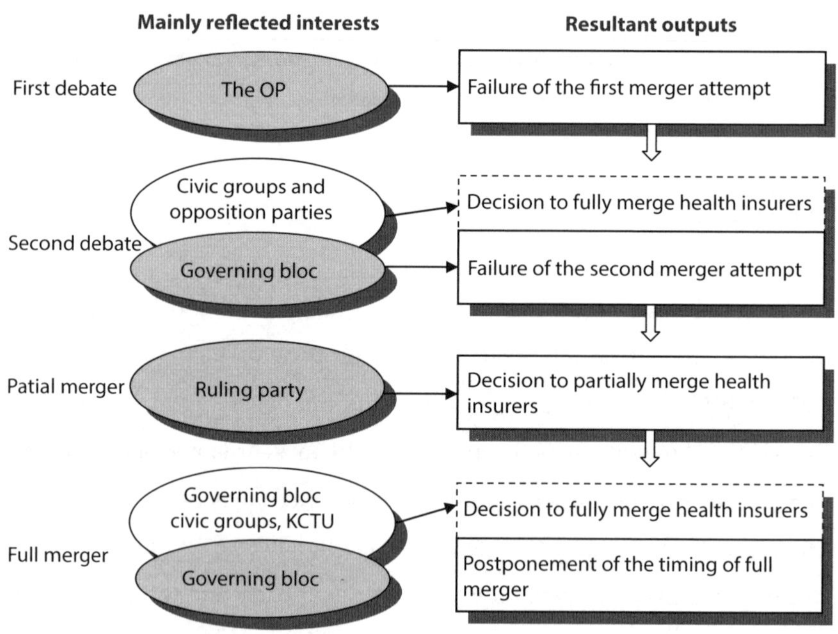

Figure 7.10 Reflected interests and resultant outputs

Figure 7.11 Distinctive characteristics of each analytical component

Although opposition parties and conservative trade unions were reluctant to see the merger, they did not actively oppose the merger itself. But then, interests of the governing bloc shone through in the second half of the debate, succeeding in delaying the merger timing, overcoming the objections of civic groups and the KCTU and the opposition GNP's wish to separate insurance funds. During this second round, the MOHW also actively participated in the debate. Figure 7.10 compares reflected interests combining them with resultant outputs and Figure 7.11 specifies the distinctive content of each component.

Chapter
8

Conclusion

1. Summary and Responses to Research Questions

The findings presented in this book can thus be summarized in six paragraphs. First, among the constituent variables of policy context, the influence of political context on institutions and policy networks was overwhelming in all the case studies. The fundamental political changes from dictatorship to democracy in the late 1980s democratised political institutions, diffused political power and widened the scope of policy networks. In addition, merger debates became a topical issue under strong political influences.

Second, institutional change was closely intertwined with political and social contexts to characterise policy networks and outputs. In this regard, institutional change in politically developing countries like Korea is largely motivated by external factors. Among institutional features, power relationships were the most salient regulators of policy networks and outputs. The severe imbalance between institutions per se and their practice was also noteworthy in a politically turbulent country. While established policies have a certain degree of inertia, path dependency is not an absolute axiom. Changes in the political context, power relations and participants' interests can create a new routes to break the established path.

Third, with the march towards democracy from the late 1980s, the basic structure of policy networks has changed from policy communities to issue networks. Political factors were critical in changing policy networks. From then on, the number of participants doubled and organised interests became actively engaged. The main debating arena also moved from the government to Parliament, and civic groups and trade unions became dominant actors in advocating the merger of health insurers.

Fourth, since the late 1980s the merger debates have become a politically sensitive issue by the initiation of civic groups and opposition parties. Many political actors united to articulate their interests. Civic groups and trade unions made use of the issue to strengthen their political power. In the 1990s it became an important symbol for social policy reform, widely drawing the attention of politicians and civil society. Needless to say, this change greatly impacted policy networks and outputs.

Fifth, of the various components and variables of the analytical framework, participants' interaction patterns were the most direct factor in characterising policy outputs. Network participants are not passive actors who are unilaterally determined by context, institutions and network structures. They enjoy a certain degree of autonomy to filter and reinterpret their constraints.

Finally, although the four major components seem to follow a linear sequence of policy context, institutional features, policy networks and policy outputs, their relationship is actually highly interactive. While the preceding components can have the constraining power on those that follow, constraints are not deterministic. But in contrast to one of the initial hypotheses, reverse influences are very weak and trivial in many cases.

This book has regarded policy-making as a complex, dynamic and political process, being developed under a set of contextual and institutional constraints, and has introduced new institutional and policy network perspectives into a main theoretical framework. Accordingly, the analytical framework was established by combining four major components — policy context, institutional features, policy networks and policy outputs. Specific variables and indices were also developed and research questions were addressed to adapt the analytical framework to empirical analysis.

Throughout, this book demonstrated the huge impact of policy context on institutional change and policy network characteristics. Institutional features were also significant in constraining policy networks, while policy networks shaped the content of policy outputs. Reverse impacts between the four components were also considered, although such relations did not prove to be particularly robust.

Empirical analysis of four case studies attempted to answer six research questions. The first question, relating to the usefulness of the analytical framework, was positively answered by confirming the adequacy of the framework in examining the dynamics of health politics. This book established a comprehensive analytical framework by combining new institutional and policy network perspectives and connecting them to the policy context (as an influencing factor) and policy outputs (as a result). The framework was able to examine the complexity of the two decades of health politics. In particular, the framework was seen to be robust in comparing the changes of policy context and institutions and their influence on policy networks and outputs across time.

In answer to the second question about the influence of policy context on institutions and policy networks, this book has confirmed the big impact of policy context on both components, irrespective of the cases studied. The political context, particularly, was crucial in shaping the features of institutions and policy networks, largely due to the politicised nature of the debate.

The third question addressed institutional constraints on policy networks. Among the variables constituting institutional features, the power relations between political organisations exercised strong constraints over policy networks and as a result on policy outputs. But where decision-making rules mattered, it was more important to understand the practical operation of the rules than the rules per se, because in many cases, there were discrepancies between the rules and their operation. Previous policies influenced interaction patterns as an established path, even though the influence was neither absolute nor permanent.

The fourth question sought to investigate attributes of policy networks and dominant actors. The analysis has highlighted the fundamental changes in policy networks and dominant actors from the second debate, as progress towards political democracy quickened. Policy networks changed from being closed policy communities to open issue networks. Changes in the political context and subsequent institutional change provided the momentum to change policy networks. Dominant actors also changed from governing blocs to civic groups and trade unions.

The fifth question referred to the relationship between policy networks and policy outputs. Through the empirical analysis, this book has demonstrated the defining impact of policy networks, particularly in terms of interaction patterns, on shaping policy outputs, regardless of the cases analysed. Even though interaction patterns were constrained by context, institutions and network structure, they are not unilaterally determined. Participants had the discretion to choose their preferred option.

In response to the final question, this book has confirmed the interactive relationship between the four analytical components. In particular, the ordinal influence of political context, power relations, network structure, interaction patterns, and policy outputs was salient.

2. Theoretical and Practical Implications

In light of these findings, important implications can be outlined.

1-1. Policy context, particularly the political context, is critical in characterising institutions and policy networks. Democratisation generates balanced power relationships and democratic political institutions, and such institutional changes, in general, produce open issue networks. In Korea, political democratisation from mid-1987 has transformed policy networks into open issue networks. Thus, understanding the policy context and its impact on institutions and policy networks is vital to adequately explore policy dynamics, and in this regard, it is necessary to combine perspectives of policy determination and policy networks.

1-2. Social and political contexts are closely intertwined. Notably, the vitality of civil society is directly affected by the degree of political democratisation. In Korea, civil society has been greatly empowered since 1987 with the progress of political democracy, and a vitalised civil society has accelerated the democratisation of politics and policy-making. Thus, connecting political and social contexts is imperative to fully understand general policy contexts.

2-1. The basic institutions of the political system — particularly the Constitution and politics-related laws — prescribe the power relations between political agencies in general. In addition, the power relationship, as a macro institution, greatly affects the practical operation of decision-making. In many cases, there is a big difference between decision-making rules per se and their real operation. Participants do not respect rules and many veto points are not carried out. Accordingly, an urgent study of the practical operation of institutions is needed as well as the study of institutions per se.

2-2. The power relationship between political organisations also greatly affect policy networks along with political context, by constraining network participants and their resource dependence. Arguably, the democratic political system and balanced power relations tend to make policy networks more open and fluid. But they do not directly decide the shape of policy networks, because they are rearranged by leading participants. Thus, it is necessary to develop a framework to understand the interaction between power relations, interests and resource dependency.

2-3. Institutions have a tendency to persist. In particular, culturally embedded institutions like decision-making rules require time to change. The ringi system as an intra-department decision-making mechanism has been preserved, and inter-departmental and parliamentary decision-making rules have remained unchanged. They were inclusive and democratic from the start, as decision-making rules in Korea largely followed Western ideas. In many cases, operators of institutions have no need to change formal institutions, as they can arbitrarily manage them in a politically transitional society where a sharp discrepancy exists between formal institutions and reality. However, despite the relative stability of decision-making rules, their practical operation has fluctuated according to differing power relations and the preferences of those setting the rules.

2-4. In politically turbulent countries like Korea, it might be more important to seek out the causes of institutional changes from the power and interest relationships between policy actors rather than from internal factors intrinsic to institutions. The change in the health insurer system was largely attributable to interest conflict and the relative power resource between those in favour or against the merger. Additionally, political events provided a policy window. In this regard the combination of historical institutionalism with the concept of Kingdon's (2003) policy window may be useful in explaining policy dynamics in turbulent politics.

2-5. Established policies also have a tendency to persist. For this reason, Korea's health policy-making has demonstrated incremental changes, albeit against the backdrop of a sudden change in the policy context. But the main reason for maintaining current policies is attributable not to the inertia of institutions per se, but more to the interest relationship surrounding them. Beneficiaries of current policies wish to maintain established policies (Ikenberry, 1988: 224), whilst losers try to alter them. In the case studies, the multiple insurer system was an established policy and opponents of the merger had vested interests in retaining it. For this reason, combining the policy network perspective with new institutionalism is advantageous in examining the relationship between established policies and policy actors' interests.

3-1. When the policy network is divided into network structure and interactions, the former operates as a constraint on the latter. For example, participants' practical interests in the issue and their resource dependency regulate interaction strategies to a considerable degree. But, in some cases, the issue network type interaction can occur even under the network structure of policy communities. Participants can select diverse strategies of interaction under the constraints of such a network structure.

3-2. The sensitivity of policy actors' interests to the issue is highly influential on deciding the scope and numbers of participants and the pattern of interaction. The more sensitive the issue is, the more participants engage in the debate and the more radical and diverse the interaction patterns are. Although the merger issue is related to healthcare policy, physicians and pharmacists did not actively engage in the debates, as it was not so sensitive to their occupational interests. Thus, the sensitivity or vitality of an issue to relevant actors' interests is another variable to be analysed in reviewing policy-making dynamics.

3-3. Participants must be able to trust each other to maintain policy networks and to work together for their mutual benefit (Keast et al., 2004: 366). When participants keep their word and their behavioural patterns are predictable, mutual trust can be established. But in most cases, network participants in Korea distrusted each other and easily broke promises in pursuit of self-interest. For this reason, policy networks in Korea have usually been unstable and turbulent. In the case studies, the ruling party tore up its parliamentary agreement in the second debate to recommend a presidential veto, and the governing bloc under the Kim Dae-jung administration postponed the scheduled full merger even before its enforcement.

3-4. Sabatier and Weible's (2007) 'advocacy coalition' and Kingdon's (2003) 'policy window' are helpful concepts to understand the internal dynamics of policy networks. In the case studies, merger proponents built advocacy coalitions from the late 1980s to effectively promote the merger. Regarding the policy window, the presidential election in the partial merger debate and the alternation of governing power in the full merger debate were important political events, which enabled proponents to dominate policy networks. Also, quantitative network analysis can be used in analysing participants' interaction, i.e. the frequency of interaction, in order to add a quantitative explanation to the qualitative traits of the policy network perspective.

3-5. The venue in which an issue is debated can also affect the nature of policy networks. While the debates in Parliament tend to generate an issue network, the government-centric debates have a tendency to be more closed and stabilised. In essence, parliamentary decision-making processes are much more turbulent than governmental ones. In the case studies, the network structure in the first debate was closed and interaction patterns were largely institutionalised amidst the government-centric debate. Then, policy networks were transformed and became closer to issue networks from the second debate, within a Parliament-centric debate.

3-6. Despite changes in politics and power relationships, agreement from the government or the strong ruling party is necessary to formulate or change policies. Change of policies or institutions is unlikely without agreement from the governing bloc, even against a democratic backdrop. The first merger attempt foundered due to opposition from the OP, while the second debate was stopped by the President's veto. In contrast, the success of the partial merger was only possible because the ruling party changed sides and campaigned for the merger. The full merger was also achievable because of leadership from the new governing elite. Thus, the willingness and interest of the governing bloc should be closely examined to better understand institutional change and policy dynamics.

In addition, the President's capacity to control the governing bloc is also important in shaping policy outputs. When the President has little control, policy-making tends to be turbulent and policy outputs unpredictable. Accordingly, whether the debates occur in the latter or earlier part of a presidential term might be important for exploring policy dynamics. Also, policy change is more probable when the change initiators' needs are combined with political opportunities such as presidential elections and a power handover.

4-1. Understanding the influence of policy outputs on policy networks and policy implementation is also required. Until now policy outputs have been regarded as a dependent variable decided by the policy context and policy-making. But researchers need to examine the interactive relationship of how policy outputs affect policy networks backward and policy implementation forward. Policy outputs are not only the result of policy-making but also another starting point in the policy process. In this respect, the analytical framework of this thesis, based on the concept of interactive relationships between the four major components, can effectively add to existing perspectives on policy-making.

4-2. Policy outputs in the debates have been the result of a gradual change in existing policies. To a degree, incremental policy change is inevitable in circumstances where many confronting interests actively engage in the debates. As incrementalism in decision-making theory contends, mutual adjustment has been necessary to alleviate conflicting interests (Hill, 2014: 149-50).

3. Towards a Better Understanding of Policy Dynamics

This book introduced three components, which have previously been applied independently, as the constraining factors on policy outputs and observed these components interactive and dialectical relations. The motivation was based on the belief that the reality of policy dynamics cannot be properly understood without analysing interrelated components. This book has demonstrated the interactive relationship between the four main components suggested in the analytical framework through the comparative case studies on health reform. Thus, it is surmised that this book can contribute to more vividly describing the dynamics of health politics in politically turbulent countries like Korea.

This book should be supplemented with future research, given some limitations of the current research. First, efforts to develop more detailed and tangible concepts and variables should be continuously pursued both theoretically and methodologically. Currently, researchers have difficulty in finding common ground on concepts and variables when they seek to study policy context and institutions. There is also a need to discover more specific and systemic variables to better understand policy networks and policy outputs.

Second, more delicate theoretical attempts to amalgamate new institutionalism and the policy network perspective should be further explored. By resorting only to the policy network perspective, researchers may encounter difficulties in exploring the institutional constraints on policy-making. In turn, the new institutional perspective without the assistance from the policy network framework may fail to sufficiently explain the inter-dependency between institutions and interaction patterns.

Third, more work on the combination of sub-institutional perspectives is recommended for future research. Of the three strains of new institutionalism, the urgency of fusing historical and rational choice institutionalism has been confirmed in this book. A full examination of institutional dynamism is impossible with only a single perspective on institutions.

Fourth, there is still a need to develop more discernible criteria to distinguish context, institutions and structure. Researchers currently debate over the conceptual broadness of these ideas. Even among institutional and policy network theorists, there are uncompromising disputes over the distinctions and sequence between the concepts of institutions and structure. Accordingly, further research to develop clearer variables between related concepts should be pursued.

Fifth, other theoretical concepts, including those of advocacy coalition, policy windows, political opportunity and network analysis, might also be amalgamated into the analytical framework developed by this book in future research.

Sixth, an effort to promote both the objectivity and generalisation of research findings is imperative. Lower levels of objectivity and difficulties in generalising findings are long-standing disadvantages of new institutionalism, the policy network perspective and the case study approach. This book has tried to increase research objectivity by devising an elaborate analytical framework and employing mixed research methods. But in the future, quantitative methods, like survey research, can be added even for limited variables like participants' interests in the issues. Above all, a wider collection of data and deeper levels of interviewing ought to be conducted to upgrade the objectivity and explanatory power of empirical research.

Seventh, regarding the comparison of case studies, this book has focused on a longitudinal comparison within the same specific area of health policy. But other types of comparison can be made in the future. Cross-sectional comparison between different policy sectors may be possible, enabling researchers to compare the impact of the nature of policy areas on policy networks and outputs. Comparison of social policy with economic one is an example. The differences or similarities between sub-level policies within a broader policy area may also be explored.

Eighth, the extent that a policy issue is sensitive to relevant policy actors might be explored as another component to the analytical framework. This book partly confirmed the fact that the sensitivity of the agenda might influence the number of participants. Focused studies based on specific variables like the difference between the political system or power relationship can also be carried out. By focusing on specific variables, researchers can analyse a single case more profoundly.

Finally, the concept of policy outputs as a final choice of policy-making can be extended to the concept of policy outcomes by linking policy-making to an implementation stage. That is, the analytical framework of this book can be adapted to explore policy outcomes and impacts, by extending its research scope.

Abbreviations

CCEJ	Citizens' Coalition for Economic Justice
DLP	Democratic Liberal Party
EPB	Economic Planning Board
FKI	Federation of Korean Industries
FKTU	Federation of Korean Trade Unions
GNP	Grand National Party
HCRC	Healthcare Reform Committee
KCTU	Korean Confederation of Trade Unions
KEF	Korean Employers Federation
KMA	Korean Medical Association
KMIC	Korea Medical Insurance Corporation
KTC	Korea Tripartite Commission
MDP	Millennium Democratic Party
MHSA	Ministry of Health and Social Affairs
MIIPB	Medical Insurance Integration Planning Board
MOHW	Ministry of Health and Welfare
MSPC	Medical Security Promotion Committee
MSRC	Medical Security Reform Committee
NCHIU	National Conference for Health Insurance Unification
NCMII	National Conference for Medical Insurance Integration
NCNP	National Congress for New Politics
NCSIR	National Conference for Social Insurance Reform
NDRP	New Democratic Republican Party
NFMI	National Federation of Medical Insurance

NHIA	National Health Insurance Act
NHIC	National Health Insurance Corporation
NKP	New Korea Party
NMIA	National Medical Insurance Act
NMIC	National Medical Insurance Corporation
OP	Office of the President
OPM	Office of the Prime Minister
PPD	Party for Peace and Democracy
PSPD	People's Solidarity for Participatory Democracy
PUC	Presidency Undertaking Commission
RDP	Reunification Democratic Party
ULD	United Liberal Democrats

Bibliography

Abrutyn, S. and J. H. Turner (2011), 'The old institutionalism meets the new institutionalism', *Sociological Perspectives* 54 (3), pp. 283-306.

Anderson, J. E. (2015), *Public Policy-Making: An Introduction*, Stamford, CT: Cengage Learning.

Béland, D. (2005), 'Ideas and social policy: An institutionalist perspective', *Social Policy and Administration* 39 (1), pp. 1-18.

________ (2010), 'Policy change and health care research', *Journal of Health Politics, Policy and Law* 35 (4), pp. 615-41.

Blom-Hansen, J. (1997), 'A new institutional perspective on policy networks', *Public Administration* 75, pp. 669-93.

Bomberg, E. (1998), 'Issue networks and the environment: explaining European Union environmental policy', in D. Marsh (ed.), *Comparing Policy Networks*, Buckingham: Open University Press.

Börzel, T. A. (1998), 'Organizing Babylon: on the different conceptions of policy network', *Public Administration* 76, pp. 253-73.

Breen, M. (1998), *The Koreans: Who they are, What they want, Where their future lies*, London: Orion Business Books.

Bridges, B. (2001), *Korea after the Crash: The Politics of Economic Recovery*, London: Routledge.

Bulkeley, H. (2000), 'Discourse coalitions and the Australian climate change policy network', *Government and Policy* 18, pp. 727-48.

Buzo, A. (2002), *The Making of Modern Korea*, London: Routledge.

Choi, Jong-kyun (2003), *Democratisation and the Political Welfare Reform: The Develop-*

ment of Public Pensions and National Health Insurance in Korea, 1961-2002, Unpublished PhD Dissertation, Kent University, UK.

Chun, Chang-bae (2005), *Two Paths of Health Care Reforms: Korea and the United States*, Unpublished PhD Dissertation at the Hankuk University of Foreign Studies.

Chun, Chang-bae, Soon-yang Kim, Jun-young Lee, and Sang-yi Lee (2009), *Health Systems in Transition: Republic of Korea*, Copenhagen, Denmark: World Health Organization.

Cnudde, C. F. and R. J. McCrone (1968), 'Party competition and welfare policies in the American states,' *American Political Science Review* 62 (December), pp. 1220-31.

Cobb, R. W. and C. D. Elder (1983), *Participation in American Politics: The Dynamics of Agenda-Building*, Baltimore, MD: The Johns Hopkins University Press.

Cochran, C. E., L. C. Mayer, T. R. Carr, N. J. Cayer, and M. Mckenzie (2003), *American Public Policy*, Belmont, CA: Wadsworthy/Thomson.

Collins, N. (1995), 'Agricultural policy networks of the Republic of Ireland and Northern Ireland', *Political Studies* 43, pp. 664-82.

Cope, S. (2001), 'Analysing criminal justice policy-making: towards a policy networks approach?', in M. Ryan et al. (eds.), *Policy Networks in Criminal Justice*, Basingstoke, Hampshire: Palgrave, pp. 1-20.

Coxall, B. (2001), *Pressure Groups in British Politics*, London: Longman.

Daugbjerg, C. (1998), *Policy Networks under Pressure: Pollution Control, Policy Reform and the Power of Farmers*, Aldershot: Ashgate.

Davaki, K. and E. Mossialos (2005), 'Plus ça change: health sector reforms in Greece', *Journal of Health Politics, Policy and Law* 30 (1-2), pp. 143-67.

Dawson, R. E. and J. A. Robinson (1963), 'Inter-party competition, economic variables, and welfare policies in the American states', *Journal of Politics* 25 (May), pp. 265-89.

Derthick, M. (1979), *Policy-Making for Social Security*, Washington D. C.: the Brookings

Institution.

Dorey, P. (2005), *Policy Making in Britain: An Introduction*, London: SAGE Publications.

Dowding, K. (1995), 'Model or metaphor?: a critical review of the policy network approach', *Political Studies* 43, pp. 136-58.

Döhler, M. (1991), 'Policy networks, opportunity structures and neo-conservative reform strategies in health policy', in B. Marin and R. Mayntz (eds.), *Policy Networks: Empirical Evidence and Theoretical Considerations*, Frankfurt am Main: Westview Press, pp. 235-86.

Dye, T. R. (1966), *Politics, Economics, and the Public: Policy Outcomes in the American States*, Chicago, IL: Rand McNally & Company.

________ (1998), *Understanding Public Policy*, Upper Saddle River, NJ: Prentice-Hall.

Easton, D. (1979), *A Framework for Political Analysis*, Chicago, IL: The University of Chicago Press.

Enroth, H. (2011), 'Policy network theory', in M. Bevir (ed.), *The SAGE Handbook of Governance*, London: SAGE Publications, pp. 19-35.

Fawcett, P. and C. Daugbjerg (2012), 'Explaining governance outcomes: Epistemology, network governance and policy network analysis', *Political Studies Review* 10 (2), pp. 195-207.

Fenton, J. H. (1966), *People and Parties in Politics*, Grenview, IL: Scott, Foresman.

Gil, Hong-keun (2000), *The State and the Policy Process in Korea: State Capacity and Labour Policy in the Transition Period, 1962-1997*, Unpublished PhD Dissertation, Kent University, UK.

Goodin, R. E. (1996), 'Institutions and their design', in R. E. Goodin (ed.), *The Theory of Institutional Design*, Cambridge: Cambridge University Press, pp. 1-53.

Grant, W. (2000), *Pressure Groups and British Politics*, New York, NY: St. Martin's Press.

Groenendijk, N. (2001), 'Multi-level governance, network governance and fiscal federalism theory', the paper presented at Multi-level Governance: Interdisciplinary

Perspectives, Halifax Hall, Sheffield University, UK.

Hague, R. and M. Harrop (2001), *Comparative Government and Politics: An Introduction*, Basingstoke, Hampshire: Palgrave.

Hall, P. A. (1986), *Governing the Economy: The Politics of State Intervention in Britain and France*, New York, NY: Oxford University Press.

________ (1992), 'The movement from Keynesianism to monetarism: institutional analysis and British economic policy in the 1970s', in S. Steinmo et al. (eds.), *Structuring Politics: Historical Institutionalism in Comparative Analysis,* Cambridge: Cambridge University Press, pp. 90-113.

Ham, C. (1999), *Health Policy in Britain*, Basingstoke, Hampshire: Palgrave.

Heclo, H. (1978), 'Issue networks and the executive establishment', in A. King (ed.), *The American Political System*, Washington, D.C.: AEI.

Heclo, H. and A. Wildavsky (1974), *The Private Government of Public Money*, London: Macmillan.

Heo, U. and T. Roehrig (2011), *South Korea since 1980*, New York, NY: Cambridge University Press.

Heywood, A. (2002), *Politics*, Basingstoke, Hampshire: Palgrave.

Hill, M. (2003), 'Social policy and the political process', in P. Alcock et al. (ed.), *The Student's Companion to Social Policy*, Oxford: Blackwell Publishing, pp. 167-72.

________ (2014), *The Public Policy Process*, Harlow, Essex: Pearson Education Ltd.

Hoare, J. and S. Pares (2000), *Korea: The Classic Introduction*, London: Kegan Paul.

Hudson, J. and S. Lowe (2004), *Understanding the Policy Process: Analysing Welfare Policy and Practice*, Bristol: The Policy Press.

Hwang, Kyung-moon (2010), *A History of Korea*, Basingstoke, Hampshire: Palgrave.

Ikenberry, G. J. (1988), 'An institutional approach to American foreign economic policy', in G. J. Ikenberry et al. (eds.), *The State and Foreign Economic Policy*, Ithaca, NY: Cornell University Press.

John, P. and A. Cole (1998), 'Sociometric mapping techniques and the comparison of policy networks: economic decision making in Leeds and Lille', in D. Marsh (ed.), *Comparing Policy Networks,* Buckingham: Open University Press, pp. 132-46.

Jones, B. (1998), *Politics UK*, London: Prentice Hall.

Jordan, A. G. and K. Schubert (1992), 'A preliminary ordering of policy network labels', *European Journal of Political Research* 21, pp.7-27.

Jordana, J. and D. Sancho (2005), 'Policy networks and market opening: telecommunications liberalisation in Spain', *European Journal of Political Research* 44, pp. 519-46.

Keast, R. et al. (2004), 'Network structures: working differently and changing expectations', *Public Administration Review* 64 (3), pp. 363-71.

Kickert, W. M., E.-H. Klijn, and J. M. Koppenjan (1997), 'Managing networks in Public Sector: findings and reflections', in W. M. Kickert et al. (eds.), *Managing Complex Networks: Strategies for the Public Sector*, London: SAGE Publications, pp. 1-13.

Kihl, Young-whan (2005), *Transforming Korean Politics: Democracy, Reform and Culture*, New York, NY: M. E. Sharpe.

Kim, Hun-jin (2003), *An Analysis of the Policy-Making Process of the National Health Insurance Scheme in the Republic of Korea*, Unpublished PhD Dissertation, Edinburgh University, UK.

Kim, Soon-yang (2011), 'The political dynamics of policy networks and advocacy coalitions in South Korea's healthcare policymaking', *Korean Journal of Social Welfare Studies* 42 (4), pp. 61-102.

________ (2015), 'An analysis of South Korea's policy responses to economic crises in 1997 and 2008', *Korean Policy Science Review* 19 (2), pp. 1-29.

Kim, Sun-hyuk (2000), *Democratization in Korea: The Role of Civil Society*, Pittsburgh, PA: University of Pittsburgh Press.

________ (2010), 'Civil society and democratization in South Korea', in C. K. Armstrong (ed.), *Korean Society: Civil Society, Democracy and the State*, Abingdon, England: Routledge, pp. 53-71.

Kingdon, J. W. (2003), *Agendas, Alternatives and Public Policies*, New York, NY: Longman.

Knoke, D., F. U. Pappi, J. Broadbent, and Y. Tsujinaka (1996), *Comparing Policy Networks: Labour Politics in the US, Germany and Japan*, Cambridge: Cambridge University Press.

Koelble, T. A. (1995), 'The new institutionalism in political science and sociology', *Comparative Politics* 27 (2), pp. 231-45.

Koo, H. (2007), 'Engendering civil society: The role of the labor movement', in C. K. Armstrong (ed.), *Korean Society: Civil Society, Democracy and the State*, Abingdon, England: Routledge, pp. 73-94.

Krasner, S. D. (1984), 'Approaches to the state: alternative conceptions and historical dynamics', *Comparative Politics* 16 (2), pp. 223-46.

Kwon, Huck-ju (1999), *The Welfare State in Korea: The Politics of Legitimation*, Basingstoke, Hampshire: Macmillan Press.

Kwon, Soon-man (2003), 'Health care financing reform and the new single payer system in the Republic of Korea: social solidarity or efficiency?', *International Social Security Review* 56 (1), pp. 75-94.

Lipson, W. et al. (1995), *American Government: Politics and Political Culture*, Minneapolis, MN: West Publishing Co.

Lowi, T. (1969), *The End of Liberalism*, New York, NY: Norton.

Lowndes, V. (2009), 'New institutionalism and urban politics', in J. Davies and D. Imbroscio (eds.), *Theories of Urban Politics*, London: SAGE Publications, pp. 91-105.

Lowndes, V. and M. Roberts (2013), *Why Institutions Matter: The New Institutionalism in Political Science*. Basingstoke, Hampshire: Palgrave.

March, J. G. and J. P. Olsen (2006), *Rediscovering Institutions: The Organizational Basis of Politics*, New York, NY: Free Press.

Marsh, D. (1995), *State Theory and The Policy Network Model*, Strathclyde Papers on

Government and Politics No. 102.

________ (1998a), 'The development of the policy network approach', in D. Marsh (ed.), *Comparing Policy Networks*, Buckingham: Open University Press, pp. 3-17.

________ (1998b), 'The utility and future of policy network analysis', in D. Marsh (ed.), *Comparing Policy Networks*, Buckingham: Open University Press, pp. 185-97.

Marsh, D. and R. A. W. Rhodes (1992), 'Policy communities and issue networks: beyond typology', in D. Marsh and R. A. W. Rhodes (eds.), *Policy Networks in British Government*, Oxford: Oxford University Press.

Marsh, D., D. Richards, and M. J. Smith (2001), *Changing Patterns of Governance in the United Kingdom: Reinventing Whitehall?*, Basingstoke, Hampshire: Palgrave.

McFarland, A. (1987), 'Interest groups and theories of power in America', *British Journal of Political Science* 17 (1), pp. 129-47.

Meyer, H. D. and M. B. Rowan (2012), *The New Institutionalism in Education*, Albany, NY: SUNY Press.

Minnich, D. J. (2003), 'Corporatism and income inequality in the global economy: a panel study of 17 OECD countries', *European Journal of Political Research* 42, pp. 23-53.

Montpetit, E. (2005), 'A Policy network explanation of biotechnology policy differences between the United States and Canada', *Journal of Public Policy* 25 (3), pp. 339-66.

Nordlinger, E. (1987), 'Taking the state seriously', in M. Weiner and S. Huntington (eds.), *Understanding Political Development: An Analytic Study*, New York, NY: Little Brown, pp. 353-90.

Oberdorfer, D. (1997), *The Two Koreas: A Contemporary History*, Indianapolis, IN: Basic Books.

Oliver, A. and E. Mossialos (2005), 'European health systems reforms: looking backward to see forward?', *Journal of Health Politics, Policy and Law* 30 (1-2), pp. 7-28.

Palumbo, D. J. (1994), *Public Policy in America: Government in Action*, San Diego, CA:

Harcourt Brace Jovanovich Publishers.

Parsons, W. (2003), *Public Policy: An Introduction to the Theory and Practice of Policy Analysis*, Cheltenham, England: Edward Elgar.

Peters, B. G. (2004), *American Public Policy: Promise and Performance*, Washington, D. C.: CQ Press.

________ (2011), *Institutional Theory in Political Science: The New Institutionalism*, London: Continuum.

Powell, W. W. and P. J. DiMaggio (eds.) (2012), *The New Institutionalism in Organizational Analysis*, Chicago, IL: University of Chicago Press.

Rhodes, R. A. W. (1988), *Beyond Westminster and Whitehall*, London: Unwin Hyman.

________ (1990), 'Policy networks: a British perspective', *Journal of Theoretical Politics* 2 (3), pp. 293-317.

________ (1997), *Understanding Governance: Policy Networks, Governance, Reflexivity and Accountability*, Buckingham: Open University Press.

Richardson, J. (2000), 'Government, interest groups and policy change'. <www.nuffield.ox.ac.uk/People/sites/Richardson/Publication%20Files/Government%20Interest%20Groups%20and%20Policy.pdf, 2016.4.10.>

Richardson, J. and A. G. Jordan (1979), *Governing under Pressure*, Oxford: Martin Robertson.

Ripley, R. and G. Franklin (1991), *Congress, the Bureaucracy and Public Policy*, Homewood, IL: Dorsey.

Robinson, M. E. (2007), *Korea's Twentieth-Century Odyssey: A Short History*, Honolulu, HI: University of Hawaii Press.

Rushefsky, M. E. and K. Patel (1998), *Politics, Power & Policy Making: The Case of Health Care Reform in the 1990s*, New York, NY: M. E. Sharpe.

Sabatier, P. A. and C. M. Weible (2007), 'The advocacy coalition framework: innovations and Clarifications', in P. A. Sabatier (ed.), *Theories of the Policy Process*, Boulder, CO:

Westview, pp. 189-220.

Seth, M. J. (2010), *A Concise History of Modern Korea: From the late Nineteenth Century to the Present*, Lanham, MD: Rowman and Littlefield Publishers.

Shively, W. P. (2003), *Power Choice*, New York, NY: McGraw-Hill.

Sitek, M. (2010), 'The new institutional approaches to health care reform: Lessons from reform experiences in Central Europe', *Journal of Health Politics, Policy and Law* 35 (4), pp. 569-93.

Skocpol, T. (1995), 'Why I am a historical institutionalist', *Polity* 28 (1), pp. 103-106.

Smith, M. J. (1993), *Pressure, Power and Policy: State Autonomy and Policy Networks in Britain and the United States*, New York, NY: Harvester Wheatsheaf.

________ (1995), *Pressure Politics*, Manchester: Baseline Books.

Tat, Yan Kong (2000), 'Power alternation in Korea', *Government and Opposition* 35 (3), pp. 370-91.

Thelen, K. and S. Steinmo (1992), 'Historical institutions in comparative politics', in S. Steinmo et al. (eds.), *Structuring Politics: Historical Institutionalism in Comparative Analysis*, Cambridge: University of Cambridge Press, pp. 1-30.

Waarden, F. van (1992), 'Dimensions and types of policy networks', *European Journal of Political Research* 21, pp. 29-51.

Williams, A. (2004), 'Governance and sustainability: an investigation of the role of policy mediators in the European Union policy process', *Policy & Politics* 32 (1), pp. 95-110.

Wilsford, D. (2010), 'The logic of policy change: Structure and agency in political life', *Journal of Health Politics, Policy and Law* 35 (4), pp. 663-80.

Wong, J. (2004), *Health Democracies: Welfare Politics in Taiwan and South Korea*, Ithaca, NY: Cornell University Press.

Yishai, Y. (1992), 'From an iron triangle to an iron duet?: Health policy-making in Israel', *European Journal of Political Research* 21, pp. 91-108.

(Korean)

Ahn, Byeong-chul (2003), 'Institution and reaction of organisation: the wage policy of the MOL and the medical payment policy of the MHW', *Korean Public Administration Review* 37 (2), pp. 243-61.

Ahn, Hee-young (2001), 'A study on the equity in the process of social insurance policy implementation', *Professorial Journal of Seoul Christian University* 7, pp. 261-81.

Bae, Han-dong (2004), 'The role of NGOs in consolidating democracy in Korea', *Korean Journal of Political Science* 12 (1), pp. 393-417.

Baek, Seung-ho (2001), 'A study on the policy-making process of the integration of health insurance system', *Korean Social Science* 23 (2), pp. 151-49.

Baik, Seung-ki (2010), 'A comparative study on the health insurance integration policy by using the advocacy coalition framework', *Korean Public Administration Review* 44 (4), pp. 233-59.

Cha, Heung-bong (1991), *Comparative Social Welfare*, Seoul: Ulyoo Moonhwasa.

________ (1992), 'The development of medical security system in Korea', in Lee Doo-ho et al. (eds.), *National Medical Security*, Seoul: Nanam Publishing Co., pp. 245-357.

________ (1996), 'The policy-making process of medical insurance', presented at the Korean Academy of Social Welfare, pp. 98-108.

Chai, Jeong-min (2001), 'The structure and function of Korea's National Assembly', *Korean Journal of Political Science* 9 (1), pp. 173-209.

Cho, Chan-rye (2003), 'The conservatives and progressives in modern Korean history', in Kim Yu-nam (ed.), *The Korean Polity: Issues and Tasks*, Seoul: Hanul Books.

Choi, Jeong-won (2001), 'Characteristics and changes of the legislation process in the Korean National Assembly', *Korean Political Science Review* 35 (3), pp.129-51.

Choi, Sung-doo (2000), 'An evaluation on the policy design and feasibility of the medical insurance integration in Korea', *Korean Policy Studies Review* 9 (1), pp. 369-90.

Cho, Suk-joon (2004), *Korean Public Administration and Organisational Culture*, Seoul: Daeyoung Moonhwasa.

Chung, Chung-kil (1994), *Public Policy*, Seoul: Daemyoung Publishings.

Chung, Hong-ki and Jeong-chan Cho (2001), *National Health Insurance Law*, Seoul: Korea Legislation Research Institute.

Chung, Young-kug (2003), *The Korean Political Process*, Seoul: Baiksan Publishing House.

FKTU (1981) (1998) (1999) (2000), *Annual Report*.

Ha, Min-cheol and Gyoun-soo Yoon (2004), 'Organisations' equivocal enactment, dilemma, and institutionalisation: a case study on the institutionalisation process of the Korea Tripartite Commission', *Korean Public Administration Review* 38 (4), pp. 63-84.

Ha, Se-hun (2003), 'The dynamics of the deliberative function in the National Assembly', *Korean Journal of Political science* 10 (3), pp. 267-86.

Hahm, Sung-deuk (2000), 'Evaluation of the Korean presidents' performance based on the inauguration promises', *Korean Political Science Review* 34 (4), pp. 93-118.

Han, Suk-tae (1999), 'A study on the Confucian elements in Korean administrative culture: literature review', *Korean Public Administration Review* 33 (4), pp. 95-111.

Health Solidarity (2001), *Annual Report*.

Hong, Chul (2001), 'The conflicts of government and civil society for hegemony: 1998-2001', *Korean Journal of Political Science* 9 (2), pp. 77-97.

Jang, Hoon (2001), 'The origins of instability in Korean presidential government: the institutional, social and political origins of divided government', *Korean Political Science Review* 35 (4), pp. 107-27.

Jang, Wook-jin (2000), *A Study on the Policy-making Determinants and Policy Legitimisation*, Unpublished MA Dissertation, Korea University.

Jee, Byung-moon et al. (2001), *The New Understanding on Korean Politics*, Seoul: Pakyoungsa.

Kam, Jeong-ki (1994), *A Study on the Traits and Their Cultural Factors of Political Participation of the Federation of Korean Trade Unions*, Unpublished PhD Dissertation, Seoul National University, Korea.

Kang, Eun-sook (2002), 'Policy network analysis on policy change: Focusing on greenbelt policy', *Korean Society and Public Administration* 13 (1), pp. 103-25.

Kang, In-jae et al. (1998), *Korean Public Administration*, Seoul: Daeyoung Moonhwasa.

Kang, Kyung-keun (2004), *Constitutional Law*, Seoul: Bobmun-sa.

Kang, Moon-koo (2003), 'A critical reflection on the path of democratisation in Korea', Kim Yu-nam (ed.), *The Korean Polity: Issues and Tasks*, Seoul: Hanul Academy, pp. 226-55.

Karl, Hyun-sook (1998), *Study of Influence which the Inter-dynamic Action between Labour, Capital and State in Korean Society has on the Alteration of Social welfare Policy*, Unpublished MA Dissertation, Hanshin University, Korea.

Kim, Doh-jong and Hyung-joon Kim (2000), 'Analysis of the 16th Assembly election outcomes', *Korean Political Science Review* 34 (2), pp. 105-27.

Kim, Jae-gwan (1992), *Analysis of Arguments about Medical Insurance Policy in Korea*, Unpublished PhD Dissertation, Sung Kyun Kwan University, Korea.

Kim, Jin-sik et al. (2013), 'An analysis of policy change by using ACMS model: Focused on health insurance integration policy', *Korean Journal of Policy Analysis and Evaluation* 23(1), pp. 59-92.

Kim, Jong-dae (2000), *Don't Cover up the Truth*, Seoul: Jeonwon Moonhwasa.

________ (2002), *A New Welfare Paradigm for the People*, Seoul: ibook.store.

Kim, Jung-hai (2003), 'An institutional analysis of the Korean Presidential Office from 1963 to 2001: John Burke's model of institutionalisation and its applicability to Korea', *Korean Public Administration Review* 37 (1), pp. 225-47.

Kim, Myoung-hee (1999), *A Study on the Output of Korean Social Welfare Policy*, Unpublished MA Dissertation, Korea University.

Kim, Sam-geun (1998), *The Study on the Policy-making Process for the Unification of Medical Insurance*, Unpublished MA Dissertation, Yonsei University, Korea.

Kim, Se-keol (2001), 'Comparative analysis of labour politics in Korea and Japan: centring on the politics of social pact', *Korean Political Science Review* 35 (4), pp. 211-28.

Kim, Soon-yang (1999), 'The formation of social consensus in the process of Korean labour policy-making', *Korean Public Administration Quarterly* 11 (1), pp. 107-29.

________ (2002), 'Improving the internal decision-making process in local governments', *Korean Public Administration Review* 36 (1), pp. 193-213.

Kim, Suk-joon (2002), *Modern Korean Presidency I: Legal, political, Psychological and Institutional Analysis on the Korean Presidency*, Seoul: Daeyoung Moonhwasa.

Kim, Yeon-myung (1996), 'Medical insurance managing system and the interests of related parties', A paper presented at the Korean Academy of Social Welfare, pp. 109-21.

Kim, Young-jong (1998), 'The policy-making model of the Korean labour policy in transition period', *Korean Public Administration Quarterly* 10 (4), pp. 855-72.

Kim, Young-myung (2003), *The History of Modern Korean Politics*, Seoul: Eulyoo Moonhwasa.

KMA (Korea Medical Association) (1977) (1979) (1986) (1989), *Newsletter*.

KTC (Korea Tripartite Commission) (1999), *The Activities of Korean Tripartite Commission in 1998*.

Kwon, Young-sung (2003), *Constitutional Law: A Textbook*, Seoul: Bobmun-sa.

Lee, Doo-ho et al. (1992), *National Medical Security*, Seoul: Nanam Publishing Co.

Lee, Hong-yoon (2000), *A Study on the Participants' Role in the Process of Social Welfare Policy Making*, Unpublished PhD Dissertation, Sung Kyun Kwan University, Korea.

Lee, Jae-hee (2000), *A Study on the Change and Process of Korean Medical Insurance Policy*, Unpublished PhD Dissertation, Korea University.

Lee, Kyu-sik (2000a), 'Policy formulation of health insurance and its problems in Korea', *Korean Journal of Health Policy and Administration* 10 (1), pp. 57-94.

________ (2000b), 'The change and problems of medical insurance integration logic', in Lee Jong-chan (ed.), *The Great Debate on Korean Medical System*, Seoul: Sonamu, pp. 52-78.

Lee, Song-ho (2003), 'An analysis of four cabinet councils in Dae-jung Kim administration', *Korean Public Administration Review* 37 (3), pp. 1-22.

Lee, U-jin and Sung-joo Kim (1996), *Contemporary Korean Politics*, Seoul: Sahwoebipyeong.

Lee, Young-chan (2003), *A Study on Social Welfare Policy in Korea: With Special Reference to the Integration Policy of the Medical Insurance Scheme*, Unpublished PhD Dissertation, Kyung-hee University, Korea.

Lim, Eul-gee (2001), *The Case Study on Change of Korean Health Insurance Policy*, Unpublished MA Dissertation, Seoul National University, Korea.

MIIPB (Medical Insurance Integration Planning Board) (1998), *Understanding the Integration of Health Insurance.*

Min, Joon-ki et al. (1996), *Korean Politics*, Seoul: Nanam Publishing Co.

Monthly Chosun (1993), *Korea's President*, Seoul: Daily Chosun.

Moon, Ok-ryun (1992), *Korea's Medical Security Policy*, Seoul: Shin-gwang Publishing Co.

NCHIU (National Conference for Health Insurance Unification) (1999), *White Paper: 10 Years Struggles for Health Insurance Unification.*

NCSIR (National Conference for Social Insurance Reform) (1999), *Medical Insurance Merger and the People's Pain.*

NEIU (National Employee Insurers Union) (2000), *Annual Report.*

NFMI (National Federation of Medical Insurance) (each year), *Medical Insurance Statistical Yearbook.*

________ (1997), *The Footmarks of Korea's Medical Insurance.*

NHIC (National Health Insurance Corporation) (2001), *White Paper.*

________ (2004), *National Health Insurance Statistical Yearbook.*

NMIC (National Medical Insurance Corporation) (1999), *The White Paper on Medical Insurance Integration.*

Oh, Il-hwan (2003), 'The alternative and tasks of Korea's power structure', in Kim Yu-nam (ed.), *The Korean Polity: Issues and Tasks*, Seoul: Hanul Books, pp. 380-441.

OP (Office of the President) (1989), *The Treatment of National Medical Insurance Bill.*

Park, Eun-hong (2000), 'Structural adjustment and democracy: theory and experience', *Korean Political Science Review* 34 (2), pp. 359-75.

Park, Jung-ho (1996), *Government's Role in the Policy Process of the Korean Medical Insurance Scheme*, Unpublished PhD Dissertation, Seoul National University, Korea.

Park, Kwan-yong et al. (2001), *Unfinished Public Duties*, Seoul: Myongsol Publication.

Public Information Office (1997), *The Kim Young-sam Government's Reform.*

PUC (Presidency Undertaking Commission) (1998), *White Paper of the 15th Presidency Undertaking Commission.*

Shim, Ji-yeon (2004), *The History of Korean Political Parties: The Politics of Crisis and Integration*, Seoul: Baiksanseodang.

Shim, Ji-yeon and Meen-geon Kim (2002), 'The transformation of the electoral system: strategic intentions and their consequences', *Korean Political Science Review* 36 (1), pp. 139-62.

Shin, Jeong-hyun (2002), *The Reform of Korean Political Institutions*, Seoul: Jipmoondang.

Shin, Young-jeon (2010), 'The history of health insurance integration', *Monthly Welfare Trends* 141, pp. 4-8.

Shin, Young-ran (2004), *The Political Dynamics of decision-making Process for the Korean Health Insurance System: A Comparative Analysis of the 1989 and the 1997 Cases*, Unpublished PhD Thesis, the Hankuk University of Foreign Affairs, Korea.

Statistics Korea (1998), *The Fifty Years of South Korea's Economy and Society*, Seoul: Statistics Korea.

Won, Seok-jo (1990), *A Study on the Political Economy of Korean Medical Insurance*, Unpublished PhD Dissertation, Chung-ang University, Korea.

________ (2006), 'A study on the process of the debate on the national health insurance system integration in Korea', *Social Welfare Policy* 25, pp. 159-80.

Yang, Jae-jin (2003), 'Changes in political power and political control of the bureaucracy: the case of the Kim Dae-jung Government', *Korean Public Administration Review* 37 (2), pp. 263-87.

Yoon, Hye-mee (1984), *A Study on the Discussion Process of Unification of Medical Insurance System in Korea: With the Framework of a Group Theory*, Unpublished MA Dissertation, Seoul National University, Korea.

Yoon, Hyoung-sup et al. (2003), *Understanding Korean Politics*, Seoul: Pakyoungsa Publishing.

Yoo, Pal-mu (2001), 'The history and social role of NGOs', in Yoo Pal-mu and Kim Jeong-hoon (eds.), *Civil Society and Civil Movement* 2, Seoul: Hanul Books, pp. 187-231.

Yu, Hyun-seok (2000), 'Economic crisis and labour movement: searching for research strategy for Korean case', *Korean Political Science Review* 34 (1), pp. 135-53.

Yu, Seung-hum (1990), *Introductory Medical Insurance*, Seoul: Soomunsa.

Public documents, statements and other reports

Periodicals

Monthly *Chosun*, Monthly *Shindonga*, Pharmaceutical Newsletter, NFMI *Newsletter*, KMA *Newsletter*, KEF *Newsletter*, KPA *Newsletter*, NCMI *Newsletter*, daily newspapers etc.

Index